# *French*
## *Dressing*

# French
## Dressing

*Women, Men and Ancien Régime Fiction*

# Nancy K. Miller

Routledge
Taylor & Francis Group
New York   London

Published in 1995 by
Routledge
711 Third Avenue,
New York, NY 10017

Published in Great Britain in 1995 by
Routledge
2 Park Square, Milton Park,
Abingdon, Oxon OX14 4RN

*Routledge is an imprint of the Taylor & Francis Group, an informa business*

**Library of Congress Cataloging-in-Publication Data**

Miller, Nancy K., 1941–
    French dressing : women, men, and Ancien Régime fiction / Nancy K.
Miller.
        p.    cm.
    Includes bibliographical references.
    ISBN 0-415-90321-1  —  ISBN 0-415-90322-X (pbk.)
    1. French fiction—18th century—History and criticism.   2. French
fiction—Women authors—History and criticism.   3. Women and
literature—France—History—18th century.   4. Man-woman
relationships in literature.   5. Sentimentalism in literature.
6. Authorship—Sex differences.   7. Sex customs in literature.
8. Libertines in literature.   9. Seduction in literature.
10. Narration (Rhetoric)    I. Title.
PQ648.M55    1994
843'.5'09—dc20                                                      94-16707
                                                                          CIP

**British Library Cataloguing-in-Publication Data also available.**

# CONTENTS

Preface     ix

Acknowledgments     xiii

## I READING IN PAIRS

1   Repairing the Tradition     3

## II MEN'S READING, WOMEN'S WRITING

2   Rereading as a Woman: The Body in Practice     45

3   Men's Reading, Women's Writing: Gender and the Rise of the Novel     53

4   Cultural Memory and the Art of the Novel: Gender and Narrative in Eighteenth-Century France     69

5   1735: The Gender of the Memoir-Novel     81

## III "I's" IN DRAG

6   "I's" in Drag: The Sex of Recollection     93

7   *L'Histoire d'une Grecque moderne:* No-Win Hermeneutics     105

8   *Justine,* Or, the Vicious Circle     121

9   *Juliette* and the Posterity of Prosperity     133

## IV EXQUISITE CADAVERS

10   The Exquisite Cadavers: Women in Eighteenth-Century Fiction     147

11   Tender Economies: Mme de Villedieu and the Costs of Indifference     161

12   "Tristes Triangles": *Le Lys dans la vallée* and Its Intertext     173

13   Novels of Innocence: Fictions of Loss     187

Notes     201

Index     235

For Naomi

# PREFACE

> The merit of a work derives from its usefulness or from the pleasure
> it gives, or even from both when it has both to offer.
> —Choderlos de Laclos, *Les Liaisons dangereuses*

> A distinguished writer like M. de Laclos should have two objects in
> publishing: giving pleasure and being useful. Fulfilling one is not
> enough. . . .
> —Marie-Jeanne Riccoboni, *Correspondance de Laclos et de
> Madame Riccoboni au sujet des liaisons dangereuses*

How should we teach the eighteenth-century novel?

The notion of "reading in pairs," which came to me through the
pedagogical imagination of others, had remained a theoretical one for
me until the spring of 1989 when for the first time I taught a seminar
on the eighteenth-century novel in which we looked at men's and
women's writing together as part of a single tradition. "Repairing the
Tradition," the introductory chapter to this book, is in its origins a
reflection about "teaching in pairs": the intensely rewarding experience of reading male- and female-authored novels with and against
each other. The first group of essays, "Men's Reading, Women's
Writing," works out the implications of that project at close range,
addressing the critical assumptions which have framed older discussions of ancien régime fiction. Women writers, we begin to see here, in
dramatic counterpoint to the dominant tradition, produce an acerbic

critique of the figures of seduction and betrayal that dominate the period's landscape; their novels offer a view of manners quite different from the literary criteria of mainstream (primarily French) critics and editors. The earlier articles in this book emerge from a focus on men's and women's writing (primarily men's) in their separate genealogies. The emphasis in "'I's' in Drag" falls on sexual histories and the interpretive confines of gender narratives in the novel. The readings in "Exquisite Cadavers" dwell on the proliferation of dead women whose erotic fate looms so large in ancien régime scenarios.

To call this book *French Dressing* is to conjure the various stages of literal and figurative undressing that rococo and libertine imaginations made fashionable; undoings that the elaborately layered—and gendered—productions of costume and rhetoric invariably provoked. It's meant to underline the power of public appearances in ancien régime fiction, and to foreground the stories of sexual performance central to this period's national ethos. *French Dressing,* finally, reflects upon the protocols of feeling that regulate the plots of novels by men and women writers in pre-revolutionary France.

Viewed from the crisis in sexual relations we have experienced at the end of the twentieth century, these novels support the claims that locate the inaugural phase of a certain depressingly stylish modernity in eighteenth-century France.

What price libertinage?

*       *       *

I'm grateful to Pierre Saint-Amand, who writes eloquently about the eighteenth century, for his suggestions and guidance—not all of which I was able to follow—in collecting these essays. Cheryl Morgan, Deborah Nelson, and Carina Yervasi helped me with the preparation of the manuscript; Katharine Jensen, Sally O'Driscoll, and Carina Yervasi handled the translations for materials previously published in French: I am infinitely grateful to them for their labors. I thank Sandy Petrey, the title maven, for coming up with *French Dressing,* and for other things as well.

I have a debt to certain students, whose interest in the eighteenth-century novel has been heartening. I'd like to thank the members of my Friday afternoon seminar in Cambridge (Fall 1993), "Gender and the Rise of the French Eighteenth-Century Novel," for their kindness and their wit: Peggy Ackerberg, Sharon Bhagwan, Diane Brown,

Anne Carman, Juliette Dickstein, Elizabeth Galaznik, Seth Graebner, Michele Hunter, Efthmyia Korodima, Dennis Lin, Terri Mendelsohn, Lark Di Lucia Miller, Rosemary Peters. I also want to acknowledge Katharine Jensen, Catherine Liu, and Sally O'Driscoll, who went on to make the eighteenth-century novel their own. And finally I wish to remember two students I miss. Peggy Brawer, who was my assistant for *The Heroine's Text* and whose remarks about the eighteenth century were unfailingly illuminating. Peggy died of breast cancer in 1991. And Jerry Leo, who was an outstanding participant in my 1989 seminar at the Graduate Center; he died of AIDS in 1993.

This book is dedicated to Naomi Schor. We were colleagues at Columbia (in our salad days, if I can allow myself the first of the terrible puns this title will no doubt produce) when the earliest of these essays were written. "Reading in pairs" has also meant writing in dialogue with her.

New York, January 1994

# ACKNOWLEDGMENTS

With the exception of "Repairing the Tradition" (not including the passages from "Decades": "Libertines, feminists, and readers in Paris. A Story.") these chapters have appeared elsewhere as articles. On the whole, I have limited their editing to putting the French quotations into English; to updating, incorporating, adding, or eliminating footnotes; and to correcting errors where they have been pointed out to me. I have also on occasion deleted remarks I no longer understand and clarified murky points. I have used published translations where easily available; sometimes I have modified these, otherwise I have supplied the English, staying as close to the original as possible. Further editing, while perhaps desirable stylistically, would have worked against my equally strong desire to present an endeavor embedded in its time. I gratefully acknowledge the following journals and editors for their permission to reprint:

"*Juliette* and the Posterity of Prosperity," *L'Esprit Créateur,* (Winter 1975), 413–24.

"The Exquisite Cadavers: Women in Eighteenth-Century Fiction," *Diacritics* (Winter 1975), 37–43.

"*Justine,* Or, the Vicious Circle," *Studies in Eighteenth-Century Culture,* Vol 5 (1976), 215–28.

"Novels of Innocence: Fictions of Loss," *Eighteenth-Century Studies* (Spring 1978), 325–39.

"*L'Histoire d'une Grecque moderne:* No-Win Hermeneutics," *Forum* (Spring 1978), 2–10.

"'Tristes Triangles': *Le Lys dans la vallée* and Its Intertext," in *Pre-Text/Text/Context; Essays in Nineteenth-Century French Literature,* Ohio State University Press, 1980, 67–77.

"'I's' in Drag: The Sex of Recollection," *The Eighteenth Century: Theory and Interpretation* (Winter 1981), 47–57.

"Tender Economies: Mme de Villedieu and the Costs of Indifference," *L'Esprit Créateur* (Summer 1983), 80–93.

"Men's Reading, Women's Writing: Gender and the Rise of the Novel." *Yale French Studies* 75 (1988), 40–55; rpt. in *Displacements: Women, Tradition, Literatures in French,* ed. Joan DeJean and Nancy K. Miller (Baltimore: Johns Hopkins University Press, 1991).

"1735: The Gender of the Memoir-Novel," in *A History of French Literature,* ed. Denis Hollier. (Cambridge: Harvard University Press, 1989), 436–42.

"Cultural Memory and the Art of the Novel: Gender and Narrative in Eighteenth-Century France," in *Textuality and Sexuality,* ed. Judith Still and Michael Worton. (Manchester: Manchester University Press, 1993), 89–99.

"Decades." *South Atlantic Quarterly* (Winter 1992) Vol. 91, 1, 65–96; rpt. in *Changing Subjects: The Making of Feminist Literary Scholarship,* ed. Gayle Greene and Coppélia Kahn (London and New York: Routledge, 1993); rpt. in *Wild Orchids and Trotsky,* ed. Mark Edmundson (New York: Viking, 1993), 77–97.

"Rereading as a Woman: The Body in Practice." *Poetics Today,* Vol. 6, 1 (1985); rpt. in *The Female Body in Western Culture: Contemporary Perspectives,* ed. Susan Suleiman (Cambridge: Harvard University Press, 1986).

# PART ONE

# READING IN PAIRS

# Repairing the Tradition

## I. Whose mouth, whose ring?

"I don't claim to be arguing. I'm talking about feelings: it's what we women mean by philosophy and you understand it almost as well as we do."
—Denis Diderot, *Les Bijoux indiscrets*

Like women, philosophers need novels to think.

Michel Foucault's *History of Sexuality* derives its authority from a classic of *ancien régime* fiction. "The aim of this series of studies?" Foucault asks. "To transcribe into history the fable of *Les Bijoux indiscrets*"(*HS*, 77).[1] The historian then goes on to lay out the premise of the *philosophe*'s tale. Diderot's novel narrates the powers of a magical ring, "whose stone, when turned, makes the sexes one encounters speak"(*HS*, 79). The ring, given by the good genie Cucufa to the sultan Mangogul, allows its owner to find out what the women in his kingdom are really up to. If he points the ring at a woman, he'll get to hear about her adventures. But, the genie warns, the source of these stories is not going to be their mouths. From where then, Mangogul demands to know? "By the truest part of them, and the best informed of what you want to know . . . by their jewels"(*HS*, 9).[2] Mangogul bursts out laughing at the idea of these "talking jewels," (*BI*, 9) and runs off to try out the ring on his favorite. "For many years," Foucault observes, "we have all been living in the realm of Prince Mangogul: under the spell of an immense curiosity about sex, bent on questioning it, with an insatiable desire to hear it speak and be spoken about . . ."(*HS*, 77). Foucault's post-Mangogulian gesture entails of course an interrogation of that desire, "this petition to know" (*HS*, 79), by looking at the mechanism of the ring itself, making the ring account for its practices, and thus, theoretically, demystifying its power. But as James Creech points out, there's a dangerous symmetry "between Foucault's desire to interrogate 'this jewel which is so indiscreet,' and Mangogul's desire to consult 'indiscreet jewels.'"[3] The arrangements of power that underwrite the fable itself seem to resist the scrutiny of Foucault's own will to know. "At the very moment he stands 'outside' the realms of Prince Mangogul so as to point to it . . . he in fact reproduces its organization in an uncanny way."[4]

What Mangogul thinks he has asked for is "something very simple"(*BI*, 8). He just wants to "have some fun [*quelques plaisirs*] at the expense of the women of his court"(*BI*, 8). What Foucault wants is a little more complicated: to study the way in which "each one of us has become a sort of attentive and imprudent sultan with respect to his own sex and that of others"(*HS*, 79). Thanks to the "talking jewels," "we"—in the wake of Mangogul—learn something about ourselves that gives us an edge over the unsuspecting women. The fable that gets transcribed as history is one through which men hear about women's sexuality without their consent. Made invisible by the ring, men find out what the genie thinks has never happened heretofore: that women tell the truth about their desire. Through the ring, women's sexuality is brought into language; or rather through the conventions of Enlightenment literary erotics, a philosopher imagines a female bodily discourse fantasized, elicited, and recorded for posterity. But whose? And what are the consequences of the Foucault/Diderot collaboration in this gynographic enterprise?

In "Speaking Sex," the first chapter of *Hard Core,* an illuminating study of film pornography, which begins with Diderot's fable and Foucault's foundational enlistment of its tropes, Linda Williams puts the matter this way: "important as Foucault's ideas are to a more refined understanding of sexuality's complex history and of the basic discontinuities in the cultural construction of sexualities in diverse eras, they are sometimes not as radical as they seem."[5] Indeed, at the threshold of our cherished modernity, Foucault reauthorizes a fable whose terms of intelligibility belong to a network of assumptions feminist theorists have systematically debunked for over two decades: notably the sex/gender arrangements Adrienne Rich named "compulsory heterosexuality"; and Monique Wittig, the "heterosexual contract"; compounded by the orientalist agenda which in the eighteenth-century novel makes women doubly Other, female and exotic.[6] But most important for a revisionary look at gender and power in *ancien régime* fiction is the persistent and unexamined assumption of whose pleasure and knowledge are at stake in a fiction or a history of sexuality. As Naomi Schor argues in "Dreaming Dissymmetry," "a single universal history is presumed to cover both sexes, as though History and, more important, the Historian of sexuality himself had no sex."[7] Foucault's fable turned into history remains a man's story. What would happen to Foucault's paradigm if the model were made to deal with the gendered subjects of its terms? What would happen to the universal claim if we countered it with a fable that reversed the vectors of knowledge? In other words, what would a history of sexuality written by women, with women as its subjects, look like?

Part of the excitement generated by French and American feminism in the 1970s was the project undertaken by women, and addressed to other women, to produce the discourse Mangogul tried to get at with his ring. Luce Irigaray thus imagined what would happen when "our lips speak together": we would tell another kind of story, a story precisely bound up with women's bodies and desires; in a new language structured according to the logic of another morphology.[8] Although the challenge of hearing the story of a "parler-femme," a "speaking (as) woman" struck us as decidedly modern, the question, as we have just seen, had been staged, albeit as a man's interrogation, in the eighteenth century.[9] This ostensibly parallel quest to press on the question of female sexual pleasure is what produced Jane Gallop's (unfair, as she will later admit) juxtaposition of the famous *Hite Report* (in which the researcher Shere Hite set out to record what women "are actually experiencing") with Diderot's philosophical novel.[10] Gallop likened Hite to Mangogul, banishing "all mystery which stands in the way of self-determination and control" (*TTB*, 75).

She identified instead with Mirzoza, the sultan's favorite mistress, who in her reading emerges as a counter power. At the end of the novel, Mangogul takes advantage of Mirzoza and finally gets the jewel of his "sleeping beauty" (*BI*, 10) to speak; it turns out that she only has her love for him to confess. On the strength of this demonstration, she gets him to give the ring back to the genie. This exchange led Gallop to conclude: "The entire baroque path of the novel is but a deferral of this confrontation with the voice of the loved woman's desire. The sexual/scientific imperialism of *Les Bijoux indiscrets* is thus no simple, successful subjugation of woman's resistant mystery to light, truth and wordly authority" (*TTB*, 77). Gallop's valuing of the mistress's power seems to buy into Diderot's fantasia of couples therapy, Enlightenment style.[11]

When Gallop reprinted her 1977 essay "Snatches of Conversation" in her book *Thinking Through the Body* (1988), she framed and criticized its positions autobiographically: having emerged from an earlier—graduate student—identification with men, and having "'passed,'" she then tried to imagine herself "authorized by virtue of her doctorate" becoming "an academic speaker *as a woman*" (*TTB*, 71). Gallop also confessed to her surprising repression of Foucault's analysis of Diderot's fable: "My rationalization for this omission was that I was writing in a feminist context and that those theoretical names [also those of Irigaray and Lacan] would alienate my readers" (*TTB*, 89).

The editors of *The Powers of Desire* (1983), a pioneering and influential anthology, seem to have made an analogous move though for different, American feminist reasons: they mention Foucault, and credit his enterprise as a powerful tool in the investigation of sex and "modern social institutions," but they pull back from his project to the extent, they explain, that it leaves women in the position of "'the sex'"; the object of "obsessive male discourse from St. Augustine to Philip Roth."[12] Noting the ambivalent take of many American feminists on French theory (they bring up Foucault the better to drop him), Schor makes the point that in the subsequent volumes of the *History* Foucault recognizes the place of women, albeit in their relation to the male subjects of his inquiry. However, as she then acknowledges, "alterity" is, of course, not specificity."[13] It will fall to women to theorize the question of women's difference. This is not simple. As the editors of *Powers of Desire* remark, "When feminists try to celebrate female sexuality, we find that men have been there first, rhapsodic and mythic about virgins, mothers, and whores. It is hard to throw off their obfuscating enthusiasm."[14] What desire means to women themselves is the great question of female-authored novels in *ancien régime* France, even if posed from the place of the second sex to which they have been assigned. In these novels, women are the subjects of sexual knowledge and the history of their alterity is part of the story they have to tell. It's also what they've been reading.

Throughout the century, women writers refuse to locate their subjectivities within the domain of libertine power and knowledge. The feminist project I begin to sketch out here is the charting of that refusal. I've named the modality of this remapping "reading in pairs." To repair our sense of the literary tradition it seems necessary to reject the dominant monologic (Mangogulian) tradition and replace it with a dialogic one. This means, however, that we will encounter asymmetry everywhere. The challenge is to make a productive sense of it. In 1748, for instance, Diderot published *Les Bijoux indiscrets*, Boyer d'Argens, *Thérèse philosophe*, and John Cleland, *Fanny Hill*. In 1747–48, Samuel Richardson published the multi-volumed *Clarissa*, whose heroine, in dying, refused the plots written for her. In 1747, Françoise de Graffigny published the slim volume of *Lettres d'une Péruvienne* in which the emblem of the heroine's subjectivity is the Inca *quipu*, which Graffigny translates into an instrument of cultural mastery—*her* magic ring—that allows her to write her way out of the predictable meanders of sexual plot I've called "the heroine's text." We're still waiting for a literary history that can make sense of these competing narratives of gender and desire and hold them together.

## II. Whose hand?

But if my taste did not preserve me from dull and tasteless books, my luck saved me from the obscene and licentious. . . . What is more, luck so favoured my modesty in this respect that I was more than thirty before I even glanced at one of those dangerous works

which even fashionable ladies find so embarrassing that they can
only read them [with one hand].
— Jean-Jacques Rousseau, *The Confessions**

The asymmetry between the traditions of men's and women's writing
can be easily tracked in publishing patterns. Typically, women's novels of the *ancien régime* are published separately and maintained in
print erratically.[15] Men's novels often stay in print longer not only
because of their more stable position in the canon; they are often kept
before the public eye in anthologies. In 1993 the publishing house
Laffont brought out an anthology in their inexpensively priced
Bouquins collection called *Romans libertins du XVIIIe siècle*.[16]
Presenting the works of eleven authors, it contains three of the novels
also anthologized by Etiemble in the Pléiade's 1966 *Romanciers du
dix-huitième siècle: Crébillon's Les Egarements du coeur et de
l'esprit*, Duclos's *Confessions du Comte de***, and Vivant Denon's
*Point de Lendemain*.[17] In both anthologies, the novels of worldliness—a young man's initiation into the complications of gendered
relations among the Parisian élite—exist side by side with licentious
and more frankly pornographic tales like *Thérèse philosophe*.

Unlike the covers of the Pléiade, which are canonically austere, typically graced by an author's photograph, or a subdued engraving,
Bouquins, as its slangy name suggests, goes for a more popular style
of marketing. On the cover of *Romans libertins* is the detail of a
Boucher painting, *A Woman Fastening Her Garter, with Her Maid*.
In the full painting a woman is sitting next to a fireplace with her legs
spread, fastening her garter, as she completes the process of dressing.
She is looking to her left at her maid who, with her back to the viewer, is selecting items for her mistress to wear. There is some debate
about whether this painting is "more than a simple genre scene":
does it depict "the occupations of a courtesan" or is this a portrait of
Mme Boucher?[18] The jury is still out, but for our purposes here, the
ambiguity (whore or wife) is interesting enough. More to the point,
however, is what gets emphasized in the detail. Cut off at the waist,

---

*In the Penguin translation, first published in 1953, Harmondsworth, and that contin-
ues to be reprinted, the English reads "that they can only read them in secret" (48).
The French reads: "qu'une belle dame de par le monde trouve incommodes, en ce
qu'on ne peut, dit-elle, les lire que d'une main." *Les Confessions* (Paris: Garnier-
Flammarion, 1968), 76.

the woman is reduced to her legs and hands. A tabby cat lies on the floor between her legs, playing with a small ball of wool. In the reduction of the detail used in the publicity campaign during the summer of 1993 for the collection, the woman becomes a single leg. The cat's tail flicks her ankle; her hands tie the garter around her knee. Underneath her legs, the advertising copy proclaims: "Libertinage is a current of thought."[19] (The anthology was advertised between two portraits: Seneca's noble gaze, with the caption, "Stoicism is an art of happiness"; and Françoise Sagan's equivocal glance, "Sagan, a certain smile.") This elegant crotch shot—the cat visually foregrounds the pussy hidden behind layers of white petticoats—is given intellectual substance on the back cover. The selling point here is not sex but brains, or at least, brainy sex: "what can be read here is the essential of libertine production in the Enlightenment. The freedom of thought and imagination of these authors has its equivalent only in the absolute mastery of a language scintillating with intelligence, beauty, and desire." The editor, author of this blurb, has done a thorough review in his introduction of the history of the term *libertine,* as well as of the dominant evaluations of the literature that has been grouped under this label. In the eighteenth century, the term, he writes, "refers mainly to dissolute behavior and the transgression of moral rules; libertinage is allied with eroticism, as well as with egoistic fulfillment, the will to power, and the portrayal of an exhausted society seeking in pleasure an end in itself." All of this seems a fair enough summary; and yet it avoids the equally legitimate question that libertine literature poses to a feminist reader: fulfillment on whose terms?[20]

What does the front cover mean to the back copy? In his long critical introduction Raymond Trousson notes that in the representation of the social relations between the sexes whatever symmetry seems to exist between them proves to be illusory. And he underlines one of the crueler ironies of gender relations within the androcentric fictions of libertine activity, the so-called power of women which derives from their role in "launching" young men in the world: "Because fashion is in the hands of women, it's necessary to be launched by them; and they, paradoxically, will do their best to train those who will become the enemies of their sex."[21] But despite the astuteness of his analysis—and he has the grace not to call the heroines (or the authors) of these novels feminist[22]—he lets the misogyny as the shaping force of libertine vision stand. What he can't seem to imagine is an outside to this world.

A British reviewer of the anthology, "Up the *ancien régime*," emphasizes Trousson's belief in the literary merit of the works he has assembled.[23] He rehashes the dominant interpretive views of libertine literature: "libertine literature was a game; . . . it was a form of slumming for readers weary of good taste; . . . it was also a business; . . . libertine authors showed no respect for religion . . . ;" and finally that "these novels constitute a truly political and indeed revolutionary literature which prepared for 1789 by discrediting both Church and State." He then concludes that in the end Trousson subordinates these generalizations to a claim for "elegant libertinage as a literary ideal": "Here was the last flowering of the aristocracy, a mix of medieval chivalry and seventeenth-century preciosity, a final affirmation of true nobility by a class which no longer had a role in society. Its later, less aristocratic forms . . . maintained the same hostility to sentiment and exclusive love, but in cruder, utilitarian terms of pleasure and sensuality." The reviewer, David Coward, who had until this point refrained from offering his own reading of this literature directly, now takes a position: "It is an interesting case, and Trousson makes it well. Yet the reader of these admirably edited texts will find it hard to avoid the conclusion that, either way, libertine literature did to the *ancien régime* what *le père* Dirrag does to Mlle Eradice with a remnant of St. Francis's girdle on page 591."

I of course immediately flipped the book open to page 591 to see what was going on that could summarize the effects and social meaning of this varied literary production. In a scene from the first part of *Thérèse Philosophe,* Thérèse gets to watch Mademoiselle Eradice being instructed in spiritual exercises. Hidden behind a panel, Thérèse avidly follows the proceedings through a hole in the wall. After being spanked, Eradice kneels on the floor leaning with her arms on the step of her prie-dieu, her head on her arms. Her dress is raised to her waist thus creating a "luxurious perspective" of two openings: her spiritual adviser devours them with his eyes, unsure which of the two "embouchures" to choose. "One was a tempting morsel for a man of the cloth, but he had promised pleasure, even ecstasy to his penitent."[24] He ends by choosing the "canonical path," penetrating the innocent Eradice with the "so-called rope." After enduring a good deal of motion with the "remnant of St. Francis's girdle," Eradice finally begins to understand what "heavenly rapture" means, and praises, as she reaches the heights of pleasure, good St. Francis and his "cordon."

So what did libertine literature do to the *ancien régime?* Which opening did it choose in order to provide a pleasure its classy readers could take in while pretending to receive instruction? If libertine literature screwed the *ancien régime*—literalizing its favorite tropes—did it screw men and women indifferently? When we resist the figure of Eradice bottom up as an economical metaphor for the *ancien régime* on its knees—like Diderot's "talking sexes"—and think for a moment of women as historical subjects of pleasure they might have scripted, we get to pose a different set of problems, one modeled along the lines of Joan Kelly-Gadol's famous reformulation of women's place in history, "Did Women Have an Enlightenment?"[25] What did the *ancien régime* mean for women? What did it do *for* them?

Women readers like Thérèse (and her contemporary Fanny Hill) have learned to philosophize by watching scenes like this one between Eradice and Father Dirrag. But was this the only way for them to get pleasure in the *ancien régime?* Were female libertines only the subjects (or objects) of male-authored fiction, and what should we make of their claims to pleasure?[26] In her essay on women erotic writers, Lucienne Frappier-Mazur makes the claim that the "first French erotic novel to be signed by a woman . . . appeared towards the end of the revolutionary period in 1799."[27] This certainly seems true: in the eighteenth century, erotic (or libertine) fiction as we know it was wholly male-authored. Did women writers remain entirely unaffected by the powerful influence of the libertine novel? The contents page of a forthcoming volume of the Pléiade, *Erotiques et Libertins* lists four anonymous late period texts in addition to the male-authored ones, so perhaps a surprise is in store.[28] ("Anon," after all, has so often been a woman.) Still, unless new research discovers that some of these anonymous authors of libertine fiction were in fact women, we must conclude that women's response to libertine plots was one of silence—but only if we understand the experience of the literary production of novels to be the same for women as for men and therefore for the results to be identical in kind. Women writers did more than bide their time, waiting for the revolution, however, and their response to the range of libertine works, primarily Riccoboni's, though many others as well, was to write fictions that present a critique and a refusal of libertine sensibility, which is also to say of its narrative models. Will their writing ever be deemed worthy of collection in a Pléiade edition comparable to *Romanciers* and *Erotiques?* "To the French," Jane Kramer writes in a witty essay called "Paris: Le Discours," "literature means precisely those titles that Gallimard prints across the delicate, gold-line spines of the Editions les Pléiades."[29] It's alas still hard to imagine the French reading women's writing in the eighteenth century *as literature.*

In "The Seductions of Women," Jane Miller eloquently identifies the ways in which Foucault's modeling of sexuality reinforces the power arrangements that infect the relations between women and men in narrative and constrain women's literary range:

> Foucault, who taught us to think about sexuality in terms of public discourses and their relation to power, contributed, nonetheless, to a tradition which offered the libertine as a kind of libertarian, hero, free spirit and individualist. That tradition focused on women only in so far as they were the generalized object of male desire; thus narrowly determining women's scope for choice and resistance within narratives of seduction and ignoring the account of events they might have given themselves, if asked. . . .

> It has above all been difficult for women to write of seduction and of seductive men and seducers within a tradition which has measured the seducer's claim to general sympathy or disapproval in terms of his stealing another man's property and thereby contravening civil law, divine law, or both. . . .

> It is necessary to unravel actual women's stories of seduction from the falsetto productions of men, as a first step towards challenging those accounts of sexual relations and sexual differences which have established them as natural, universal, even eternal relations and differences, when they are always in fact historically specific and are, moreover, controlled as practice and discourse by men, in their own interests.[30]

Women writers saw libertine freedom for men as unfreedom for themselves as women and as authors (no matter how much they resisted the word); the constraints of propriety that made for lack of symmetry between the sexes in the novels played a shaping role in the poetics of the emerging tradition. As one of my students recently queried, what would *Crébillon fille* have written? In the 1730s, rather than document the worldly doings of her own salon, Tencin, for example, turns to the "historical" setting of an earlier period.

In 1757 Marie-Jeanne Riccoboni published a novel entitled *Lettres de Mistress Fanni Butlerd*.[31] What makes this novel, Riccoboni's first, so extraordinary is its representation of female sexuality. Written after both *Les Bijoux indiscrets* and *Lettres d'une Péruvienne*, Riccoboni makes the epistolary novel the vehicle of a feminist erotics. In an essay called "Going Public: The Letter and the Contract in *Fanni Butlerd*," in which she analyzes the woman writer's relation to the public sphere, Elizabeth Cook writes: "Both in the sexual and the representational realm, Fanni takes responsibility for—and pleasure in—her actions. A celebration of autonomy as well as of sexuality, her post-coital letter records the joy of deliberately satisfying the beloved's desire by the free gift of the self: 'I did not give in: a moment of delirium did not throw me into his arms; I gave myself: my favors are the fruit of love, the prize of love.'"[32] The continued presence of a rhetoric of femininity in which a woman "gives" herself to a man should not blind us to the boldness of this work, unique in the century for its assertion of female sexual autonomy. More startling, perhaps, although equally revisionary, is Riccoboni's reworking of Diderot's fable. In scenes of what Cook calls "magically assisted voyeurism," Fanni hides herself in Alfred's bedroom by virtue of a ring, which like the genie Cucufa's, allows her to watch while invisible herself. "In these fantasies," Cook comments, "Riccoboni deliberately inverts images of male domination and, playing with themes of illusion and disguise, undermines the traditional gendering of the active/passive hierarchy, though without relinquishing her identification with feminine qualities of *délicatesse*."[33] Unlike Mirzoza, who dreads the ring's power to invade the private space of her body and proves to be a faithful and accommodating mistress, Riccoboni's heroine jubilantly uses the ring to turn her gaze onto the body of what turns her on. When the object of her desire proves to be unworthy of her libidinal investment, she goes public with her rage, violating the codes of propriety which require that female eroticism remain a reluctant response to male desire, and the consequences of sexual betrayal, the subject of private shame. Although, as Susan Lanser comments, "it's revenge without improvement," the revenge emerges from the elaboration in novel form of female sexual fantasy and empowerment, that as Katharine Jensen argues, "takes control . . . over the epistolary tradition of female emotional and sexual vulnerability"; together fantasy and revenge combine to provide the terms of a startling feminist provocation.[34]

How can we understand Riccoboni's appropriation of this trademark of the *conte licencieux?* Is this the work of a libertine author? Is this a case of reverse ventriloquism?[35] Of a woman writer writing like a man?

When we think about the different ways in which the magic ring functions in both novels, separated by barely a decade, we begin to have a framework for talking about the dialogic nature of the novel in eighteenth-century France. Riccoboni writes as a feminist, and her novel constitutes a reply both to *Bijoux indiscrets* and to the famous *Lettres portugaises*. It more generally establishes the terms for an anti-libertine discourse that resists by its values the plots of a wide range of novels in which the hero makes his way through women as he makes his way in the world: Crébillon's Meilcour, Duclos's Comte de***. Thus, in the same letter in which Fanni details the mutuality of the sexual pleasure enjoyed with her lover, she also introduces a doubt about the future of their shared joy, of which the ultimate proof is the simultaneity of its expression: "He's writing to me while I'm writing to him . . ." (FB, XXXVI). This is the epistolary version of Barthes's dilation on the figure "I-love-you," on what it would mean if two spoke their love at once: "I hallucinate what is *empirically* impossible: that the two profferings be made *at the same time:* that one does not follow the other, as if it depended on it."[36] But the moment of conviction is short-lived: "Ah, be careful, be careful, dearest Alfred, my life's happiness or unhappiness is in your hands! . . . Heaven forbid, if ever a little less vivacity appeared in your style . . ." (FB, XXXVI). The seeds of the novel's denouement are planted in that flash of anxiety. Thus, Riccoboni provides here mid-century—and more dramatically still in *Lettres de Juliette Catesby*—a female-authored language of feminist protest. In a variety of tones, Riccoboni, as a woman writer, identifies the unequal power arrangements that flow from an unchallenged male aristocratic privilege and that Laclos dramatizes for his own ends toward the end of the century.

I wonder, then, whether we shouldn't see Laclos's inclusion of his correspondence with Riccoboni in the 1787 edition of his novel as uneasy acknowledgment of the lessons he learned from the author he so confidently chides. Imitation and influence in the eighteenth century cut both ways.

### III. Libertines, feminists, and readers in Paris. A Story.*

> Ideally, one would be Simone de Beauvoir, smoking with Sartre at the Deux Magots, making an eccentric domestic arrangement that was secondary to important things and in their service. One would be poised, brilliant, equipped with a past, above the fray, beyond it, foreign not domestic. (And ideally Sartre would look like Albert Camus.)
>
> —Rachel Brownstein, *Becoming a Heroine*

### 1962–1968

*It's 1962. I've just turned twenty-one in Paris. For my birthday, my roommate at the Foyer International des Etudiantes has given me a copy of the* Lettres portugaises, *which she has inscribed with a message that invites me to consider how wonderful it is to be like the* religieuse portugaise—*young and passionate*—*and concludes: "dis 'fuck you' à tous les garcons [she was learning English from the Americans who ate downstairs at the Foyer's student restaurant] et aime-les." This edition of the letters, in which the typeface imitates handwriting, is illustrated by Modigliani drawings of women looking unhappy, or at least withdrawn poignantly. Modigliani is an artist whose images of elongated women I find entrancing. I am knocked out by these letters. They are written, I believe then, by a real Portuguese nun, Mariana Alfocarado, seduced and abandoned by a real, if anonymous, Frenchman, and obsessing about it. I identify*

---

*What follows in italics is excerpted from my essay "Decades," as it appears in *Wild Orchids and Trotsky*, ed. Mark Edmundson (New York: Viking, 1993).

*completely, even though I'm of course not Portuguese (not to mention a nun). I have only begun to meet Frenchmen myself and I can tell already that I'm out of my depth.*

*I'm also studying for my M.A. with the Middlebury Program in Paris and taking a year-long seminar on Laclos. Antoine Adam, an authority on the early history of the French novel, standing in front of the lectern in a huge amphitheater of the Sorbonne, produces a weekly lecture on* Les Liaisons dangereuses. *I'm supposed to write an essay on it; the choice of topic is up to me. The program has assigned me a tutor to oversee the writing. I'll call him M. Souilliez. He lives on a dark street in the Latin Quarter, on a steep incline, somewhere near the Sorbonne, maybe behind the Pantheon. It's April. A first draft of the* mémoire *is long overdue; I haven't begun the outline (the outline, "le plan," is at the heart of the French educational system). I have spent Christmas in Italy with an American boyfriend on a motorcycle, and Easter vacation with my roommate at her home in Tunisia where I have discovered, among other things, the art of leg waxing with lemon and sugar. I don't know how I'm going to write this essay, let alone an outline for it.*

*In despair I go to see the tutor one evening in his apartment. We sit in the living room and talk about* Les Liaisons dangereuses; *we talk, that is to say, about sex. I am inwardly panicked because I cannot come up with an essay topic, so I try to appear worldly and unconcerned, and with studied casualness hold forth on sex and love, and men and women. Suddenly, I get an idea: I'll write on the women in the novel, how each of them is betrayed by the images others have of them and that they each have of themselves. I sit at a table opposite M. Souilliez and start to make an outline. I'm inspired, excited. As I write, he gets up and walks around the room. I forget about him— I'm so happy that I at last have an idea! Then as I sit at the table, I feel a hand on my breast. M. Souilliez, standing behind my chair, has reached down and slipped his hand through my blouse around my left breast. I stop writing.*

*Despite the fact that I realize the moment I feel the hand feeling me that I have been chattering away about precisely these kinds of moves in the novel, it hasn't really occurred to me to make the connection between seduction (not to say sex) and M. Souilliez. I am now nonplussed. I try to imagine that in the* Liaisons' *cast of characters I'm* the sophisticated Madame de Merteuil, not the ingenue Cécile, even though I feel a lot more like a schoolgirl than a libertine (that's Cécile's problem in a nutshell, of course). I don't want to have to go to bed with M. Souilliez (he's "old" and not, I think, my type) but I also don't want a bad grade. The hand is still moving around inside the blouse. I remove the hand and sigh. "Oh monsieur," I say, pausing, and hoping for the world-weary tone of the Marquise in my best American jeune fille French, "j'ai déjà tant d'ennuis sans cela."

He goes no further, shrugs (in a Parisian gesture which seems to mean either: it's your loss or you can't blame a guy for trying), and lets me leave. I race down the stairs out into the street and up the Boulevard St-Michel to the Foyer. When I get back to my room, I begin to wonder how much harm I've done myself. I finally write the essay—"Women and Love in Les Liaisons dangereuses: the Betrayal of Images"—and wait for the grade. The comments in the margins alternate between, "b" bien, and "md," mal dit. In general, I seem to have more insight than argumentative force. I take too long getting to the point: "what you say is true and interesting, but what's happened to your outline?" ("Le plan") I expect the quotations to do the work of commentary (they should play only a supporting role). And my favorite: "Never hesitate to be clear." In the light, I suppose, of these weaknesses, and despite a very nice overall comment (he thinks I'm smart), I get a mediocre grade on the essay (my own fault, I tell myself, for doing it all at the last minute; it really wasn't very good, anyway).

In 1968 when, having returned to New York, I decided to apply to graduate school, I went through my box of "important papers" and discovered the M.A. essay. I looked at the grade on the title page and it suddenly seemed to me—correctly, as it turned out—that the number grade (French style) was the equivalent not of the "B" on my transcript, but an "A"; the number had been mistranscribed. In 1968, it still didn't dawn on me to be angry about M. Souilliez's hand down my blouse. By then, flirting with a libertine incarnation of my own (I took the sexual revolution seriously), I congratulated myself instead, Merteuil-like, for having played the right card (didn't I get an "A"?). Recently, I ran into an old friend I knew when I was first living in Paris. I asked her if she remembered my scene with the tutor. "Oh yes," she said, "at the time we thought that sort of thing was flattering."

## 1969–1977

*I'm in graduate school at Columbia and feminism is in the streets—at least in a mainstream kind of way.*

*August 26, 1970 is the first annual nationwide "Women's Strike for Equality." Friends and I join the march down Fifth Avenue to celebrate the fiftieth anniversary of suffrage. Kate Millett publishes* Sexual Politics *and makes the cover of* Time Magazine. *At Town Hall, it's Germaine Greer (*The Female Eunuch *came out in the States in 1971) and a panel of women critics and writers vs. Norman Mailer. Mailer can't understand why women would become lesbians. After all, he opines, men can do to women what women do to each other—90%—and then some. In disgust, Jill Johnston walks off the stage and embraces her lover—to Mailer's despair: "C'mon Jill, be a lady"—in sight of the audience.*

*There is, in general, lots of writing and talk about female orgasm, how many (multiple, preferably), and what kind.*

*In January 1971, after reading an article by Vivian Gornick in the* New York Times Magazine *about consciousness-raising groups, some friends and I start our own. At our first meeting, we are amazed by our commonalities. In particular, we talk about how we don't want to be like our mothers, who, we feel did not know what they wanted. What do we want? The specifics are not clear but the aim is to take charge of our own lives. It is nothing less than a fantasy of total control: not only having what we want, but on our own terms and our timetable. The point of the group as we see it is to help each other bring this about, not to be victims.*

*What does this mean for graduate school? In graduate school, where the men are the teachers and the women the students, it's harder to say when things begin (certainly not in courses); it's more about things coming together—personally. One day, the man who was to be the second reader of my dissertation, an eighteenth-century specialist and a man in his sixties, takes me aside to issue a dire warning: "Don't try to be another Kate Millett"—*Sexual Politics *was originally a Columbia English department Ph.D. thesis—"she wasn't first rate to begin with." This man, who had co-edited a popular anthology on the Enlightenment, taught a course on eighteenth-century French literature (from the anthology) in which, to see whether we* *had done the reading, he would pull questions out of a hat and match them with some hapless student. This had something to do with why I didn't want him as my advisor. But he did tell great stories: in fact, the account he gave of Julie de L'Espinasse's life, the way a real woman (and a great letter writer) "died of love," sealed my fate: Of course I was going to "be" in the eighteenth century.*

*In June 1972, fortified by our ongoing weekly discussions in the group, I take the plunge. I'm going to get serious about my work: write the dissertation. I buy an electric typewriter, second-hand filing cabinets on 23d Street, and a door that when placed on top of them makes a desk. I also declare my thesis topic: "Gender and Genre: An Analysis of Literary Femininity in the French and English 18th-century Novel." In those days in the Columbia French department this is called a stylistic structural analysis. I am going to analyze nine novels according to the principles of narratology and rhetoric: Propp and Greimas, Riffaterre and Genette, Barthes and Kristeva. I am going to do this, I say, as a feminist.*

*I had become a feminist and a structuralist together. That's a little condensed: this happened at the same time, but on separate tracks. Feminism, for me meant the group, Ms. Magazine, feminist fiction, and a whole set of what today we might more portentously call cultural practices. It meant a revolution in relationships—between women, between women and men—and one's perception of the real—in material and symbolic terms, even if we didn't talk that way. Feminism had to do with our lives. And yet despite pockets of local activity—the annual Barnard "Scholar and Feminist" conference, the occasional undergraduate offering—the academic institution was impervious to the dramatic changes occurring in social relations wrought by the events of '68 and by feminism. Affirmative action began officially in 1972, but its immediate effects were almost invisible; the tiny number of tenured women at Columbia remains virtually unchanged since the early seventies.*

*In 1972, as I remember things, the phrase "feminist criticism" was not yet an acknowledged working category, at least not on the fifth floor of Philosophy Hall where formalism reigned supreme. There was literary theory (what the good people did) and there was feminism (Kate Millett, English departments). I liked to think that feminism and criticism worked together. After all, I used to argue, both are modes of critique: the one of the ideology that regulates the relations between men and women in culture and society; the other, of its own blinding assumptions about literature and art. It's hard to see now, but in the early seventies structuralism, as it was understood in American universities, like feminism seemed to mean a break with a reactionary past: men's club style. (In 1972 the name of the Men's Faculty Club, noted for its elegant Ladies' Lounge—the wives had to go somewhere, after all—was changed to the Faculty House.) For us, as beleaguered but ambitious graduate students, this "science of literature" was exciting; it provided a new language and a dream of transparency to sustain us in what we saw as a long struggle against "them." I can still remember the moment when, in a study group, I understood Saussure's model of the sign: never again would I confuse the word and the thing; literature and the world; sign and referent; signified and signifier (little knowing that Lacan had already turned this upside down, not to mention Derrida). This epiphany about the processes of signification was on a par only with the thrill of discovering binary oppositions and how they organize symbolic and social universes. Lévi-Strauss delivered the truth of this fact in person in the Barnard College gym in 1972 (post-structuralism, with a whole new set of emphases, had already unsettled structuralism in France, but colonials necessarily live according to belated cadences). What I mainly remember from this event was the conviction (Lévi-Strauss's, then rapidly mine) that binary oppositions were embedded functionally in the brain. For me, it all went together perfectly with Beauvoir's magisterial analyses of the polarizing operations that opposed man as Same to woman as Other (Beauvoir herself, of course, relies heavily on Lévi-Strauss's paradigms), and even, since everything made sense in these vast systems, with the lowly housewife's "click" (the sign that she had deciphered the codes of domestic oppression) that Jane O'Reilly dissected famously in Ms. Whatever the cultural material, structuralist models of analysis rescued you from the murk of ambiguity (not to say personal confusion) and privileged authority (the variously tweeded "we's" of a fifties legacy), and feminism showed you what to make of what you found. Between the capacious categories of narratology and the stringent lines of feminist hermeneutics, there was no text the new "we" couldn't crack. It was a heady moment.*

Is it true that there was no problem in articulating feminism and structuralism together? Yes and no. It's probably that combination of enthusiasms that British reviewers of the book my thesis finally became—The Heroine's Text (1980)—found so deadly: structuralist jargon and feminist ideology. I kept seeing the same story everywhere, they complained. Well, yes, that's the whole point (which American academics—at least the feminist ones—generally got): heroines either die (it's true that Madame de Merteuil survives, but she's exiled and hideously disfigured) or marry (sometimes both, like Rousseau's Julie). The objections to my language (I called these endings "dysphoric" and "euphoric") and approach (plot summary, as the unkinder put it) bothered me less (even if they were insulting and sort of true) than a certain feminist refusal of the project for "ideological" reasons. There were those who felt that all formalism was male, hence incompatible with feminist analysis, and that the task of feminism was to respond to the issues of "real" women. In that sense I was indeed guilty as charged. Women were strikingly absent from my dissertation. When I chose the expression "literary femininity" I meant it to mark my distance from anything real and to sound theoretically advanced (to ward off the ambient disdain that "working on women" generated): women in fiction, but with an emphasis on narrative; female destiny, with an emphasis on plot. This was my way of showing (again) my difference both from Kate Millett, the incarnation of "strident" feminism, and from the mode of "images of women" that had already begun to emerge in English studies. Any historical considerations were necessarily foreclosed. On the one hand, the historical seemed like an antiquated belief in the referent, on the other, the invocation of the historical as the truth value of literature, the dominant mode of eighteenth-century studies, was the very thing I wanted most to escape from and oppose.

In 1972 my corpus, as we then called it, was made up entirely of respected male authors, major figures (with the exception of the bad boys Sade and Cleland, forgiven because of outrageousness and sex), and famous books. It was the canon, although the term wasn't current at that point. And women authors? The entire time I was a graduate student, during lectures, reading for seminars, for the thesis, I never once asked myself the question of female authorship, despite the fact that I must have read some women writers for course work *or exams: Marie de France, Louise Labé, Marie-Madeleine de Lafayette, Germaine de Staël (the last two known then of course as Mme de . . . ). Besides, by the time I started writing my dissertation, the Author (male) w̄as Dead, intentions a fallacy, and all I cared about was The Text. I blamed—if I blamed—texts for the representations of women, not authors. And not even texts: texts were prisoners of ideology just as men were prisoners of sex.*

*After my thesis defense, it was reported to me that the sole woman on the jury (one of Columbia's classic tokens) had praised me for "sitting on my feelings." I've never been absolutely sure what that meant: that I was tautologically angry because feminist, but my writing was cool and "scientific"? Or that through the elaborate veils of my narratological tables she could tell I really cared. About what? About the logic of "female plot" that killed off heroines—exquisite cadavers as I called them in my first article—at the story's close?*

*What I really cared about then, I think, had as much to do with my own fate as with the fictional destiny of women in the eighteenth-century novel. At stake—if buried—in the ponderous prose of my structuralist feminism was the story of my plot: my own "coming to writing"—"as a woman"—to invoke the language of a feminist literary criticism that was to flower after the mid-seventies. Despite the hierarchies and abuses of academic conventions, I saw writing a dissertation as something radical, but also literary: as becoming the heroine of my life. Despite the so-called feminization of the profession, my getting a Ph.D. in the early seventies felt like a violation of gender expectations. In 1961, having gathered my ideas about appropriate intellectual and domestic arrangements in the America of the late fifties, it seemed natural for my college boyfriend to get a doctorate (even if that was hardly his—nor indeed our generation's idea of creative accomplishment); I was slated to get an M.A. and teach high school French, unless, of course—my mother's fifties fantasy for me—I married very well and got to be a woman of leisure who spoke French only in Europe. When, a decade later, I started writing and saw the pages pile up on my desk—a lot of the time spent at my desk involved admiring the height of the chapters—it seemed miraculous: as though someone else were responsible for producing the work. The man I lived with at the time, who had mixed emotions about my passion for the enterprise, did a drawing of me sitting with my hands*

*thrown up in the air, as if in astonishment, watching the pages—pro-*
*duced by my cat pounding away at the typewriter—fly upward with a*
*life of their own. But when my typist met me with the final version of*
*the manuscript, I burst into uncontrollable tears on Broadway at*
*116th Street: I suppose that's part of what I was "sitting on" during*
*the defense . . . .*

## 1978–1989

*By the fall of 1978, when, after having taught my first course—a*
*graduate seminar—on (French) women authors, I wrote "Emphasis*
*Added" (the second of my essays on women's writing), I had both*
*regressed to and returned from the Portuguese nun. I had fully lived*
*out Simone de Beauvoir's analysis of the* grande amoureuse—*the*
*woman hopelessly and desperately in love—and changed literatures. I*
*wrote this essay, which takes its examples from Lafayette's* La
Princesse de Clèves *and Eliot's* The Mill on the Floss, *in total soli-*
*tude, in the aftermath of a story with a Frenchman that had turned*
*out badly (let's just say that I had renunciation thrust upon me).*
*When I discovered—by teaching the letters in a course on women*
*writers—that the Portuguese nun was really a man (a literary hack)*
*in drag, I was more embarrassed at my ignorance, I think, than dis-*
*appointed. Besides, I didn't need her anymore: I didn't need to be in*
*love to write. That was half of the story; the other half was falling in*
*love with the Princess of Clèves: the heroine and the novel.*

*When I say that I fell in love I mean both that this book swept me*
*away and that it took me somewhere. Working on "Emphasis*
*Added" six years after starting to write my dissertation was like a*
*second coming to writing. The dissertation was still sitting on my*
*desk waiting to be revised, transformed (one hoped) into the tenure*
*book. It seemed to me that I needed to do another kind of writing in*
*order to talk about women writers; but the old task demanded its due*
*and the two projects were at odds with each other. As it turned out, it*
*was writing the new essay that allowed me to finish the old book, to*
*finish off a certain past with the flourish of an epilogue. Those few*
*pages are the only part of that book I can still bear to read.*

*I wrote the epilogue to* The Heroine's Text *in a single sitting, in*
*rage against an anonymous and extremely hostile (female) reader's*

*report. I wish—or I think I wish—I still had a copy of the report. As I recollect it, the reader complained—among other things—that I didn't seem to realize that the novels I analyzed were written by men. This felt at the time an outrageous objection to make to me, of all people! Still, I had to ponder the remark and it led me to make the point explicitly at the close of the book: that these novels were written by men for men through the double fiction of the female reader and her heroine. It also led me to think about my complete failure to consider what difference women's fictions would have made to my argument about the limited arrangements of closure that I called the heroine's text. That was a point less easily fixed. It seems to me now that a lot of the energy that fueled my writing after the epilogue came from a desire for reparation: how could I not have taken female authorship into account from the beginning?*

The answer to that question is autobiographical, but not uniquely mine. We read as we are taught to read—generationally, and within the history of our sexualities. Judith Okely, in her book on Simone de Beauvoir, describes her encounter with Laclos's novel in 1960 when she was a foreign student in Paris, *before* having read Beauvoir:

> Eventually I stopped "going out with men." In those days the anatomical rules for "nice girls" separating "petting" from penetration seemed so ridiculous that I chose abstinence. One man had presumed I was "experienced" when I had accepted his invitation to stay at his place after my hostel closed. He'd told me there were two beds. So extreme was my ignorance of the mechanics of sexual intercourse that for a while I was convinced that he'd "taken" my virginity in my sleep! Such naivety was not unusual for girls of my era. Over breakfast he made me read aloud the seduction scene from Laclos's *Les Liaisons dangereuses*. . . . Since an English girl in Paris was regarded as exotic and amoral, there were ample opportunities to lose one's ignorance. Moreover, there was not the public vocabulary to label for ourselves the treatment we received as sex objects.[37]

Okely makes no further comment on her exposure to the *Liaisons*. (Had she already read Laclos's novel? Did she go on to read it?) She instead continues the narrative of her dilemmas as an "eighteen-year-old virgin of 1960 who had not yet read de Beauvoir."[38] And she looks back with dismay at the path that tempted her, "self-immolation" to a great artist: "The masochistic self-sacrifice which intoxicated the bourgeois girl of that era was all too well documented in *The Second Sex*."[39] We knew what we didn't want from the fifties; it was harder, on the cusp of the sixties, to imagine what the decade's social upheaval would mean for our lives *as women*.

In a brilliant essay on the relative powers Merteuil and Valmont exercise in Laclos's novel, "Valmont—or the Marquise Unmasked," Marina Warner (a few years younger than Okely and I are) comments in a parenthesis on her reaction to reading the novel as an adolescent:

> The tyranny Mme de Merteuil exercises over Valmont can be thrilling to women, as much as Don Giovanni's boldness. (At the age of sixteen or seventeen, when I first read the novel, I too wanted that kind of power, in kind and degree.) But one has to take care with this type of lure: a fantasy of control will always seduce the disenfranchised.[40]

The *Liaisons,* as I wrote in my twenty-one-year old (no longer a virgin, but barely) categories of 1962, offers images of women all of which turn out to be fatal to the women who embrace them. I solved the dilemma of identification—which of these women could I possibly be?—by trying them all on: the American girl, alone, like Cécile, in a room with a strange man, and not sure what to do; the seductive marquise who could play at being the characters *she* read about in novels; the passionate Présidente who immolated herself to the happiness of a man who had figured out how to turn her on. None of them of course worked for long: I rapidly outgrew Cécile's naiveté; I wasn't cynical enough to not get caught in my own power games; I didn't manage to die of love. Nonetheless, I kept trying for a long time—even after reading Beauvoir, who of course turned out to be more complicated sexually than anyone dreamed in the 1960s—and failing to discover any form of power or autonomy.

Had I had read Lafayette, or Beauvoir, before reading Laclos, would it have made a difference? The *Liaisons* was in many ways the novel of the sixties, as *La Princesse de Clèves* was the novel of the seventies; for me, but also for a whole generation of critics. In the "Brief Word" Roger Vadim tacked on to his *Liaisons dangereuses*

*1960,* he emphasizes the movie's contemporaneity: its relation to the emergent "new species of liberated young girl." Walking toward the viewer, an overcoat thrown over his shoulders, smoking a cigarette, Vadim comments, in heavily accented English, on the mimetic, yet fictional quality of his movie. Like the publisher of the novel, the director needs to deal with the relation between representation and social reality as a way of forestalling censorship. Nonetheless, the movie created a terrific brouhaha. Produced in 1959, it wasn't released until the following year when a big court battle determined the director's right to his vision. Defended by François Mitterand, then a young lawyer associated with "left" causes, Vadim was vindicated on the grounds of artistic freedom; it's not clear that the defense of the film had anything to do with Juliette de Merteuil's right to sexual liberation.[41] After all, like Laclos, Vadim found it necessary to disfigure his heroine, thus marking out symbolically and visually the boundaries of female entitlement.

In the more recent film versions of the novel, Stephen Frears's 1988 *Dangerous Liaisons* and Milos Forman's 1989 adaptation, *Valmont,* Merteuil loses face but her beauty is left untouched. When Glenn Close takes off her makeup in the final scene, she's still gorgeous. But what this says about how to read *Les Liaisons dangereuses* today in our own *fin de siècle* is not entirely clear. As Marina Warner observes, ". . . it is a tenet of the new, mythologized female sexuality that even the coolest, blandest, and most cerebral of women can be possessed of insatiable desires which will impel them to stop at nothing in their hunger for gratification. Hence the casting of Glenn Close in the 1980s; in the late 1950s, the choice fell on the convincingly night-prowling Jeanne Moreau."[42] Frear's Merteuil survives, but like the Mother she evokes, she is framed and blamed.[43]

Like Christopher Hampton's play, which emphasized the continuities between Laclos's "eighties" and our own, both movies in their different ways (though *Valmont* is significantly more cheerful) point to the hopelessness of the gender wars, to the intractable plots of sexual difference that we—in our dominant cultural myths and representations—cannot seem to keep ourselves from rehearsing: compulsive heterosexuality.

How should we understand the erotic anxieties behind this culture's national devotion to sexual self-display?

## IV. Dressing

> By her tender silence, the Marquise authorized all my actions; final-
> ly, touching her everywhere and wherever I wanted, and seeing that
> no obstacles were opposed to my desire, I threw myself on her with
> such insistence that I obtained the last favor with my sword still at
> my side and my hat under my arm.
> —Duclos, *Les Confessions du Comte de* * * *

Stephen Frears's *Dangerous Liaisons* closes, but also opens, with
Merteuil looking at herself in the mirror. At the beginning of the film,
during the credit run, the camera moves away from the detail of her
beautiful, mobile face to shots cross-cutting her dressing with the
morning ablutions (aided by six servants) performed—or endured—
by her male counterpart, Valmont. They are equally fabricated and
made up. In fact, the last stage of Valmont's self-construction emphasizes, even more than Merteuil's ultimately more familiar feminine
cosmetology, the artifice necessary to the aristocratic ideal: he holds
the cone mask over his face while a servant blows powder on his hair.
When he lowers the cone, we have our first glimpse of his gaze and
direct experience of its effects: the face of masculine privilege.

But this symmetry between the man and the woman, members of
the same class, believers in the same codes, proves to be unstable, as
it necessarily will in modern heterosexual culture. (As Vadim put it in
his "Brief Word," a man who has many mistresses is a Don Juan, a
woman with many lovers is, in his words, "a trollop.") Though as
I've said, the ending of Frears's film resists the gesture of disfiguration
(Merteuil gets to keep her literal face while losing her figural one), it
reinforces nonetheless the violent gender discrimination at the end,
which is also to say the center, of Laclos's novel.

At the end of the duel in the snow—perhaps a wink at Vadim's
winter sports location—when Valmont, dying, turns over the packet
of blood-stained letters to Danceny, it is in part to set the record
straight and to seek revenge. It is as, if not more important to close
ranks between men against the woman who beat them—in epistolary
genius—at their own game, only to defeat herself. "Be careful of the
Marquise de Merteuil," Valmont manages to say, "in this affair we
are both her creatures." Although images of Tourvel in his arms flash
across Valmont's consciousness as he duels his life away, and

although his last words are "for her," it's essential to remember to whom they are spoken, and what behavior they follow.

Missing from all three films—although strictly speaking he is named and plays a bit part in Vadim's—is Prévan. But his importance to understanding the gender arrangements that structure the closure of the *Liaisons* is central. Mme de Volanges makes the point clearly in letter CLXXIII to Madame de Rosemonde.[44] After describing the way in which Merteuil is booed at the Comédie Italienne, an episode of public reprobation whose spirit is rendered poignantly by Frears, she goes on to narrate the appearance of Prévan on the scene:

> For there to be nothing lacking to her humiliation, her ill luck would have it that M. de Prévan, who had showed himself nowhere since his adventure, entered the small drawing room at that moment. As soon as he was observed everyone, men and women, surrounded and applauded him; and he was carried, as it were, before Madame de Merteuil by the public who made a circle around them. . . . This situation, so ignominious for her, lasted until her carriage was announced; and at her departure the scandalous hootings were redoubled. It is dreadful to be a relative of this woman. That same evening M. de Prévan was welcomed by all the officers of his corps who were present and no one doubts that he will soon regain his post and his rank. (*LD*, CLXXIII)

The fact that the restitution of Prévan, whose reputation Valmont vainly warned her about, takes place precisely in Merteuil's face, is further corroboration, if it were needed, of the way in which gender asymmetry functions in *ancien régime* fiction. Prévan's practice of unsafe sex proves not only to be collectively applauded and socially sanctioned but a form of gender consolidation: the officers of Prévan's corps identify with him, whereas Merteuil's cousin can't bear to be related to her.

In this sense, I think, it's the pairing of Merteuil and Prévan as mirror images of each other rather than the Merteuil/Valmont couple that provides the clearest model of the stakes of sexual difference. In an earlier letter, we recall, Mme de Volanges had singled out the two letters that the public found particularly shocking (*LD*, CLVII); one was the autobiographical letter (*LD*, LXXXI), the other, her narrative of the deception wrought on Prévan (*LD*, LXXXV). (In case we

miss the point, the publisher footnotes the numbers of the missing letters.) Volanges claims that she can't see how the letter about Prévan
could possibly be true—i.e., how or why Merteuil would have played
such a dangerous game (thus agreeing with Valmont); it doesn't
strike her as plausible. The two letters are further commented on by
Danceny when he writes to Mme de Rosemonde, explaining what he
thinks she ought to make of the letters he is putting in her hands (LD,
CLXIX). He takes on himself, without consulting her, the necessity of
publishing those two letters, leaving her with the copies. Taken
together those two letters supply a condensed account of the workings of male aristocratic privilege in eighteenth-century French fiction
and its foundational resistance to any sort of "feminist" challenge.
No wonder Riccoboni picked up her pen to protest, and Laclos's
friend Duchasteller picked up his to comment: "One has never seen a
man complain that his sex was being done a wrong or an injury; now
one can't say anything bad about a woman, real or imaginary, without all the others sounding the alarm" (LD, 901).

## V. Talking Sexes

"May you one day prove that you love me!"
    With these words she lowered her eyes, as if she were ashamed of
having said so much. . . . I urged her tenderly to look at me: she did
so. We gazed at each other.
                    —Crébillon fils, *Les Egarements du coeur et de l'esprit**

Professional lovers generally avoid breaking completely with the
women who are no longer loved. One takes on new ones, and one
tries to keep the former ones, but most of all one must remember to
add to the list.
                    —Duclos, *Les Confessions du Comte de****

What of the *Liaisons* in the nineties? In Hampton's play, Merteuil
imagines pleasure as usual in the new decade: "I dare say we would
not be wrong to look forward to whatever the nineties may bring.

---

*Translation by Barbara Bray. *The Wayward Head and Heart* (New York: Oxford
University Press, 1963).

Meanwhile, I suggest our best course is to continue with the game."[45] The guillotine and the various unfoldings of the Revolution put an end to these specific games of *ancien régime* sex; Merteuil would not have made it into those nineties intact. Is anyone still playing today?

In a poll entitled "Sexy pas sexy!?" that appeared in a popular mainstream magazine called *Actuel,* readers were asked to rank films, books, songs, politicians, and the like, according to their sexiness.[46] The *Liaisons* ranked first (the list included all of Baudelaire, Henry Miller, Sade, George Sand's *Lettre à Musset,* etc.). For French readers, it seems, the evocative power of Laclos's novel remains strong as a literary and social reference; it embodies the legacy of a certain eighteenth-century language in which the codified relations between the sexes stand in—stylishly—for human interaction and psychology. We could say that *ancien régime* libertinage functions in the contemporary French imaginary as the emblem of a certain, modern national (hetero)sexuality.[47]

A best-seller in the summer of 1993, *Les Hommes et les femmes,* an exchange between Bernard-Henri Lévy, philosopher, and Françoise Giroud, writer, editor, publisher, and the woman appointed to head the Ministry on Women created in 1974, was reviewed by Catherine Clément with the title, "Les princes de Marivaux."[48] The review casts Giroud and Lévy as two "experienced seducers": the Marquise and the Vicomte. Clément, clearly taken with the book and its project, underlines its crucial point of agreement between the two interlocutors: "sexual liberation is over, broken off because of AIDS, and French society falls back on 'the solid values of feeling.'"[49] Post-feminist, post-Marxist, and even post-Sollers, Clément picks up on their nostalgia; her own shows her the way. Meanwhile, Lévy and Giroud worry—differently—about the new puritanism among the young.[50] Could it happen in France? If it does, it will be blamed (it already has been) on the Americans, and their attachment to what the French call *in French,* the "politically correct."

In 1993 these matters were taken to heart in a spate of commentary in the United States on the elaboration of a code to guide sexual encounters between students at Antioch College. This response to the problem of date rape on campus was analyzed with predictable bad faith in the *Comment* section of the *New Yorker.*[51] To the question of who will benefit from the new rules, comes the answer: "Jaded male libertines. For by not merely recommending but actually mandating chatter during foreplay, the Antioch rules are perfect for men whose preferred method of seduction is to sweet-talk women into compliance. The rules don't get rid of the problem of unwanted sex at all; they just shift the advantage from the muscle-bound frat boy to the honey-tongued French major."[52] (This analysis may be just what's needed to reverse the trend of declining enrollments in French in the nineties.) The piece ends with a plea for tolerance and remarks about how "new ideas about dignity and autonomy and style require new approaches to sexual relations."[53] But the new here seems remarkably dependent on very old models: notably, the invocation, however jokily, of the "jaded male libertine" and strategies of seduction. As Eric Fassin perceptively remarks in an *Op-Ed* column in the *New York Times:* "What the consensus against the Antioch rules betrays is a common vision of sexuality," that has its origins in a "conventional situation, perceived and presented as natural: a heterosexual encounter with the man as the initiator, and the woman as gatekeeper. . . . "[54] These conventions underwrite the ideological frames of the eighteenth-century novel, even though libertine heroines convert their defense against incursion into seduction strategies of their own.[55]

What kind of "new ideas about dignity and autonomy and style" might the objects of the classic libertine seduction have in mind today in Ohio, or even in New York or Paris?[56] And what literary models might she have in eighteenth-century novels? Fassin's vision of social change in which "women may express demands, and not only grant favors"[57] sounds remarkably like Fanni Butlerd's announcement cited earlier: "I did not give in: a moment of delirium did not throw me into his arms; I gave myself: my favors are the fruit of love, the prize of love." As it turns out, however, the expression and fulfillment of sexual wishes do not necessarily change the conventions of the heterosexual plot which underpin the social order. Riccoboni's novels stage the imaginative expression of women's sexual demands; they also demonstrate the prerogative of "jaded male libertines" (are there any other kind?) to recontain that sexuality within power arrangements harmful to women. Heroines protest but the system remains intact.

## VI. Redressing

Mme de Lafayette was always my mistress and my guide; the honor
of approaching her, following her, even at some distance, is the
praise I would like to deserve, and that would be a flattering reward
for my feeble attempts.
—Mme Riccoboni, Letter to the *Mercure de France* (1768)

Before Madame Riccoboni began writing, the novels of Abbé
Prévost enjoyed a great reputation; but those of Madame Riccoboni
made the reading of those novels impossible, and no work in this
genre will cause *Lettres de Milady Catesby, Ernestine, Jenny,
Amélie,* etc. to be forgotten. Who could compare the tragic adventures of an *Homme de qualité,* the heavy and diffuse *Cleveland,* and
even the boring *Doyen de Killerine* with these charming works?
—Mme de Genlis, *De L'Influence des Femmes
sur la littérature française* (1826)

If libertine novels (generally memoirs) are famously involved with
sequence, the repetition of stylized events—choose, pursue, seduce,
break—that must be enacted in order, novels of sensibility (generally
epistolary) dwell on consequence: the emotional, social, and physical
effects of seduction. The painters of the eighteenth century delight in
representing these unhappy outcomes. Greuze's nubile girls weep
over dead birds, droop over shattered mirrors; whole families fret
over broken eggs.[58] Letters are returned; sorrow repays pleasure in
spades. Fragonard's decorative panel, "Abandonment," seats the
heroine at the foot of a long column: the picture of despair, her hand
resting listlessly in her lap, she gazes mournfully into the distance;
while above her, at the the top of the column, Cupid points: "He
went thataway." Men suffer too, of course. The male mourners—Des
Grieux, Comminge, Saint-Preux—shed tears over the women they
have loved and lost, sometimes twice. (Even Valmont, depending on
which movie version you watch, ends up suffering when he discovers
that he went too far.) They get left for good.

In addition to getting left, girls and women sometimes get pregnant. Aside from Julie's first pregnancy, which she hopes will force
her father to let her marry Saint-Preux, finding yourself pregnant is
not often good news. (And, of course, Rousseau's good girl miscar-

ries along with the plot of rebellion.) Arguably, the most violent instance of unwanted pregnancy is to be found in Lafayette's *nouvelle historique, La Comtesse de Tende,* published posthumously in 1724. The Countess finds herself pregnant by her lover. When he dies nobly in battle, she tells her husband, who is aggrieved despite not having treated her well during their marriage. She gives birth prematurely and the baby dies. Shortly after the death of her infant son, the Countess expires with a sense of extraordinary joy. Her husband, we learn, received this news with joy himself. From the Countess's point of view, but also from her husband's, this is the best possible outcome. The Count never remarries. It's hard to imagine a more condensed and eloquent account of consequence.

The presumably wanted pregnancy in Isabelle de Charrière's *Lettres de Mistress Henley* (a short novel published in 1784) also provides a dramatic ending to domestic drama. The story ends before Mistress Henley gives birth, but the prognosis is grim. Now that she is well into her pregnancy and exhausted, she explains to her friend (and publisher), her letters will cease, and she will either have become "reasonable" (become what her husband wants her to be) and "contented," or she will no longer be. In the peculiar sequel (not authored by Charrière but sometimes thought to be at the time) called *La Justification,* the second Mistress Henley dies in childbirth. A contemporary reviewer found this a bit overdone as a way of providing a denouement to the drama of marital incompatibility: "That's certainly taking things tragically."[59] Given the bitterness of what has come before in Charrière's bleak domestic fable, I don't think it is such a bad solution.

Mr. Henley's reaction to Mrs. Henley's pregnancy (*he* will decide whether or not she should nurse[60]) proves to be the last straw in the couple's—Mr. Right's and Mrs. Wrong's—disintegrating marriage. However we choose to read Charrière's vision of women's possible fulfillment in marriage generally, there's no mistaking the failure of this one. When the heroine affirms in a letter to her friend, "I think many women are in my situation,"[61] it seems fair to take this as a feminist protest against domestic arrangements across the board.[62] We should also remember Charrière's enlistment of La Fontaine's own fable of conjugal dissatisfaction in her epigraph: "I've seen no happy marriages." But meanwhile, can this marriage be saved? Would having a child rescue its partners from their war? (Mr. Henley has a little girl from a previous marriage, whose education Mrs. Henley tries to take on, but this too fails to produce an emotional connection: "No . . . , she's not my child, she's yours."[63]) There's a fleeting moment when Mrs. Henley thinks a child might bring happiness; or rather, the excitement produced by her fantasy child carries her into a future of fulfilling expectations: "Soon I thought of my son or daughter only as a prodigy of beauty, whose brilliant talents, cultivated by the most stunning education, would excite the admiration of the whole surrounding country, nay all of Europe."[64] Does it matter whether it's a boy or a girl: "My daughter, lovelier yet than Lady Bridgewater, chose a husband among the noblest in the kingdom. My son, were he to take up arms, became a hero and commanded armies: if he gave himself to law, he would be at least Lord Mansfield or chancellor; but a permanent chancellor whom the king and people could no longer do without. . . ."[65]

How should we understand this painfully conventional vision of generational bliss? The beautiful girl destined for a storybook husband, the accomplished boy whose future lies in the world. By the end of the story, of course, these hopes are dashed, since the dysphoria of the couple narrative overrides the mother-to-be's euphoric tableau. Charrière, I think, turns away from the temptations of what Michael Warner has called "repro-narrativity," the presumption of heterosexual self-replication that makes for the naturalization of family plots.[66] It's precisely the unexamined legitimacy of the family and male authority within its domestic arrangements that Charrière, as well as Lafayette, Tencin, and Graffigny before her, refuses. Now it's also true that with the exception of Rousseau the scene of children and family is not one that compels the imagination of eighteenth-century novelists, male or female.[67] So we shouldn't perhaps make too much of this one. And yet the stillborn silence of this tale's despair has to give the feminist reader pause. If a child of one's own (and rarely has a more poignant portrait of stepmothering's disappointments been sketched in fiction) is offered as the only fictionally acceptable way out of a deadlocked marriage (as opposed, say, to a real-life self-invented career as a novelist or salonnière), and that project fails to come to fruition, then what indeed could remain for a woman to live for?

Curiously, the question of the child-as-future leads us back to the annoying ending of *Juliette Catesby*. Why does Riccoboni end that novel with marriage? Why does Juliette forgive Ossery? Let me try to answer that question by another detour to Laclos's *Liaisons*. At the end of *Valmont*, Forman, whose adaptation plays most freely with the novel, has a pregnant-by-Valmont Cécile marry her boring husband, Gercourt, as she was meant to. As she walks down the aisle, she exchanges knowing looks with Mme de Rosemonde, to whom she has already announced the news and who is delighted that her nephew's progeny will live to continue his spirit. Although in real-life arrangements of aristocratic couples in *ancien régime* France this was doubtless a common enough occurrence, it is not the stuff of female-authored plots (no more than it was Laclos's, who, playing hide and seek with censorship, had Cécile miscarry and end her days in a convent, appropriately covered with shame and blame).

I'm interested in speculating about the future of the dead heroine's child, the daughter of Jenny Montfort. Let's say that this novel is not about "happily ever after," but about showing how much women don't want to marry, about how disappointing marriage inevitably is, given the current arrangements between the sexes. Friendship is better, not to mention letter-writing and flirtation; the erotic is all in foreplay. Jenny Montfort loses her virginity and gets pregnant at the same time; neither is wished for.[68] Because Ossery, despite the forgetfulness that leads him to take advantage of his best friend's sister, is a noble fellow, he has to marry her and give his daughter a legitimate destiny: "Ah, what tender feelings she would owe her father, if she ever knew at what cost he gave her his name!" (*JC*, XXXV)[69] (I like to think that because he hasn't forgotten whom he's really in love with, he also names his daughter after the woman he meant to marry.) In the novel Juliette claims that if Ossery had told her what had happened, instead of disappearing without a word, the two of them could have become friends: "Friendship," she maintains, "would have bound us together with sweet chains, so dear to noble hearts" (*JC*, XXXVI). This would have made for a more innovative plot. Juliette could have "loved his wife" and played godmother to little "Juliette." She would have retained her complete freedom, writing to Henriette, and finishing her work as *moraliste*.[70] The two women—Juliette and Jenny—would have been friends and companions.[71] Instead, Juliette ends up as a stepmother with a husband dangerously, if proleptically, inclined to Henleyisms—"Juliette Catesby is no longer" (XXXVII); even though the legitimacy of his authority is somewhat undercut by Juliette's continued correspondence.

We're left, then, with the question of a little girl's future. What will it be like for Juliette Ossery (née Catesby) (not to mention Milord Ossery) to watch little "Juliette" Ossery (Jenny Montfort's little one) grow up?[72] A daily, living reminder of the fateful forgetting. All may be forgiven, but how can all be forgotten? This has some of the flavor of the haunting of her sister's and former lover Oswald's marriage arranged by Corinne, who, we recall, teaches her niece Juliette (named after one of her great roles) to play and sing just like her. It also resonates with the mimicry of Claire's Henriette who looks uncannily like her dead aunt Julie. What will Juliette write to her friend Henriette?[73]

Reading backwards and forwards, we can see these little girls as liminal figures, miniature heroines of plots not yet written for them, ciphers of plots they, perhaps, will write themselves. Riccoboni, mid-century, toys with the conventions that do not bode well for the future of girls. Charrière, post-Revolution, smashes them; Staël, at the threshold of Romanticism, exploits them for an outrageous revenge on the part of an extraordinary heroine: reparation for having wanted what the man (whose embedded memoir, like Ossery's, tells a tale of masculine weakness) is incapable of giving her. These novels by women writers thus present problems, not solutions, swerves and negotiations, not revolutions. Their entanglement with the sexual and domestic plots already available to them provides the measure of the difficulty revising will entail. The narratives of masculine inadequacy—of husbands and lovers who don't seem to get it—demonstrate, through the device of embedded memoirs, how limited our gender stories have been for men as well as for women.

By what right do we as readers ask for more?

We've only begun to imagine more interesting futures for girls.


## VII. Readdressing, or Safer Sex

Come, Déterville, come learn from me to economize the resources of our souls and the benefits of nature. Renounce tumultuous feelings, those imperceptible destroyers of our being. Come learn to know pleasures innocent and lasting, come enjoy them with me.

You will find in my heart, in my friendship, in my feelings, all that can compensate you for the ravages of love.

—Graffigny, *Letters from a Peruvian Woman**

What do women want? What, for that matter, do men want? At the beginning of Duclos's *Les Confessions du comte de*\**, the narrator explains to a younger (male) member of his family how happy he is to be living in the country away from the agitation of the world. He explains that he has new values and new pleasures, now that he shares his solitude with "a faithful friend, who . . . in making up for everything prevents [him] from regretting anything" (*LC*, 181).[74] This friend, who has transformed his life, is announced in the masculine: "un ami." At the end of the novel, however, we will learn that this male friend is in fact a woman, Mme de Selve, who, as her name suggests, has saved him providentially from women. He explains how, like his illustrious precursor, Augustine, he finally changed his fornicating ways: Selve showed him the light. But even his feelings for her were not enough to get him to give up his bad habits:

> It wasn't reason that was to bring me back and cure me of my errors; I was to become disgusted of women by women themselves. Soon I found nothing appealing in dealing with them. . . . I couldn't find a mistress who didn't resemble one of the ones I had already had. The whole sex had become nothing more than a single woman for whom my taste was jaded [*usé*]. (*LC*, 263)

The justification given for the novel-as-list in which the professional lover goes from woman to woman is its sociological value: through women one can report on the social text. Parisian women belong to "different classes" that have "little to do with each other" (*LC*, 201). But they all have something in common: "they all have pleasure as their object" (*LC*, 201). So it's not so surprising that in the end that object erodes the differences between them. All the same. If all women are only one woman, and pleasure with her has become

---

*Translated by David Kornacker. *Letters from a Peruvian Woman* (New York: The Modern Language Association of America, 1993).

dulled, what's left for the heterosexual plot of the novel of manners? A woman who isn't a woman. A woman who is a man. Together the man and the woman live in friendship, although their friendship is consolidated by marriage. Once they marry, however, gender adjusts: "I find the whole universe with my wife who is my friend [*amie*]" (*LC*, 264). Duclos's narrative ends according to the denouement Crébillon announced in his preface to the *Egarements:* "We will see [the man] finally, in the last part, restored to himself [*rendu à lui-même*], and owing all his virtues to a good woman."[75] What is a man restored to when he is restored to himself? To an identity purged of sexual desire and free of women's bodies. To a secular solitude of self-mastery in which, presumbably, he writes a memoir for his cousin, who will in time come to understand how "a friend [*ami*] can make up for [*dédommager*] the world," and become a good in itself.

In a variant ending, which has led some critics to make the claim that Duclos's novel is feminist, the narrator cites Mme de Selve's essential difference: "Madame de Selve made me see the value [*quel prix*] a reasonable woman is."[76] He then adds some general remarks about the unfairness of blaming women for behaviors which the culture at large supports by giving women such an inadequate education. Most important, he adduces a famous comment of Ninon de Lenclos's to support his case: "'I've thought since childhood about the uneven distribution of qualities that exists between men and women. I saw that we had been granted what is most frivolous, and men had reserved for themselves the right to the essential qualities, and from that moment on, I made myself a man,' and she did it well."[77] Thus, these two exemplary fictions of libertine *Bildung* state as their goal the making of man into himself, through the love of good woman, who is really a man in drag, like a man by virtue of her reason.

Why can't a woman be more like a man? Why not skip the women altogether and just bond between men?[78] (This was the always deferred fantasy of *Manon Lescaut.*) And if this is the lesson of the libertine novel, who and what is it for? Men in these novels compete with and perform for each other's admiration: a "second seduction."[79]

The novel of male experience addresses itself to a reader like the narrator and his narratee in gender and class: The Marquis de Renoncour identifies with Des Grieux, then Des Grieux tells him his tale of woe; Duclos's Count, as we've just seen, keeps his story within the family; Versac lectures Meilcour on the "science of the world," maxims drawn from his vast experience of wordliness—what Susan Winnett calls "a how-to narrative, a tale of how to keep up the appearances in whose terms the next generation will discover for itself the same old plots"[80]; and at the end of the century, in another genre, Valmont gives Danceny the letters of his exploits (Merteuil thus doesn't get to make a memoir out of his letters after all). This knowledge is destined for a reader who has something to learn and who can do something with that knowledge. The libertine novel, Claude Reichler argues,

> . . . makes of its reader [*son lecteur*] the subject of an initiation. . . . Wanting in its own way to *instruct and please,* a libertine poetics ends up producing . . . a new imaginary investment of desire in a reader destined to pursue the fiction of a voluptuous project. Isn't this precisely the phenomenon that Rousseau designates in his condemnation of those novels that ladies, he says crudely, "read with only one hand"?[81]

We encounter here a familiar conundrum of gender and reading in discussions of the eighteenth-century novel. How does the targeted male reader whose desire and education are at the imaginative heart of these novels become Rousseau's beautiful masturbating lady?[82] The logic is puzzling. If women are, as Naomi Segal puts it, the "unintended readers" of narratives of desire "about" them, how and where do they enter these narratives?[83]

The novels are addressed to a reader who through resemblance and identification can model himself on the narrative poetics libertine fiction enacts. The male reader takes his place in the pedagogic chain described by the male critic/poetician. But it's women who—supposedly—get turned on. The fiction is persistent: Diderot's Zima, addressed on the first page of the *Bijoux,* as a potential reader of the very text we are reading by virtue of her activities as a fan of Crébillon and Duclos (*Le Sopha* and *Les Confessions* have been discovered under her pillow); and of course Merteuil got herself in the mood by Crébillon's *Sopha,* as well as Rousseau's *Héloïse,* not to mention La Fontaine. Male writers, it seems, need to conjure the titillation of fictional women readers—and female narrators—to please their audience. (It works wonders for their critics and editors.)

Meanwhile, cured of women and of desire, Duclos's Count finds friendship and happiness with his "ami." Many égarements later, Meilcour is restored to himself. Des Grieux and Tiberge, *his* "fidèle ami," hook up again in the New World and return home together to the family estate, putting the vast detour of passion behind them as they leave the perfect dead woman in the ground.[84]

In the aftermath of heterosexual initiation, what happens in comparable novels by women writers? Are they in fact comparable to the novels of the dominant tradition?

At the end of Graffigny's *Lettres d'une Péruvienne*, Zilia extends her rejected suitor Déterville an invitation to share in the pleasures of friendship. Like Duclos's Count, and in much the same language—both use the verb "dédommager" to account for the benefits to be gained by choosing friendship over love—Graffigny's Princess remembers the past and, in the future, prefers friendship to love: it lasts longer. Only here's the difference: the Count is a reformed rake, Zilia, a chaste heroine. From his solitude, Duclos delivers memoirs of a jaded masculinity; from hers, Zilia constructs a new femininity at home in the library, uninterested in "home." More conventional than Graffigny's, Duclos's ending conjoins friendship and marriage; hers separates them. Graffigny's heroine will share her solitude with her friend, not with a husband.[85] Even when marriage is offered as closure, as in the vexing case of Riccoboni's *Juliette Catesby,* female friendship recontains the marriage: the last words of the novel—"tendre amitié"—attest to the strength of the bonds between women. Friendship in the feminine is also marked out in the full title of the novel: *Lettres de Milady Juliette Catesby A Milady Henriette Campley, Son Amie.* The thread of a connection between female friendship and the exposure in public of private dissatisfaction, if tenuous in Riccoboni's novel, is taut in Charrière's. The power of women's connections to supercede the disappointments of marriage is explicit—if a fiction—in the title of Charrière's bitter tale: *Lettres de Mistress Henley, Publiées par son amie.* As publisher/editor the female friend prevents the woman from disappearing into wife, whatever the outcome of her plot.[86] Going public with these letters is a way of saying the personal is the political, epistolary style.

Midway through the last letter of *Fanni Butlerd*—the letter which appeared anonymously in the public papers as a form of advertisement for the novel to come—the heroine protests indignantly against male privilege and in the double standard that allows men to treat women differently from the way they treat each other: "Oh, who are you, men? Where do you get the right to fail to show women the respect you insist upon amongst yourselves? What law of nature, what convention in a state ever authorized this insolent distinction?" (*FB*, CXVI). Fanni thus generalizes her pain and she addresses her rage to men as a class. This apostrophe—which continues to escalate: "Ferocious monsters"—on behalf of women as a class is the mark of a rhetoric that refuses the very principles of libertine economy, an economy based on a solidarity between men.[87] "Almost all sexual discourse—from the writings of Denis Diderot to hard-core film," Linda Williams argues, "has been spoken by men to other men," and listened in on by women.[88] Riccoboni's first novel begins as a letter "A Un Seul Lecteur" (To A Single Reader). It ends by joining that reader to his gender.[89] But the fiction of her address depends on another solidarity: that of the women who participate in the performance of the heroine's identity, the readers who share the values of the fiction they have just read. The other side of the apostrophe is the voice that utters it, and that voice turns away from the familiar calculus of libertine seduction, in which each woman imagines that she will have "the sweet certainty of pleasing and retaining" her lover: "la douce certitude de vous plaire, de vous fixer" (*FB*, CXIII). Feminist discourse may play with male address; it does so, however, from the place of women. Unlike the universe of Laclos's novel in which women pride themselves on not being like other women, in Riccoboni's world heroines—however much they pride themselves on their superiority—never fail to recognize their common bonds.

Toward the end of the novel Fanni explains the repugnance she feels at her lover's proposal that she remain his mistress when he marries the socially advantaged woman he claims not to love. She begins by wondering, rather pointedly, how he can fulfill his sexual obligations without feeling. This split, she says, is technically a lot easier for women, since they can fulfill their conjugal duties without "their senses being engaged." (It's just this split that Merteuil bragged about exploiting, only to opposite ends: faking frigidity.) But could he perform without feeling, would that lessen her resistance? She returns to her initial reaction, to the horror of "sharing what one loves"; she doesn't want to "look for traces on [his] mouth of kisses another would have left there"; his caresses would leave her cold (*FB*, CXII). Thinking it over, she finds the offer offensive not only to herself but to the other woman: "By what right would I cause another woman the pain that I feel? Why would I want to distress a woman who hasn't offended me?" (*FB*, CXIII). It's this sense of solidarity *between women* that leads Fanni to go public with her private pain, not hope for an egalitarian exchange with any man.

And so it goes. Women between men. Men between women. Libertine or feminist, of manners or sentiment, eighteenth-century novels confirm over and over that men and women don't speak the same language, don't want the same things; not even, perhaps, each other. Heterosexual plot falters on disgust, or despair. Friendship is the consolation of lust and longing; writing, the remedy for rage turned inward. The only safe sex, finally, is remembered or deferred. Or one's own.

# PART TWO

# MEN'S READING, WOMEN'S WRITING

# REREADING AS A WOMAN
## *The Body in Practice*

*"Would it not stand to reason that men and women read differently, that there must be a fundamental disparity between what they bring to, do to, demand from and write about texts? And if we do read differently, is it not necessary to figure out how and where we do so? To what extent is the 'body of scholarship' on any given author really two bodies?"*

These questions, formulated by Susan Winnett as the rationale for a special session at the 1983 MLA conference called "Reading and Sexual Difference," are the pre-text and context of what follows. I have chosen to address the question of sexual difference literally (to the letter, as it will emerge), taking its terms, for the purposes of argument, as a question of identity tied to a material body circumscribed by and in the *practice* of reading and writing. The plan for the session paired a male and a female reader with a single text. Peter Brooks and I worked, though not together, not reading each other beforehand, on *Les Liaisons dangereuses;* J. Hillis Miller and Julie Rivkin, on *The Egoist* (both novels considered by some to be written by male feminists). The first part of my title picks up on the section in Jonathan Culler's *On Deconstruction,* entitled "Reading as a Woman." The second part of my title seeks to reground to strategic ends the "hypothesis of a female reader" that Culler importantly foregrounds to situate feminist criticism in the contemporary critical landscape.[1]

Feminists have no sense of humor, as Wayne Booth has shown. In a celebrated moment at a symposium organized by *Critical Inquiry* in 1981 on the "Politics of Interpretation," Wayne Booth, then President of MLA, came out as a male feminist, or at least as an admitted "academic liberal," and embraced the "feminist challenge" to *reread,* recognizing what "many feminist critics have been saying all along; our various canons have been established by men, reading books written mostly for men, with women as *eavesdroppers.*"[2] Taking Rabelais as the authorial example to illustrate his point, Booth addressed the question of ideology and aesthetic response; of sexual difference and the pleasure of the text:

> When I read, as a young man, the account of how Panurge got his revenge on the Lady of Paris [as you recall, he punishes the lady for turning him down by sprinkling her gown with the pulverized genitals of a bitch in heat; he then withdraws to watch gleefully the spectacle of the assembled male dogs of Paris pissing on her from head to toe] I was transported with delighted laughter; and when I later read Rabelais aloud to my young wife, as she did the ironing(!), she could easily tell that I expected her to be as fully transported as I was. Of course she did find a lot of it funny; a great deal of it *is* very funny. But now, reading passages like that, when everything I know about the work as a whole suggests that my earlier response was closer to the spirit of the work itself, I draw back and start thinking rather than laughing, taking a different kind of pleasure with a *somewhat* diminished text.[3]

Booth's account of his conversion experience is of course important and gratifying for a feminist critic;[4] but what I want to take off from here is not so much his self-conscious reading *as a man,* as his staging, within the scene of his own discourse of a woman's point of view, his placing of a "voice," however muted, that he finds absent from Rabelais's, and Bakhtin's, dialogics.[5] Mr. Booth does not tell us how he knew which parts his wife did not find funny, or why. But let us guess that listening to this story from a book "written mostly for men," Mrs. Booth felt a bit like an eavesdropper, like a reluctant voyeur called upon to witness a scene of male bonding (a man and his

46

best friends) which excluded her. Or perhaps, as a woman (reader), she put herself, for a moment, in the Lady's place.

To reread as a woman is at least to imagine the lady's place—to imagine while reading the place of a woman's body; to read reminded that her identity is also re-membered in stories of the body.

Like the young Mrs. Booth, the ironing notwithstanding, I too can easily tell when I am supposed to find something funny. I can tell, read to or reading, when I am expected to be transported, as "fully transported" as those we might think of as the *dominant responders* (or "dr's")—one's husband, one's teachers, the critics; though clearly I am not nearly so good a sport. So let us now turn to a less "carnivalesque" but equally witty example of the canon; to the epistolary novel of the Enlightenment in which every reader is perforce an eavesdropper, or rather a voyeur reduced to the scopic delights that may be derived from reading someone else's mail.

In letter XLVII of *Les Liaisons dangereuses* the Vicomte de Valmont explains to his correspondent, Mme de Merteuil, that while making love to Emilie, a courtesan, he writes a passionate love letter to Mme de Tourvel—the woman in the novel he is trying to seduce—literally, or so he would have the Marquise believe, on Emilie.[6] Writing vividly "to the moment," Valmont codes his "undressed" physical exertions in the rhetoric of "dressed" amorous discourse:[7] "I have scarcely enough command of myself to put my ideas in order. I foresee already that I shall not be able to finish this letter without breaking off," etc. Double meanings follow upon each other like a rigorously expanding metaphor; and the foreseen interruption of the inscription occupies (neatly) the blank space between paragraphs. The performance over, Valmont forwards the letter—XLVIII in the volume—to Merteuil, leaving it open for her to read, seal, and mail (he wants, he says, to have it postmarked from Paris). Emilie, the woman as desk, and the first reader of the love letter, Valmont recounts, "a ri comme une folle"; she "split her sides laughing." "I hope you will laugh too," Valmont adds, by way of preparing Merteuil's response to his text and its context: his one-man show.

Readers, on the whole, have responded to the optative and been amused. In an essay entitled, "The Witticisms of M. de Valmont," Georges May observes:

Doubtless many readers will find this instance of Valmont's sense of humor particularly intolerable, and will rebel at this display of poor taste. To them this long series of double meanings will not endear the Vicomte, nor make him in any way more charming. But *willy-nilly*, as they read this letter, *they will become a party in his conspiracy*, for the simple reason that they will understand the hidden though transparent meaning of the letter, to which the addressee, Mme de Tourvel, cannot but remain blind. Moreover, these morally inclined readers who, to be sure, will condemn Valmont on elementary grounds of decency, *will also have to appreciate*, on a *strictly intellectual or even perhaps esthetic level*, Valmont's remarkable though devilish intelligence and his enviable mastery of stylistic devices.[8]

This model of double reading, which opposes the "morally inclined" to the "strictly intellectual or even perhaps esthetic," and valorizes the victory of the latter, since it implies a narcissistic alliance between two hegemonic modes ("enviable mastery"), describes very nicely the plight of the feminist critic of whom it is regularly said, as Booth imagines it will be said of him: "I've lost my sense of humor or I don't know how to read 'aesthetically.'"[9]

In a more recent work on Laclos, the double reading becomes triple and the aesthetic grounds, hermeneutic. Glossing letter XLVIII and in particular the coding of the *scriptus interruptus*—"I must leave you for a moment to calm an excitement which mounts with every moment, and which is fast becoming more than I can control"—Ronald Rosbottom concludes: "This is a blatant example of *double entendre*, amusing and well done; it demands a rereading, and maybe even a third reading, at first to laugh, and then to wonder."[10]

The third reading then wonders about the transmission of information in the novel, the ways in which the novel insists upon "the process of signifying," and takes as its subject, "how things mean."[11] But it might also wonder whether it is really the perception of the double register in itself—"the very table on which I write, never before put to such a use, has become in my eyes an altar consecrated to love"—that compels complicity. It seems, rather, that the appeal of the letter derives from a masculine identificatory admiration for Valmont's ability to do (these particular) two things at once. This is of course not to deny that to conjoin in representation activities not normally conjoined is textually arresting: like that of Aesop's master, who, to save time, pissed as he walked, as Montaigne relates in "Of Experience"; or *a contrario,* Gerry Ford, of whom it was said, in the cleaned-up version, that he could not walk down the street and chew gum at the same time. But I do want to insist (at the same time) on both the specific referents of Valmont's conjunction, and the sexualization that privileges the letter writer over the letter reader, conflating, predictably, virility and authority.[12]

Let us move now from the ways in which sexual difference can be said to structure the scene of production, the actual production of reading material, to the scene of reception, the reading of the letter, and the glossing of its text.

We should recall that the dominant trope of the act of novel-reading in the eighteenth century is the figure, or allegory, perhaps even the fact, of the *lectrice,* the woman reader reading. *Les Liaisons dangereuses* provides us both with the standard model, Mme de Tourvel—the beleaguered heroine in a story she does not understand, reading, as fortification against the plotting hero, volume two of *Christian Thought* and volume one of *Clarissa;* and the model ironized, Mme de Merteuil. The super woman reader who would be (male) author (early in the novel she proposes to write Valmont's memoirs in his place), the marquise instead rereads from Crébillon, Rousseau, and La Fontaine to prepare for her part in the fiction she embodies but cannot represent in letters; or rather, which she at the end represents as truth at the cost of disfiguration.

The tropology of the woman reader reading is also evoked in the novel's frame when the Editor rehearses his "anxiety of authorship" with a particular emphasis on the reception of the work by a female readership.[13] Despite the ironic tone, the Editor's expression of anxiety here, may, I think, usefully be construed as an anxiety for female authorization which in turn veils Laclos's desire for recognition *by men* of his status as (stand-in for) a penetrating writer; a social theorist rewriting Rousseau. Thus in his prefatory moves, the Editor invokes the sanction of a "real" woman reader: a good mother, who, having read the correspondence in manuscript, declares her intention (in direct quotes) to give her daughter the book on her wedding day. This singular "already read" fantasized wishfully as a collective imprimatur—"if mothers in every family thought like this I should never cease to congratulate myself for having published it"—consoles the Editor for the more limited readership he "realistically" imagines for his collection.

Like Emilie, the bad daughter (*la fille*), the first woman reader, the good mother, has a sense of humor, even wit: *de l'esprit*. But are they *reading as women?* Put another way, what would it mean to place oneself, to find one's place as a woman reader within a phallic economy that doubly derives female identity through the interdigitated productions of the penis and the pen? Thus, on the one hand, the body-letter receives the sperm-words, she is the master's piece, the masterpiece;[14] and on the other, she figures as metaphorical "woman," disembodied because interchangeable—I hope you will laugh too.[15]

If we follow out the privileged hermeneutic chain, Emilie, Merteuil, me, you (all of us narratees doubled into whores by the act of reading itself), it seems fair to claim that the female reader of this novel is expected to identify with the site/sight, topographical and visual, of her figured complicity—like that of the classical *lectrice,* Mme de Tourvel—within the dominant order. Tourvel is the "immasculated" reader, who is "taught to . . . identify with a male point of view . . . Intellectually male, sexually female, one is in effect, no one, no where, immasculated."[16] What is it possible for a woman to read in these conditions of effacement and estrangement, in a universe, to return to our previous discussion, where the rules of aesthetic reception and indeed of the hermeneutic act itself are mapped onto a phallomorphic regime of production?

The third reading I evoked earlier might not so much ponder the impossibility of fixing meaning, or admire the text's "modernity," as interrogate the particular kind of phallic modeling that attaches itself to the very process of encoding and decoding, or vice versa. A third reading might wish instead to reevaluate the reciprocities of sexual and scriptional practices, and rethink a metaphorics of writing and reading that figures, and at the same time paradoxically *grounds,* "woman" as material support for a masculine self-celebration; a metaphorics that specularizes the double entendre—which we might freely understand as the trope of interpretation itself—as the couple man/woman (man over woman) and fetishizes the superscription of the masculine. (This might also be thought of as a working definition of the canon.) But even a third reading produces for me not only a "*somewhat* diminished text," and a "different kind of pleasure," to return to Wayne Booth's formulation but finally an acute desire to read something else altogether and to read *for* something else.

In closing, therefore, I want to evoke another (almost) eighteenth-century author, and another—and for me more congenial—staging of the scene of reading, writing, and sexual difference. I am referring to the famous moment in Jane Austen's last novel, *Persuasion,* when Captain Wentworth drops his pen. "While supposed to be writing only to Captain Benwick," and while eavesdropping on a conversation between his friend Captain Harville and the heroine Anne Elliot about men's and women's inconstancy and constancy, Captain Wentworth, in a room full of people, writes a love letter.[17]

The pen falls as Anne sets forth what we have come to call the sex/gender arrangements of our culture: the division of labor that grants men, among other things, the professions, and women, the private world of feelings. Here a woman figuratively picks up the pen, as Austen's heroine decorously but specifically protests against that troping of the spheres, against the penmanship of the hegemonic culture: "Men have had every advantage of us in telling their own story. Education has been theirs in so much a higher degree; the pen has been in their hands. I will not allow books to prove anything."[18] The "histories" from which one quotes to prove one's point were all, as Captain Harville is quick to grant, written by men. In *Persuasion,* which recycles the epistolary and retrieves its earlier (more Rousseauian) desire for the proper destination, Wentworth delivers his letter by hand, its "direction hardly legible to Miss A.E.———."[19] And we read with her: "While supposed to be writing only to Captain Benwick, he had also been addressing her!"[20]

To miss this letter is to run the risk of believing that the pen is nothing but a metaphorical penis, even though we know, as we stand here ironing, that has never been entirely true.[21] For if Valmont writes to (and on) women in order, ultimately, to be read by men—other libertines, literary critics, etc. (women are, we know, always and merely the cover and site of exchange for this founding homosocial contract)[22]—then Wentworth, "at work in the common sitting room," as Gilbert and Gubar have persuasively imagined him, "alert for inauspicious interruptions, using his other letter as a kind of blotter to camouflage his designs" (much like "Austen herself")[23] writes, I would argue *as a woman* to a woman in order to be read by women.[24] (Paradoxically, this shift in address is made possible by the historical development of the female readership in the eighteenth century, whose authorization, we saw, the Editor of the *Liaisons* anxiously and ironically hypothesized in his preface.) By having Captain Wentworth both drop his pen because of the sound of a woman's voice, and write a love letter in dialogue with the claims of her discourse, Austen, I think, operates a powerful revision of the standard account: she puts the pen in the hand of a man who, unlike Valmont (or Lovelace) wishes to have his feelings for the other "penetrated."[25] This wish for transparency, however nostalgic, may be said to deconstruct the familiar logic of the body as parts, and by that move writes the possibility of a body beyond parts; a body, therefore, through which the stories of sexual difference would have to be figured otherwise.

# MEN'S READING,
# WOMEN'S WRITING
## Gender and the Rise of the Novel

The latest enemy of the vitality of classic texts is feminism.
—Allan Bloom, *The Closing of the American Mind*

I will begin with the matter of a footnote.

About six hundred pages into Frances Burney's nine-hundred-page novel, *Camilla,* the heroine receives the visit of the ebullient Mrs. Mittin. Mrs. Mittin eagerly tells Camilla the story of her getting to know Mrs. Berlinton.

> I happened to be in the book shop when she came in, and asked for
> a book; the Peruvan Letters she called it; and it was not at home,
> and she looked quite vexed, for she said she had looked the cata-
> logue up and down, and saw nothing she'd a mind to; so I thought
> it would be a good opportunity to oblige her, and be a way to make
> a prodigious genteel acquaintance besides; so I took down the
> name, and I found out the lady that had got the book, and I made
> her a visit, and I told her it was particular wanted by a lady that
> had a reason; so she let me have it, and I took it to my pretty lady,
> who was so pleased, she did not know how to thank me.[1]

Burney's 1796 novel was republished by Oxford University Press in 1983 in an edition established by Edward A. Bloom and Lillian D. Bloom. Their footnotes are abundant and carefully documented. Thus on this passage, for "book shop" they offer: "obviously a circulating library. In *The Southampton Guide* (6th ed., ca., 1801, pp. 74–75) [the story takes place in Southampton] there is a description of such a library: 'T. Baker's nearly seven thousand volumes, forming a more general collection of useful and polite literature than is usually found in circulating libraries. The books are lent to read, at 15s. the year, 4s.6d. the quarter, and 5s. for the season."[2] As someone who rarely does this kind of research herself, I love having access to information provided with such detail. The precision of it—4s.6d. the quarter— feeds the fantasy (which I think it must remain) that one might be able to reconstruct the material contexts of a past of reading.

Despite the seduction of its details, this is not the footnote I'm after. The note in question comes (next in sequence) to explain the title of the book requested, the "Peruvan Letters": "Mrs. Mittin meant," the editors inform us, "either Charles de Secondat Montesquieu's *Persian Letters* (trans. 1722) or George Lyttleton's *Letters from a Persian in England to his Friend in Ispahan.* In her ignorance, she failed to distinguish between Persia and Peru."[3] The failure to distinguish between Persia and Peru, however, may not be an either/or affair. In their eagerness to identify one woman novelist's readings, *Camilla*'s editors missed another's writing: Françoise d'Issembourg d'Happencourt de Graffigny's *Lettres d'une Péruvienne* (1747), which were being translated in England as the *Peruvian Letters* as late as 1782.[4]

I am, it might seem, placing a heavy burden on an academic detail: why Burney (or Lyttleton, for that matter), and not Graffigny? Nonetheless, because the uneven inclusion of proper names in the set of common references that shape collective legacies is a symptomatic expression of broader cultural choices, I want to retain this instance of omission as the point of departure for a reflection on the vicissi- tudes of canon-formation.

In this essay, I will be dealing more specifically with the ways in which the reading and writing practices of a given period are record- ed, reformed, gendered, and forgotten. I will take as my particular focus the critical discourse that comes to place in literary history a dominant current in eighteenth-century fiction: the novels of manners that obsessively represent what Joan Kelly called "the social relation of the sexes."[5]

> Men have this way of forgetting . . .
> —Marie-Jeanne Riccoboni, *Lettres de Milady Juliette Catesby*

In his wonderfully erudite and still timely study on the eighteenth-century novel, Georges May makes the observation that the "history of the French novel remains to be written." "The volume devoted to the eighteenth-century novel," he adds, "is especially lacking,"[6] and he wonders about this missing piece of literary history. Twenty-five years after the publication of May's *Le Dilemme du roman au XVIIIe siècle,* despite several excellent books on the novels of this period, the task, I think, still lies before us, if, by a history of the French novel, one has in mind a history that includes women's foundational role in its development. As a feminist critic concerned with imagining the volume devoted to the eighteenth-century novel still to be written, I find myself twenty-five years later returning to May's introduction (and the long chapter, "Feminism and the Novel") for a place from which to begin again, for, among other things, a gendered account of authorship: men *and* women writers. Thus, in a roll call of novelists publishing between 1715 and 1761, he names (in this order): Prévost, Marivaux, Crébillon, Duclos, Tencin, Graffigny, and Riccoboni and characterizes them as the "least forgotten" writers of this period (3). The inclusion of women's names as a matter of course (even among the least forgotten) may not be taken for granted in 1963 or today.

In "Classical Reeducation: Decanonizing the Feminine," Joan DeJean shows how anthologies in seventeenth- (and eighteenth-) century France served as a kind of "continuing education" for adults "who wished to keep abreast of the literary scene"; anthologies were organized pedagogically not only to supply literary material, but to shape a generation's taste by supplementing its ideology.[7] Let us turn now to what I see as a modern version of this mode, René Etiemble's collection of eighteenth-century prose fiction in the 1966 two-volume Pléiade, *Romanciers du XVIIIe siècle.*[8] I have chosen this volume precisely because, as Etiemble himself argues, the Pléiade edition constitutes a form of recognition meant to assure a posterity of reading. The Pléiade edition "of itself" confers legitimacy and provides authorizing versions of the included texts.

Of May's list, Etiemble includes only the male writers, to which he adds others. Now, Etiemble has read Georges May and concurs with his position that one needs a history of the eighteenth-century novel; that it is wrong to justify ignorance of the general reading public who see in the novel only Balzac and Stendhal, instead of Rétif, or Duclos, or Crébillon, and miss the eighteenth century completely. But nowhere in the preface and introduction, both of which demonstrate an acute self-consciousness about the grounds for inclusion and exclusion at work in the anthology, and a sympathy for what he calls the "human reference" (R, 2:xx), does the critic refer to the writers central to the production and formation of the very fictional forms he has collected for a sophisticated reading public ("aux gens cultivés," R, 1:8).

Etiemble explains that a reader who wants a more complete picture of the evolution of the genre ought to "reread" *other* works not included in his volumes (not included, because unlike his selection, these have received their own individual Pléiade "consecration"). Readers, he specifies, are to *return* to the novels of Montesquieu, Marivaux, Diderot, and Rousseau, interweaving them in chronological order along with his choices if they are to have a complete picture; more than "a glance of what the French novel becomes in the eighteenth century" (R, 1:7). Thus, despite Etiemble's awareness of the importance of women writers of this deconsidered form in the seventeenth century—he names Scudéry and Lafayette (R, 1:7)—and his admiration for Georges May's mapping of the terrain, neither Graffigny, Tencin, nor Riccoboni, for example, figures in this "tableau" of the French novel. Why was Etiemble, who is not beyond a major saving operation in this anthology, not moved to make a case for women writers? Why Sénac de Meilhan, or Cazotte, and not Riccoboni or Tencin? Nothing indicates whether Etiemble read any of the women's novels I'm thinking of; read them and rejected them. (In an earlier critical overview of eighteenth-century prose writers, he mentions in passing Tencin's Les Mémoires du comte de Comminge and Graffigny's *Lettres péruviennes* [sic] without any evaluation.[9]) What concerns me here are the effects produced by his passing over women writers in silence.

To be sure, one could argue that the category of the "woman writer" was not a vivid one in 1966. Or rather that the category of "la romancière" very precisely left the question of the specificity of women's writing either moot or intact.[10] One could also more pointedly suggest that what attracts Etiemble to his corpus is the lure of identification, a form of "reading as male bonding" that Susan Winnett, in a shrewdly theorized essay on "narrative and the principle(s) of pleasure," identifies as a "homoaesthetic subtext," a set of assumptions that follow from a "legalized, entirely male circuit of desire."[11] Etiemble, for his part, seems drawn to the form of male memoir epitomized in Louvet's *Les Amours du Chevalier de Faublas*. From the list of "si j'aime le *Faublas* c'est . . ." let us retain this formulation: "It's in particular because of the slightly disreputable women who work at satisfying Faublas for the amusement of the well-endowed reader" ("C'est à cause en particulier des femmes un peu moins honnêtes qui s'emploient à combler Faublas, pour l'amusement du lecteur bien constitué" [R, 2:xxv]). Although, to be fair, this invocation of the well-endowed (red-blooded might be a better translation) reader is not Etiemble's only explanation for his textual preference, it is difficult to resist the impression that his evaluation of Crébillon, Duclos, Denon, and company is finally inseparable from a highly masculinist mode of critical pleasure (very specifically, reading as a French, relentlessly heterosexual, terminally misogynistic though always elegant and gallant, male [R, 2:xxvi]): in a word, reading like a man.

I want to suggest further that if Graffigny, Tencin, and Riccoboni do not appear on Etiemble's screen, it may also be because in addition to their status as women writers (hence their general invisibility), they specifically produce *feminist writing* on the same subjects. These fictions of dissent call into question the fulfillment of the virile subjectivities that typically structure libertine texts, by which I mean here the recollections of a man's life as a list of encounters or the obsession of a single passion, like *Manon Lescaut*. This particular plot of heterosexual engagement provides the basic psychosocial design of the memoir-novel, one of the two dominant novelistic forms in the eighteenth century. Feminist fictions take another, harsher, and less jubilant view of the sexual and social stage of human relations; and in these novels female subjectivity is the figure, not merely the ground of representation against which the tropes of masculine performance display themselves.

In *Subject to Change* I make the claim that it is important to locate any poetics of feminist writing in relation to a historicized national and cultural production; indeed that a "poetics of location" is the only way to work against the universalizing tendencies of a monolith of "women's writing."[12] Although the individual works that I treat there range in time from *La Princesse de Clèves* (1678) to *La Vagabonde* (1910), I draw implicitly on the powerful body of eighteenth-century women's texts for my general understanding of this writing. The novels of women writers in eighteenth-century France may be characterized by what Rachel DuPlessis has called a "poetics of critique";[13] more specifically I focus on the *figuration* of dissent from the plots of the dominant tradition that marks these fictions. In these eighteenth-century novels—most dramatically, perhaps, Riccoboni's *Lettres de Mistress Fanni Butlerd* and *Histoire du Marquis de Cressy,* and Tencin's *Mémoires du Comte de Comminge*—the conventional sex/gender arrangements that underwrite masculinist stories (the complacent fantasies of the "roman-liste," for instance) are vividly undermined.[14]

In this sense, then, in order to understand the patterns of inclusion and exclusion that shape the history of the novel in France, it is not sufficient to speak simply of men's or women's writing. Retained for posterity among the eighteenth-century novels devoted to the social relations of the sexes is, we might more usefully say, libertine and not feminist writing. Put another way, at an angle to the notion of a literature of "worldliness," we want to emphasize the differentiation of the viewpoint from which the world (and its discursive domains) is perceived, entered, and experienced.

To understand the history of the French novel, especially as it played itself out in the eighteenth-century fictions of manners which in so many ways made the nineteenth-century realist novel possible, it is crucial to perform two gestures: first to restore feminist writing to the body of fiction that becomes the novel; second, to reread the texts retained by literary history through this supplemented and redoubled vision.

Flaubert was writing the new novel of 1860, Proust the new novel of 1910. A writer must bear his date, knowing there are no masterpieces in eternity, only works in history; and that they survive only to the extent that they have left the past behind them and announced the future.

—Alain Robbe-Grillet, *Pour un nouveau roman*

Let us consider a recent example of the old literary history; unlike the Etiemble volumes, this is not an anthology, but another legitimatizing instance of eighteenth-century letters, a mainstream exercise in cultural diffusion: the volumes published in 1984 by Arthaud, specifically the volumes of *Littérature française,* volume 5, *De Fénelon à Voltaire,* and volume 6, *De L'Encyclopédie aux Méditations.*[15]

The problem of inclusion and exclusion in these manuals, by which I mean the difference in treatment of men's and women's writing, is related to a problem of category and definition: the men appear in the table of contents of volume 6 with their names under the large headings: "Great Works, Great Authors." Except for Staël (and she is part of an ensemble along with "Benjamin Constant et le groupe de Coppet") no women's names appear in the table of contents, or in the bibliographical sketches at the back of the book. But in both volumes the hidden bodies are there, of course, slotted into the subset of a literary historical category: the sentimental novel, in volume 5, under "Forms and Genres." Under the promising heading "Toward a New Novel," Tencin and Graffigny are located within the subheading "le roman des coeurs sensibles," the novel of (and for) feeling hearts. In volume 6 the category is called "le roman sensible" and includes two pages of critical comment on Riccoboni. Despite a certain grudging admiration for her "portraits of women" (*LF,* 6:214), in the end the authors of the manual find that Riccoboni's work does not meet the standards of the male model: Riccoboni, less talented than Richardson and Diderot as a novelist of everyday life, fails to create the illusion of reality through a judicious use of detail (Riccoboni "ignore le pittoresque" [*LF,* 6:216]). And at the end of the century, we find in a short list Krudener, Charrière, Cottin, Staël ("Staël elle-même"[!])— servile imitators, "who borrow from Rousseau their characters, situations, settings and the means of moving their female readers, for these women are addressing a female audience" (*LF,* 6:221).

Although in their analyses of the production, distribution, and consumption of books the authors of the manual rarely distinguish by gender, they note the role played by education in the formation of a reading public and the fact that women are excluded from the scenes of knowledge: with a few exceptions, they observe, women are not seen as fit for studying serious subjects: "women are granted the novel, the frivolous genre, without anyone suspecting that it is to them that the novel will owe its surprising development" (*LF*, 5:45). Unfortunately, this acknowledgment of the material conditions of literature and its paradoxical relation to women's social inferiority stops there and congeals into a commonplace. It does not take the next step to reflect upon its own categories of analysis, categories that by their language—"Great Works, Great Authors"—return women to invisibility, to the clichés of the *lectrice:* of a female reading public on the one hand, and of women writers as inferior imitators of a perfected male-authored model and novel of the feminine to boot—Richardson and Rousseau.

In their unexamined adherence to the masterpiece codes of the dominant tradition according to which they (re)construct a male genealogy, the Arthaud editors fail to see women writers, on the one hand, as the continuers of a powerful tradition of seventeenth-century women writers, and on the other, as the producers of new forms and new reading practices. I cannot stress too heavily the degree of canon *de*formation this failure of vision represents.[16]

What we need in order to write a history of the eighteenth-century novel are some new ways of thinking about what goes on in a "republic of letters," restoring its heterogeneity and reopening the question for criticism of the relations between social values and literary forms. Although I am specifically concerned here with what Jane Tompkins calls the "cultural work" performed by women's writing and with the social values defining women's place that subtend a national literature at a given historical moment, the implications of such an emphasis in fact require a reimagination of the whole picture: the mix of writing that has been sorted out to become the narrow and fixed literary tradition we study, write about, teach, and pass on.[17]

There's no cause for alarm. I'm not going to talk either about the play *Cénie,* or even about the *Lettres péruviennes,* works that were somewhat appealing in their time and that are completely passé today. I'm going to talk mainly about Voltaire; Mme de Grafigny

brings us into his home and helps us to discover him in a rather new
or at least very natural light. (Monday, 17 June 1850)

—Sainte-Beuve, *Lettres de Madame de Grafigny,*
*ou Voltaire à Cirey*

Let us reconsider now the case of Mrs. Mittin's mistake. Graffigny's
*Lettres d'une Péruvienne* is a novel that, like most women's writing
in France, enjoyed tremendous popularity when it was published, and
in this case even a certain posterity: thirty editions, including ten in
English and Italian, until 1777, and then continuous publication until
1835. Despite its contemporary critical recognition (the "*Lettres*
*d'une Péruvienne* was one of the most widely read books in the eighteenth century" [*LF,* 6:210]), the novel rarely appears in the standard
accounts of eighteenth-century fiction, nor until recently has it been
collected in standard editions. Unlike many female-authored novels,
however, the *Lettres d'une Péruvienne,* had a reprieve of sorts. In
1967 an Italian scholar, Gianni Nicoletti, brought out a critical edition of the novel, which had not been republished since the early
nineteenth century.[18] And in 1983, more important perhaps, a paper-
back edition, based on Nicoletti's work, was published by Garnier
Flammarion, in a collection of epistolary novels. This volume has
made it possible for the first time to teach the novel as a matter of
course. Will this be the case?

Despite the work's material availability, without a rethinking of
the value paradigms that have overdetermined our reading habits,
without a critical reflection about the act of women's writing as a
type of cultural intervention, it is not at all clear that the *Lettres*
*d'une Péruvienne* will emerge from the margins to be read alongside,
for example, the Persian ones. The very fact of classifying the novel
for publication as a love-letter novel ("romans d'amour par lettres")
maintains the hierarchy of classifications that, as we saw in the discourse of the Arthaud manual, trivializes female authorship.

The reconstructive project of reading women's writing, then, necessarily involves textual strategies that acknowledge the peculiar
status of this literature in the library: there, but in opposition to the
"already read," the *déjà lu* of the canon—"underread," the *sous lu,*
cut off from the kind of historical and metacritical life that characterizes the works of dominant French literature. Learning to read

women's writing entails not only a particular attentiveness to the marks of signature that I have called "overreading"; it also involves "reading in pairs" (or, in Naomi Schor's coinage, "intersextually").[19] By this I mean looking at the literature of men's and women's writing side by side to perceive at their points of intersection the differentiated lines of a "bicultural" production of the novel—Persian *and* Peruvian—more complicated than the familiar, national history of its tropes.

In a long review essay on Fanny Burney's *Cecilia* (1784), Laclos elaborates a comparative (French and English) and gendered poetics in which he makes the claim that women are particularly well suited to novel writing because the genre requires the three skills of "observing, feeling, and depicting."[20] "[Women's] education," Laclos writes, "their existence in society, all their praiseworthy qualities, and if one must tell all, even some of their flaws, promise them successes in this career that they would, in our view, seek vainly in every other" (*LR*, 501). Laclos explains that he doesn't have the time to develop his theory (readers can supply their own examples) but moves instead to situate Burney in his survey of the field: "Among the women whom one could cite as having placed themselves beside [*à côté de*] our best novelists [*meilleurs romanciers*], there would be few more distinguished and more surprising than the Author of the Work we are going to review" (*LR*, 501). What I suggest here is that, writing literary criticism toward the end of the eighteenth century, Laclos reads women's writing through a set of clichés of femininity that leave the category of novelist masculine and originary: for Laclos the class of novelists is male. Thus, despite the high praise he has bestowed upon *Cecilia,* despite the relation of contiguity—*à côté de*—that ground his rhetoric, in the end, Laclos replaces Burney's novel within a clearly ranked and conventionally gendered hierarchy of difference: "Finally, we think that this novel must be counted among the best works in this genre, with nevertheless the exception of *Clarissa,* the novel in which one finds the most genius, *Tom Jones,* the best constructed novel, and *La Nouvelle Héloïse,* the most beautiful work ever produced under the title of the novel" (*LR*, 521).

In this move from metonymy (the aleatory contacts between writers) to metaphor (the fixed relations between the sexes) we have the principle of selection that guides most anthologies of literary history.

Laclos had already elaborated the logic of this poetics of gender in his exchange of letters with Riccoboni. In the correspondence between Riccoboni and Laclos that followed the 1782 publication of the *Liaisons dangereuses,* to Riccoboni's critique of Laclos's representation of women—notably of the portrait of Madame de Merteuil in which, in her words, he would have "decorated vice with attractive features"—Laclos replied by inviting readers to turn to the "charming tableaux" of Riccoboni's own novels for more "gentle feelings." In his self-justification and explanation for the difference between his fictional universe and hers, Laclos, in what by then is a commonplace in eighteenth-century critical commentary, returns to the eternal nature of women and men for supporting evidence:[21] "women alone possess this precious sensibility, this easy and cheerful imagination that embellishes everything it touches, and creates objects as they should be: but . . . men, who are condemned to a harsher labor, have always acquitted themselves well when they have rendered nature exactly and faithfully!" (*LR*, 688).[22]

In "Idée sur les romans" (1800) Sade writes literary criticism according to the same principles, indeed proclaiming in a parenthesis women's generic superiority to men: "as if this sex, naturally more delicate, more suited to writing novels, could not in this genre lay claim to many more laurels than we."[23] Praising the works of Gomez, Lussan, Tencin, Graffigny, Beaumont, and Riccoboni for "honoring their sex," he names "Graffigny's *Lettres péruviennes,*" which, he goes on to assert, "will always be a model of tenderness and feeling, like [the letters] of Mylady Catesby, by Riccoboni; they will eternally serve those who only aspire to grace and lightness of style. But let us return to the century where we left it, pressed by the desire to praise the lovely women who in this genre taught men such good lessons."[24] For Laclos the category of writer remains the male universal against and from which the woman as novelist is judged; he also assumes the role of *critic*.

Almost two centuries after Laclos's and Sade's closural moves of putting the woman in her place, Delon et al., we have seen, make the same gesture. In each instance the protocol that regulates the social relations between the sexes takes the place of—at the very least displaces—literary criteria. What grounds the reproduction of this discourse?

In "[Why] Are There No Great Women Critics? And What Difference Does It Make?" Susan Lanser and Evelyn Beck raise the question of the "*woman critic*" and ask what difference to the history of critical discourse her voice might make.[25] Lanser and Beck do not conclude about the judgments of women theorists, but they imagine that their poetics would constitute a "challenge to traditional generic classifications."[26] In the absence of a history of women's critical writing (not to say a self-consciously feminist poetics), we can begin by turning to the prefatory moves of a woman writer who situates her work in relation to an already gendered literary history.

In the original preface to *Evelina*, Burney begins with a paragraph almost identical in its language to the beginning of Laclos's review article (*LR*, 499). Writing as a man, Burney, like Laclos, observes that "in the republic of letters, there is no member of such inferior rank, or who is so much disdained by his brethren of the quill, as the humble Novelist."

But in the detail of her editorial remarks she places her authorship in this fraternity somewhat differently. Despite the powerful models of Johnson's "knowledge," Rousseau's "eloquence," Richardson's "pathetic power," Fielding's "wit," and Smollett's "humour," Burney will not pursue, she explains, "the same ground which they have tracked." Unlike the other arts, where "a fine statue, or a beautiful picture, of some great master, may deservedly employ the imitative talents of young and inferior artists," "in books," she argues, "imitation cannot be shunned too sedulously; for the very perfection of a model which is frequently seen, serves but more forcibly to mark the inferiority of the copy." In her conclusion, however, she backs away from any implications of self-promotion in these poetics. "I have, therefore, only to intreat, that my own words may not pronounce my condemnation; and that what I have here ventured to say in regard to imitation, may be understood as it is meant, in a general sense, and not be imputed to an opinion of my own originality, which I have not the vanity, the folly, or the blindness to entertain."[27]

In the preface to her letter-novel, Graffigny, in the familiar ironic style of eighteenth-century philosophical discourse, like Burney, also raises the problem of imitation. In what I see as a similar defense of new ground, and what beyond the canonical tropes of authorial modesty I "overread" as a claim for the originality of a woman writer, she invites the public of novel readers to decipher another story. Writing as an editor-publisher of letters translated from the original, Graffigny regrets the power of prejudice that leads "us" (the French) to scorn other nations, notably the Indians, "only to the extent that their customs imitate our own, that their tongue resembles our language."[28] As feminist critics "we" might today reinterpret this utterance—"we recognize what mirrors and mimes us"—as a historical gloss on the status of women's writing in the dominant culture: the canon retains what it knows how to read, when it recognizes its own idiom.

By locating her subject of difference in writing and language in France (as opposed to the precursor's "Oriental" scene of the seraglio) and by placing her at the end of her fiction retired from the world in solitary study in the library, Graffigny stages another reading of Enlightenment categories. In the construction of her Peruvian other, Graffigny produces not so much minor fiction for "coeurs sensibles" as a minority literature of protest which of necessity demands to be read in majority context, against what we have learned to see as the monuments of the dominant culture. "The work of a woman," Myra Jehlen has argued, "—whose proposal to be a writer in itself reveals that female identity is not naturally what it has been assumed to be—may be used comparatively as an external ground for seeing the dominant literature whole."[29] The effect of reading from this point of view that "in itself" challenges the complacency of the "normative universal" is a displacement of the positionings of identity that keep the canon alive.

As a provisional answer to the question of canon-formation as it might be posed in eighteenth-century French studies, then, I want to summarize the three points I have been arguing for in this essay. First, that in the range of works that make up the packaging of "the eighteenth-century novel," the very categories that traditionally have defined this corpus serve as effectively to suppress a wide range of women's writing by narrowing its project; when, for instance, women's novels are placed in the category of the sentimental (for "coeurs sensibles") and not read, as men's writing conventionally is, as realistic fictions of social life, what results is a radical impoverishment of the complexity that characterizes literary exchanges in the eighteenth century.[30] My second point is that the exclusion of these voices of critique from a highly dialogic sociality is naturalized through a critical discourse of male bonding; flattered by the mirrors of his own representation, the masculinist critic sees himself, say, in Faublas. This narcissistic identification both emerges from and reinscribes a general ignorance of (and resistance to) female and feminist traditions of writing and rewriting that did not wait for Rousseau or Richardson to take shape. Finally, in order to register the heterogeneity of the cultural record of writing that becomes the history of the novel, we need to take another look within the period at the sites where the intersecting discourses on femininity (as the inflected term of the masculine-feminine couple) and fiction become—like the recklessly heterosexual couples of the social text they also articulate—permanently and dangerously entangled.

> I am convinced that the practice, as against the theory of feminist criticism has in many cases weakened the critical enterprise.
> —Richard Poirier, "Where is Emerson Now That We Need Him? Or, Why Literature Can't Save Us"

In "Woman in France: Madame de Sablé," George Eliot, filled with admiration for French women writers—especially "those delightful women of France, who, from the beginning of the seventeenth to the close of the eighteenth century, formed some of the brightest threads in the web of political and literary history"—celebrates, among others, Germaine de Staël: "Madame de Staël's name still rises to the lips when we are asked to mention a woman of great intellectual power."[31] On our way to a conclusion about the place of women writers in the literature of the eighteenth century, and a revisionary strategy for teaching their works, I will just point to the case of Staël, who represents both the culmination of a great tradition of women writers in France and a challenge—never met—to the novel of the nineteenth century. What, for instance, of *Corinne,* the great feminist novel that punctures the illusions of masculine subjectivities and creates a dramatically new voice and place for women writers?[32]

Etiemble, defending Sénac de Meilhan from obscurity, manages to work in a swipe at Staël (the only woman mentioned in the second volume). He uses the literary historian Albert Thibaudet to set her up. Thibaudet goes on about the merits of *L'Emigré* as "a figure of the cosmopolitan novel less decorative, but more lively, more moving and more true than *Corinne*." Etiemble comments: "That's a fair judgment of *Corinne*; still, despite Thibaudet, despite his *Histoire de la littérature française* where I cull these few lines, it's *Corinne* that is edited, glossed, taught, admired and pitied. Poor students! [*Pauvres potaches!*]" (*R*, 2:xxvi–xxvii). Anyone who tried to find an edition of Staël's novel in a library or bookstore before its recent republication by des femmes in 1979 and the Gallimard Folio in 1985, or looked at a reading list, in this country at least, for exams or syllabi on the eighteenth- or nineteenth-century novel will be amazed by these claims. Staël's name, however, does of course have a place in the landscape of French studies: as a writer of literary theory who created the idea of comparative literature.

Courses on women writers, either in the form of a historical survey, or by genre and period, offer a simple, if conventional way to address the exclusions of the canon. The very gesture of reconstructing the histories of women's writing provides a standpoint from which to dismember the universal subjectivity enshrined in dominant literatures. It also establishes a ground from which to address the question of the work performed by women's writing and the value one wishes to ascribe to that work. But at the same time the establishment of such a parallel history (or curriculum) runs the risk of generating, and perhaps guarantees, an even greater indifference to the question of women's writing itself on the part of those authorizers and disseminators of cultural value, who, as we have seen, are happy enough to have a women's chapter that leaves their story intact. It may be that the pleasure of this new text requires another pedagogical politics.[33] It may also be that to produce a literary history that articulates the complexities of the cultural record, it is as important to conceive a pedagogy that leaves less already in place. This would mean among other things a commitment to the practice of a gendered poetics that rereads men's texts in the weave of women's.

The question, then, of "placing" women writers in French literature must be understood finally as a double operation. If the first move inevitably takes the form of a replacement that appears to leave the field intact, or rather, subject only to minor displacements (one in the stead of the other) that respect the original body, this must not be seen as its aim. Rather, seeing the first as immediately doubled by an interrogation of the body itself, it becomes possible to start another project altogether.

# CULTURAL MEMORY AND THE ART OF THE NOVEL
## Gender and Narrative in Eighteenth-Century France

What is *le roman sentimental?*[1] Henri Coulet, in his classic study, *Le Roman jusqu'à la révolution,* puts the matter this way: "Under this heading are included, somewhat arbitrarily, novels that have different subjects and forms, but whose purpose is to depict and analyze feelings rather than to describe manners."[2] Because the history of the novel is typically seen as an evolution toward the realism of the nineteenth century, which is to say the novel of manners (*moeurs*), and because the novels of the eighteenth century are typically seen through that paradigm, to classify women's novels generically as *romans pour coeurs sensibles* is both to separate their works from the mainstream tradition to which they belong and to refuse their powers to read the world: their powers to know and describe the real.

If all women's writing tends to be included in the category of *le roman sentimental,* what of men's writing? Here, to be sure, there is greater range, but the mode that dominates—whatever the sub-genre—is that of *libertinage.* As Coulet argues for the novel before 1760 (while acknowledging the arbitrariness of the date):

> Libertine style is perhaps more a question of technique than of perspective; its prevalence in the eighteenth century demonstrates its

importance as a method of expression, but also its inconsistencies as a system of thought. There is libertinism in thinkers as different as Prévost, Marivaux, Montesquieu, Diderot and Voltaire, and one doesn't have to look far to find it in Rousseau as well. The eighteenth century as a whole recognized and proclaimed the role of the senses, and the way in which the moral is determined by the physical, and looked for a seemly language to expound this role in the feeling that was most often idealized: love.[3]

The quickest way to think about what the term libertine has signified historically for the novel is to note the extraordinary appeal—fascination might be a better word—today in France, England, and the United States of Laclos's *Liaisons dangereuses,* the acknowledged masterpiece of the genre, in the theater and as a film. It is not difficult to grasp why the term libertine should apply to the *Liaisons.* But it is important to understand what else this term means for the eighteenth-century novel. The dominant mode of fiction described as libertine, which is to say in the most general (generic) possible terms, the plot of serial heterosexual engagement seen from a male-authored and male-narrated perspective, in practice comes to include all works to which critics and literary historians *also* assign the two prime values of mimetic representation essential to the genre of the novel: the portrayal of *moeurs* and psychological analysis; a vision of social life, subjected to some form of moral judgment. These terms are not especially precise, of course, but that is exactly why they are effective. What concerns us here is the fact that for the uses of literary history, the label libertine rather than limiting a work's attractiveness by its thematics, finally relocates the work within the mainstream of what is today in France regularly called, "the national patrimony."

Thus, in the introduction to his critical edition of Duclos's *Les Confessions du Comte de\*\*\*,* Laurent Versini, categorizing the book both as a "novel of manners" (*roman de moeurs*) and a "moralist's novel" (*roman de moraliste*), describes Duclos's writing as that of an "elegant libertinage learned from Crébillon," and links him to the "tradition of the classical moralists."[4] At the same time, however, the "rehabilitation" of libertine writers, often includes a gesture of distancing from the implications of the label. In the 1977 Folio edition of Crébillon's *Les Egarements du coeur et de l'esprit,* Etiemble first tries to lift Crébillon out of the category "licentious" or worse, "coarse" to make him into a writer to be taken seriously: "Every writer is of his time, and that is how it should be—so long as he escapes by wanting to be universal. Crébillon is definitely universal in the *Egarements* because of his subject."[5] In his introduction to the 1985 Flammarion edition, Jean Dagen argues along similar lines: "It is highly problematic to define Crébillon as a libertine novelist. The 'libertine novel' is an invention of historians who, whatever they may say, take too literally a certain moralism that it would be unjust to impute only to Rousseau. Crébillon was, quite simply, what he wanted to be: a novelist."[6]

Since men's writing that under the mode *libertin*, by its universal pretensions, describes feelings as well as manners, we might also ask whether it isn't also possible that women's writing portrays manners as well as feelings? Sentimental texts by women writers produce a critique not only of the world and manners of libertine texts but of the categories of heterosexual power relations that construct them. In this sense they too can be seen as "wanting to be universal."

I'm going to take the case of two novels written within the same decade to consider both what sentimental and libertine fictions have in common—and the grounds of their differences. The texts I have chosen are Charles Pinot-Duclos' *Mémoires pour servir à l'histoire des moeurs du XVIIIe siècle* (1751), a memoir-novel, and Marie-Jeanne Riccoboni's 1759 epistolary fiction, *Lettres de Milady Juliette Catesby A Milady Henriette Campley, Son Amie.*[7] Duclos's *Mémoires* and Riccoboni's *Juliette Catesby,* like many eighteenth-century novels, represent the vicissitudes of heterosexual plot within an aristocratic setting in which the protagonists spend most of their waking hours dealing with the hermeneutic perplexities posed by the opposite sex; despite the difference of genre, they tell the story of a sentimental education that ends with marriage. More specifically, however, I have chosen to pair the two novels because by virtue of their insistence on gendered valences of memory—notably, the remembering and forgetting of sexual event—they illuminate the fundamental ambiguity of the famous "reign of women" said to characterize eighteenth-century social life. If Riccoboni's novel, which one could argue, is engendered by the various meanings of the verb "to forget" (meanings activated by a young man's sexual oversight), it also provides a reflection on what women's memory remembers for the culture.

At stake for us then in this paired reading will be a double reflection: first, what can these narratives of gender and memory, memory and sexual experience tell us about so-called sentimental and libertine modes of fiction? And second, what does sentimental or libertine memory tell us not only about the politics of literary traditions but about what might be entailed in changing them?

I begin with the Duclos because the novel's structure clearly shows the generic constraints it embodies. For me this is the main interest of the text. I could equally well have chosen his better known *Confessions du Comte de\*\*\** (1741) or Crébillon's "masterpiece" in the genre, *Les Egarements du coeur et de l'esprit* (1735–36) as instances of the social construction of masculinity under the *ancien régime*. These texts all begin with a young man's entrance into the world; his sexual initiation and social education at the hands of a variety of women.[8] Duclos details twenty-three in the "roman-liste" of the *Confessions;* here, he's down to nine. After running through the list, the hero finally settles on a virtuous woman who is truly worthy of him, with whom to live happily ever after.

The relationship between the memorial, the libertine, and the representation of *moeurs* is articulated explicitly in the *avertissement* to the reader that frames Duclos's novel: "Love, amorous intrigues, and even libertinage have always played such a large role in most men's lives, and especially those in high society [*le monde*], that a nation's customs [*moeurs*] would be hard to understand if such important subjects were left out." And the narrator explains that, "Since I intend to focus on the errors of my youth, it should not be surprising that love will play a large part" (*M,* 10–11). To say love of course, is to mean women; indeed as Henri Coulet puts it in the preface to Duclos's novel, women "have pride of place in the novel"(*M,* ii). Interestingly, then, in these three versions of the book's focus, what matters is the women; unnamed, they nonetheless inhere in the authorial project—in libertinage, in love, in "les moeurs d'une nation." For the narrator, the errors of his youth are essentially the time spent with the wrong women; women, who all ultimately will be erased from memory by the perfection of the one who is chosen at the end to end the memoir.

The purpose of this young man's recollection, and its relation to the genre of the text itself is articulated explicitly in terms of memory and sexual experience, or rather the women with whom the man has had affairs.

> It's not my intention to recall here all the women I've known; most of them seemed to forget our liaisons, and sometimes I barely remember them myself. I want to include only those relationships which had something singular about them, and I shall not forget one particular woman whom I particularly liked, but our liaison was so stormy that it was unbearable. (*M*, 104)

Missing from the list are those women who lacked the singularity to imprint forcefully on his memory; those women who like him forgot to notice what they were doing. As it turns out this particular liaison will be the last before the change of heart that brings about the end of the novel: the narrator's penultimate *égarement* before leaving his dissolute life (*M*, 109).

This summary is meant to provide a flavor of the tone and structure of this novel, in which through the reconstruction of his sexual life, a man negotiates his social and moral identity. What remains to consider is the manner in which this trajectory of self-fashioning based on the movement through women gets fixed and becomes the emblem of heterosexual union. But I want to defer consideration of the marriage trope until we get to the end of our discussion of Riccoboni's text.

If Duclos's narrator cannot remember all the women he had affairs with, Riccoboni's Juliette Catesby can't forget the man of her life. Indeed she can't forget the man whose "oubli"—as it will be ambiguously named—whose forgetting—shattered her happiness. The novel opens on Juliette's separation from the friend Henriette to whom the letters of the novel are addressed; she is leaving in order to avoid meeting again this man who, as she puts it, "for two years was always on my mind . . . and nothing has been able to make me forget him" (*JC*, I). Henriette, whose letters we as readers don't see, has written to offer a way out of the situation:

> You tell me to *forgive Milord Ossery* or *not to think about him anymore*. Forgive him! Ah, never! . . . Not think about him? . . . I

can avoid this man, renounce him, hate him, loathe him, but forget . . . Oh, I cannot! (*JC*, VI)

What has Ossery done that leads him to ask the woman he loves to
forget all about him: "Must I be reduced to wanting you to forget
me? Ah, I shall never forget you, I shall always adore you; I shall
always think about you! (*JC*, XIV). When Ossery's letter comes to
announce his departure and the rupture of their engagement, he
alludes to a "horrible secret" that he cannot reveal because it involves
another person, calls himself an ingrate, and disappears.

The reader doesn't discover the explanation for Ossery's behavior
until the last quarter of the novel when Ossery reappears on the scene
and begs for permission to see Juliette. He finally writes to give an
account of his behavior. The passages below are excerpts from a long
self-narrative, which includes a brief account of his general social
behavior. In all points, he is the antithesis of Duclos's narrator:
embarrassingly well-behaved. It is against this self-portrait—a male
memoir novel *en abyme*—and the earlier representation Juliette had
made of his charm, that the story of the *oubli* unfolds.

Ossery explains that he was on his way home when he encoun-
tered, on their return from a hunting party, some old acquaintances
from his university days; one of them, Montfort, a good friend, presses Ossery to join the group for dinner at his country estate. It's an
all-male dinner and the conversation turns to women: their beauty,
their soul, their taste and so on. The host, Montfort, claims that the
most attractive of women is the least sophisticated, and to prove his
point produces his young sister, Miss Jenny, a portrait of modesty.

The sister is rapidly ill at ease in this bachelor setting and asks
permission to withdraw. A few moments later, Ossery feels uncom-
fortable and goes to get some fresh air. Looking for his way out he
finds himself instead alone in a small room with Miss Jenny. He asks
her to show him to the garden, but since the only candle has just gone
out, Miss Jenny can't find the bell to ring for help, the two of them
start stumbling about in the dark, looking for the door, bumping into
each other, and tripping over the furniture. Jenny falls down. The
description of what then happens is the crux of the novel:

> Her fall caused mine; soon great peals of laughter showed me that
> she was not hurt. Her immoderate playfulness made an extraordi-

nary impression on me; it emboldened me: the disorder of my mind went straight to my heart. Overcome by sensual desires, I forgot my love, my integrity, laws that I had always held sacred, my friend's sister. A respectable girl appeared to me at that moment as nothing but a woman offered up for my desires, for that crude passion that instinct alone inflames. An impetuous impulse overtook me; I dared all, I cruelly abused the confusion and innocence of an incautious young girl, whose innocence caused her downfall.

I was beginning to think of my unfortunate adventure as a weakness that would soon be lost to memory, when its catastrophic consequences brought it forcefully back to me and obliged me to suffer the penalty of my lack of caution. (*JC,* XXXV)

As a result of Ossery's "weakness" Miss Jenny gets pregnant; because of what he owes the brother, Ossery feels obliged to marry her; they have a daughter; and then the young wife dies. It is as widower that Ossery returns to beg Juliette's forgiveness.

Juliette has to determine how to interpret Ossery's story before the novel can reach closure. And what follows is her *explication de texte* (italics are hers):

> ... an unfortunate adventure! this *small room* ... this *darkness* ... his boldness ... he calls this *an unhappy accident* ... *I forgot my love,* he says ... Yes, men have *this way of forgetting;* their heart and their senses can act independently; at least, that is what they claim, and by making these distinctions that they consider excuses, they reserve for themselves the option to be aroused by love, seduced by pleasure or carried away by *instinct.* How can we disentangle the genuine feeling that motivates them? (*JC,* XXXVI)

In her protest against the inequities that structure these arrangements between the sexes, Juliette underlines two important problems familiar to feminist theorists today: what to call what has happened, and what to do about it: "Les hommes ont de ces *oublis.*" Men have this way of forgetting. In his preface to the novel, Sylvain Menant describes Ossery's action as "a momentary lapse" ("un moment d'égarement")—thus remaining within Ossery's own vocabulary and the lexicon of libertinage made famous by Crébillon.[9] In one of the few full-scale studies of Riccoboni's work, Joan Stewart characterized it as "a passing infidelity," but more recently "a rape-like event."[10] In *Fictions of Authority*, Susan Lanser calls it rape.[11]

The letter in which Juliette rereads the letter with Henriette presses specifically on the implications of its language: "His *confused* mind . . . his *disordered* judgment . . . ah, what a disorder! It has certainly cost me some tears! Must I forgive him?" (*JC*, XXXVI). And the letter ends on her indecision: "Oh, I don't know what to decide!" (*JC*, XXXVI). Yet the very next letter announces: "Ah, all is forgiven, all is forgotten" (*JC*, XXXVII). The novel ends in a flurry of event a few pages later, with marriage. What are we to make of this marriage? Does it condone a rape?—or forgive a libertine lapse? For Lanser the abruptness with which the marriage is brought off and the jubilation of the husband's marital discourse—"Milady Catesby is no more; she is my wife, my friend, my mistress, the good spirit who gives me back all the blessings of which I was deprived" (*JC*, XXXVII)—undermine a straight reading of closure. Can Riccoboni's heroine by a remarkable display of *noblesse de sentiment* really have forgiven the libertine? Or if she has, must we? It is difficult to come down firmly on one side or another. Like *Juliette Catesby*, Riccoboni's first two immensely successful novels participate equally in the indictment of masculine privilege and its abuse, but end instead with female defiance and rage, including a sublimely staged suicide. *Juliette Catesby* includes too much internal commentary on men and marriage itself for us to read the ending as another complacent installment of heterosexual plot.

Let us return to our paired reading to help us evaluate Riccoboni's narrative strategy. In his desire to reform, Duclos's narrator returns to Mme de Canaples, the woman to whom he tried to make love at the very beginning of his career. At that point she was married, and unlike most of the women in the libertine world, although attracted to her suitor, even more attached to her "devoir" (*M*, 21). Mme de Canaples, when the narrator returns to her, is widowed and, in theory, like the Princess of Clèves after her husband's death, free to marry. Still, she hesitates. Her tone, the narrator explains, is that of a person not wanting to appear to "have forgotten her principles so quickly and who would like to be talked out of them"; but who is not saying no, only deferring (*M*, 136). As if to prove the Princess right almost seventy-five years later, the narrator discovers that in the interim he has also fallen in love with a poor relation of her late husband's that Mme de Canaples has decided to take under her wing. Before he can confess his dilemma, Canaples shows him she has deciphered the state of his heart and arranged a marriage for him and the charming orphan:

> So our marriage took place, and from that time on my wife has devoted her time to pleasing me; Madame de Canaples seemed to take her pleasure from ours, and it increased our joy to owe it to her, and to find in her a benefactor, a mother, a friend, a guide, and a model of virtue. The calm and happy state of affairs I am revelling in has convinced me that true happiness exists only in uniting pleasure and duty. (*M*, 148)

Through a retrospective gaze on what this experience has meant, the narrator completes a circle of self-regard: a young wife whose sole purpose in life is to please him; a maternal surrogate whose love for him is sublimated into her dedication to the couple's happiness.

Libertine or sentimental? Feelings or social analysis? Do these novels describe two different worlds? In both, the male protagonist splits sexuality from feeling and forgets about its consequences; in both marriage comes to put an end to such libertine exploits; in both the representation of the "customs of a nation" depends on the social relations between the sexes and is submitted to the moral judgment of authorial voice.[12] In fact, one could argue that all libertine texts are also sentimental. It would also be interesting to think about what Duclos's echo of Lafayette can tell us about male writers' appropriation of earlier feminist traditions. Here he takes the Princess' self-possession and transforms it into a support of male satisfaction.

Written in the decade that precedes the publication of Rousseau's *Nouvelle Héloïse*, the *novel of feeling* that in literary history marks at once the highpoint of the genre's feminization and the erasure of women writers from its history, the two texts point to an emergent bourgeois desire for a model of union between the sexes that would escape the contamination of the aristocratic model of masculine privilege and abuse. In this sense sentimental and libertine are but two sides of the same coin: Riccoboni's fictions are novels for the "feeling heart" if we include in the domain of the heart a social critique of libertine paradigms of sexual relation in which feeling is women's only power, a power that is also their weakness. Duclos's are libertine if we understand by this that the libertine paradigm of multiple pleasure only makes sense against its sentimental belief in women's singular and redemptive virtue: Mme de Canaples's self-abnegation.

And yet, if the novels explore the same territory—the stakes of gendered relations in a world of leisure and privilege—the standpoint from which this social interaction is narrated and judged produces different reading effects; point of view, we might say, ultimately constructs different readers. The construction of this differentiated readership is at the heart of canon-formation and its history is typically evaluated in the language of memory: thus, Voltaire recalling Duclos's publishing success with *Les Confessions du Comte de\*\*\**, remarks: "This isn't a book that will be handed down to posterity; it is only a chronicle of good luck, a story that goes nowhere, a novel without a plot, a work that leaves nothing to think about, and that one forgets as the hero forgets his mistresses. However, I imagine that the naturalness of the style, and especially the subject matter, have entertained young men and old ladies."[13] The only full-scale study of Riccoboni's work until recently was called: *Une romancière oubliée* (A Forgotten Lady Novelist). But that is another story.[14] For now we will deal with what the female novelist remembers.

In counterpoint to Duclos's worldly voice of masculine forgetfulness, in which as Voltaire points out, women are recollected in order for the man to recollect himself, Riccoboni's novel produces a female voice that throughout the space of the novel *remembers*. This voice attached to her past interrogates—sometimes anxiously, sometimes angrily—the consequences of being forgotten. Through the letters of one woman to another, Riccoboni tracks the movements of a female subjectivity that oscillates between forgetting and remembering, forgetting and forgiving. And in the end turns the question of forgetting's aftertext over to a community of women readers— Riccoboni's female plural "nous"—for their response: "How can we disentangle the genuine feeling that motivates them?"

*Juliette Catesby*, finally, like many novels in this tradition, also inscribes the signature of the woman writer whose material, like Riccoboni's, is precisely the story that Ossery's narrative of Miss Jenny tells. In the reading Juliette provides of his self-forgetting Riccoboni suggests another way for the story to turn out. As it stands, because Ossery's silence followed his forgetting, a dead woman lies between them. For feminist readers today, this insistence on the stakes of memory looks a lot like moral discourse on "moeurs."[15]

These problems of genre and the gendering of memory's narratives are inseparable from the relations of gender and power. In its etymology *libertine* includes the root of freedom: an exercise of mind played out in the body most often enjoyed by men, men free to forget. This freedom for women is often imagined in the eighteenth century by male libertine novelists: Laclos's creation of Merteuil is the most famous example. But as even the recent representations of that fiction show, this experiment is finally intolerable, insupportable in women. This for some is seen as a feminist point on Laclos's part. Riccoboni famously objected to his representation of Merteuil, not as an author, she said, but as a woman. And he answered by saying, he was just being a "realist": showing the way things were; that she, like other women writers, was gifted for embellishing reality: showing how things should be.

Reading Riccoboni's novel paired with Duclos's or indeed with Laclos's suggests that her acts of embellishment prove to be a powerful critique of social life in eighteenth-century France: of a libertine sociality that depends as we have seen on a separation of sexuality from feeling; a split, most importantly, that allows the one to forget the other. From the realm of feeling in which women are meant to live, the libertine view of the world is a world without memory— except, we might say, as a track record: a world of sequences cut off from meaning, from the "meaningful bodies" that women inhabit in the sentimental universe.[16] To forget these texts, by calling them sentimental, to remember only the stories they comment on, respond to, and rewrite, is not only to miss half of history, but to repress half the fictions of its cultural memory and their refusal to forget.

# 1735
# *The Gender of the Memoir-Novel*

Young people and women like novels that portray unhappy love
and that make them shed tears. The *Mémoires du Comte de
Comminge* have what it takes to make them cry.
    —Grimm, *Correspondance littéraire, philosophique et critique*

The *Mémoires de Comminges* (sic) are being read by everyone with
taste and are unanimously considered to be a well-written book.
Even if I weren't convinced of the justice of this praise, I wouldn't
conclude any the less that they deserve it.
    —Prévost, *Le Pour et Le Contre*

The *Mémoires du Comte de Comminge* were published anonymously
in The Hague in 1735. Although neither anonymous publication nor
publication in Holland was unusual in the period (as a result of censorship and the system of *privilèges* in France), the fact that Claudine
Guérin, the marquise de Tencin, who presided over a powerful
Parisian salon, chose, like Marie-Madeleine de Lafayette before her,
to publish her novels anonymously nevertheless raises critical questions about the contemporary status of French female writers and
their place in the canons of literary history. Thus the *Petit Larousse
illustré* (1986) lists Tencin under a description of her brother, Pierre
Guérin, cardinal de Tencin, archbishop of Lyons and minister of

state: "His sister, Claudine Alexandrine Guérin, born at Grenoble (1682–1749), the marquise de Tencin, maintained a famous salon and was the mother of d'Alembert." There is no mention of her writing. The structuring categories of the entry—sister to the cardinal, mother of the philosophe, *salonnière* to (male) writers and thinkers—body forth in the late twentieth century the stereotypes of what was called the "reign of women" in eighteenth-century France.

Tencin in fact wrote five novels. Three were published anonymously in her lifetime: *Comminge; Le siège de Calais* (1739); and *Les Malheurs de l'amour* (1747). The unfinished *Anecdotes de la cour et du règne d'Edouard II, roi d'Angleterre* (1766) and *Histoire d'une religieuse écrite par elle-même* (1786) were published posthumously with her signature. For thirty years after the publication of *Comminge*, the secret of its author's name was kept, although Tencin's friends Montesquieu and Marivaux (who left a famous portrait of her as Mme Dorsin in his own memoir-novel *La Vie de Marianne*, 1731), seem to have been in the know. According to a note added by an intimate to a collection of Montesquieu's published letters, Montesquieu, on the day of Tencin's death, acknowledged her authorship of novels thought by many to have been written by her nephew. Not until 1786, however, did her signature appear on the novel.

If much is known about Tencin's social and political life—she is typically described as an *intrigante* (a plotter, though this is not meant to refer to her novelistic technique)—how and why she came to writing remains a mystery. It appears that at about age fifty, having done as much as she could to advance the career of her famous brother, she invested her energies in a secret literary career and changed the population of her salon from priests to writers.[1]

The social commentator and literary critic La Harpe was one of many to describe *Comminge* as the "equal" of Lafayette's *Princesse de Clèves* (1768). Indeed, in 1804 the widely read and appreciated *Comminge* was published in an edition combining Tencin's novels with those of Lafayette and Marie-Louise de Fontaines. *Comminge* was republished at least a dozen times until 1835, after which it remained out of print until 1969. Its publication history is emblematic of the fate of eighteenth-century women's writing and of many seventeenth-century women's texts as well.

Standard literary history has placed Tencin along with Françoise de Graffigny and Marie-Jeanne Riccoboni under the rubric of the *roman sentimental,* characterizing their novels as poignant fictions of thwarted love that created both the audience for and the posterity of Rousseau's masterpiece *Julie, ou la nouvelle Héloïse* (1761). Recent feminist criticism has recast that genealogy, replacing the female writers of the eighteenth century in a strong literary tradition characterized by a recognizable narrative poetics that begins with Lafayette and continues through Germaine de Staël.

But identifying Tencin's place in this tradition, notably in relation to a powerful line of seventeenth-century precursors, is only a first step. Replacing women's writing in literary history requires a double revision: women's writing must be seen both in relation to a diachronic female tradition and in synchronic relation to the contemporaneous mix of male (and female) works. This second critical strategy involves more specifically a "reading in pairs": reading women's writing in the weave of men's, and, perhaps more radically, the other way around.

From this double perspective, we might wonder why, for her first novel, Tencin chose the model of a memoir in the masculine. The memoir-novel was, of course, an extremely popular and creative novelistic form from 1690 to 1750. The 1730s, which are generally seen as a decisive moment in the evolution of the French novel, also represent the high point of the form; its best-known examples are Prévost's *Manon Lescaut* (1731), Marivaux's *La Vie de Marianne* (1731–1741), and Crébillon's *Les Egarements du coeur et de l'esprit* (1736–1738). The memoir-novel seems to have developed in reaction to complex social and political pressures from critics and commentators both to create texts of greater narrative plausibility and to confront the competing demands of morality and realism. In contrast to the historically framed narrative modes favored in the seventeenth century, these fictional first-person retrospectives fashioned new spaces within which to represent the relations between gendered subjects and their changing social realities.

Typically the memoir-novel restages the narrator's experience of the world: from entrance into social life at adolescence, through a series of experiences in the apprenticeship of social relations (notably sexual encounters) to a detached view of that experience, generally to a disillusionment with worldly values. Although seventeenth-century female writers had authored successful and popular pseudomemoirs with female protagonists, by the 1730s the gender of recollection tended to be male.

Few female writers in the eighteenth century wrote memoir-novels. In the corpus of forty-six memoir-novels studied by Philip Stewart, for example, only three are by women (although some of the still-anonymous memoirs may have been female-authored).[2] Female writers were associated instead with the first-person feminine voices of the epistolary novel, which increasingly became the dominant form in the second part of the century; the first-person feminine retrospective was left largely to the male imagination—Marivaux's socially mobile Marianne and Diderot's ambiguous nun Suzanne are the most famous examples of the genre.

The fact that few female writers chose the memoir form in eighteenth-century France reflects in part the decline in social and political power enjoyed by dominant women in the seventeenth century. To produce a plausible retrospective fiction of worldliness required a certain indifference to the scandal of being a writing woman, and by the 1730s the protocol regulating the codes of public and private behavior for men and women had significantly curtailed the spheres of women's social autonomy and political intervention. But perhaps eighteenth-century fiction itself offers the sharpest reading of the consequences for women of going public with a female perspective on the apprenticeship of worldly life. Early in Laclos's *Liaisons dangereuses* (1782), for instance, a novel that casts a backward glance at the social and sexual intersections of the pre-Revolutionary elite, the Marquise de Merteuil, a woman of the world not entirely unlike Tencin in her remarkable mastery of social plots, imagines a *rouerie*, a sexual exploit, for the Vicomte de Valmont to include in *his* memoirs, memoirs that *she* would write and have published for him. Later in the novel, however, writing privately to Valmont, she supplies for his edification a condensed memoir of her own; this is the story of her duplicitous self-formation in the world. When the dangerous relations are unmasked at the end of the novel, the public—in the novel—is particularly shocked by the account of a woman's deliberate manipulation of social convention. Merteuil's punishment—social exile and hideous disfiguration—points very specifically to the price women pay for committing to writing the memoir of a female self whose social performance violates the prevailing social codes of masculine and feminine behavior.

Writing in 1735, Tencin had a variety of models to use for her first novel: memoirs of women by male writers writing as a woman (novels of female impersonation); memoirs of men by male authors (generally libertine novels); and third-person "historical" novels of aristocratic manners by women, in particular, the works of Lafayette and Villedieu. Tencin also had access to the first-person feminine memoirs of Henriette de Castelnau Murat, Villedieu, and, closer in time, the explicitly feminist memoir-novels of Mme Méheust, *Histoire d'Emilie* (1732) and *Les Mémoires du chevalier de . . .* (1743). By choosing anonymity but taking a man's name in the title of her memoir, Tencin produced an oblique fiction of dissent: a feminist critique of masculine privilege. Tencin's novel of male destiny interrogates the place of woman in patriarchal plots; it exposes the tradition that uses her as a pretext for male narrative, such as that of the exquisite cadaver of Prévost's *Manon Lescaut*.

The full title of Prévost's novel, *Histoire du chevalier des Grieux et de Manon Lescaut* (1731), is rarely used; even less that of the seven-volume *Mémoires et aventures d'un homme de qualité qui s'est retiré du monde* (1728–1731), to which *Manon Lescaut* was appended. But the wording of the original titles points to both the general narrative project of the memoir-novel and Prévost's role in shaping it. *Manon Lescaut* is the story of the Chevalier des Grieux as told to "the man of quality," the Marquis de Renoncour. In the "Notice" that frames the novel, the marquis presents des Grieux's story as one enough like his own for him to have considered inserting it into his own memoirs, but different enough to deserve narrative space of its own. Thus the older and wiser man of the world frames the account of the younger and authorizes the interest of that experience: "Each deed that is here reported is a degree of enlightenment, an instruction that substitutes for experience; each adventure is a model on which to form oneself; all it needs is to be adjusted to the circumstances one is in. The entire work is a treatise on morality shown entertainingly in practice" (*ML*, 19).[3] The model for formation proposed to the reader, like the relation that connects the two men's stories to each other, assumes a complicity of well-born masculine subjectivities.

Once the framing narrator has introduced the young man and provided him with the occasion to tell the story of his life, he withdraws, and the "I" who speaks tells of his undying passion for a woman, now dead, whose name in the history of the novel has displaced his. Thus, although the novel appears to belong to the eighteenth-century tradition of constructing fictional texts around a heroine's name and fate, in its narrative and in its ideology it is structured by the apprenticeship of masculine identity.

Des Grieux's story begins with a young man's entrance into the world: "I was seventeen and I was finishing my philosophy course in Amiens, where my parents, who belong to one of the best families in P____, had sent me" (*ML,* 27). Destined to join the Order of Malta, des Grieux, a younger son, takes a long detour from his rightful place in the social order by falling in love with a beautiful young woman "of common birth" (*ML,* 31). The disparities of class and circumstance—the faithful (though fallen-from-grace) seminarian and the fickle (though loving) courtesan—combine to create the pathos of opera (which Puccini and Massenet capitalized upon in the nineteenth century). The story follows the familiar sequences of illicit love punished: seduction, fleeting happiness, threat, betrayal, retribution. Despite the love that binds them, each time des Grieux and Manon set up a ménage, their domestic idyll is undermined by Manon's need for money. Des Grieux becomes a gambler, a thief, and a murderer in his efforts to fulfill Manon's desires. Finally, captured by the police and driven from the Old World by the rage of the fathers—his own and the man the young couple has tried to dupe—the couple attempts to find happiness in America. But legitimate and tranquil union is not to be the lot of the ill-fated lovers, prisoners of the state and of their desire: Manon dies of cold and exhaustion in the New World. In perhaps the most famous scene of the novel, des Grieux, after having "remained more than twenty-four hours with my lips pressed to the face and hands of my dear Manon" (*ML,* 188), breaks his sword to dig a grave for the idol of his heart, whom he has wrapped in all his clothes. Although he wishes for death, he survives and returns home with his friend, the faithful Tiberge, who has come from France to bring him help. The woman must die in order for the men to reestablish their bonds with each other.

Prévost revised the novel in 1753, and it is this edition that is most commonly preferred. The revisions include a change in the description of Manon's origins from modest to common—generally understood as an attempt to make her ambiguous behavior more palatable to bourgeois readers; a shortening of the time des Grieux spends attached to Manon's dead body, from two days and two nights to twenty-four hours; and an expanded penultimate sentence that shifts the emphasis from the dead father—the words upon which the novel originally ended—to the son's return.

Just before des Grieux reaches his account of Manon's death, he interrupts himself to address the marquis: "Forgive me if I finish in a few words a story that kills me. I am telling you of a misfortune without precedent. My whole life is devoted to weeping over it" (*ML*, 187). It is exactly this posture of the male mourner that Tencin adopts in opening the memoirs of her unhappy hero: "I have no other goal in writing the memoirs of my life than to recall the smallest circumstances of my misfortunes and to engrave them still more deeply, if that is possible, in my memory."[4] In both cases, a man's love for a dead woman engenders the memorialization of a life.

The plot of Tencin's novel is set in motion by a quarrel between two brothers as a result of a grandfather's will. Two young people whose fathers are mortal enemies meet and fall in love. Comminge decides to hide his true identity from Adélaïde de Lussan, the beautiful young woman whose name he did not know when he fell in love with her at first sight; then, once she learns the truth from him, he insists upon his right to marry her despite the paternal interdiction. His father imprisons him on the family estates, and Adélaïde sublimely decides to marry the most disagreeable man she can find in order to save Comminge's honor as a son and to free him for happiness. After the marriage, Comminge tries to see Adélaïde, who lives like a prisoner on her husband's estate, and comes to almost fatal blows with the jealous husband. But in the face of Adélaïde's resolve to endure her miserable destiny alone—"If I have not been mistress of my feelings, I have at least been of my conduct, and I have done nothing the most rigorous duty could condemn,"[5] she declares in language that echoes that of the Princess de Clèves—he abandons all hope and withdraws to a Trappist monastery, where toward the novel's end Adélaïde, freed by her husband's death, ultimately finds him. Disguised as a man, she lives among the monks until her early death.

The most famous scene in the novel is the last. Lying on the ashes, on the point of death, Adélaïde, still dressed as a monk, speaks in her woman's voice: she explains that wandering through the countryside after her liberation, she was lured into the monastery by the sound of her lover's voice singing; she followed him around secretly as he performed his spiritual exercises (in particular digging his own grave), but did not reveal herself to him because she did not want to threaten his salvation. As she expires, Comminge cries out in belated recognition and throws himself on her dead body. The monks forcibly tear him away from their final embrace but allow him to spend the rest of his days waiting for death in a hermitage, where presumably he writes the memoir of his unhappy life. Prévost, in his periodical *Le pour et le contre,* condemned the scene of the deathbed confession as an offense to plausibility, and in general the ending was criticized for not showing enough repentance and respect for religion. From 1764, when Baculard d'Arnaud adapted Tencin's novel into a successful play, *Les amants malheureux,* until well into the nineteenth century, the scene was greatly admired for its pathos and moral dimensions. By granting the lovers a moment of recognition—she realizes that he still loves her; he learns that she has always loved him—but not earthly reunion, Tencin, like Prévost, reproduces the narrative logic of much eighteenth-century fiction.

In *Manon Lescaut,* as in many other male-authored eighteenth-century novels, passion comes to challenge the class assumptions of the social order, the prejudices that bind property to propriety under patriarchal law. What, then, is the role of passion in a novel based on class identity? Like the seventeenth-century fictional model of aristocratic relations, passion in *Comminge* displaces difference from the oppositions of class to focus uniquely on those of gender. What difference does sexual difference make? If in feminist writing passion's ideal form is sublimation, then the difference within that difference is that women are superior to men; they love better without hope of fulfillment.[6]

Tencin's novel ends with her hero miserably rehearsing his second loss of the perfect woman. As Adélaïde explains in the confessional narrative of her own abbreviated memoir, her cherished Comminge, in love with her absence, failed to perceive her presence; fascinated by the fetishistic remains of their thwarted union (her farewell letter to him and her portrait, which he studies in tearful solitude), the man overlooks the woman whose sublimity he reveres.[7]

In its conclusion, the novel sharpens the critique of patriarchy by showing the ways in which the sons *as men* prove to be as blind as the fathers to the fatal embodiment of human relations. More pessimistic and more skeptical about the old realities of patriarchal authority than Prévost—whose novel finally returns the son to the land of his fathers and to his proper place—and perhaps bitter about the limits placed on the life of an exceptional woman forced to operate through men in it, Tencin's fiction represents the end of the line.

# PART THREE

# "I's" IN DRAG

# "I's" In Drag
## *The Sex of Recollection*

1669 saw the publication in France of a slim volume of correspondence often taken to be the origin or at least the intertextual model of
a certain kind of eighteenth-century novel. Published anonymously
and announced as "an accurate copy of the translation of five
Portuguese letters which were written to a gentleman of quality, who
was serving in Portugal,"[1] it was a one-way correspondence of love
letters entitled *Lettres portugaises traduites en français,* or, as it is
generally referred to in English, *The Letters of a Portuguese Nun.*
The history of the reception of the letters is the history of a debate
over origins, authorship, and authority that is documented in the
introduction to the Garnier edition of the letters and that I will not
rehearse here. I will, however, begin my discussion by citing the
opening moves of that text—"The Enigma of the Portuguese
Letters"—because it reveals an important translation or displacement
of what I take to be the more interesting riddle: why were these letters written by a man as a woman to himself and then thought to be
written by a woman?

> Whether for reasons of modesty [*pudeur*] or appearances [*préjugés*],
> the great works of the seventeenth century that stage the passions of
> love directly and without a mask are anonymous: we don't know
> what the respective participation of Mme de Lafayette, La

Rochefoucauld, and Segrais is in *La Princesse de Clèves;* exceptionally, twenty-five years after his death, a kind of miracle revealed the name of the author of the *Illustres françaises;* and finally, the most surprising case, three hundred years after the publication of the *Lettres portugaises,* editors of library catalogues still do not know under what name to file their author, nor even to which literature, French or Portuguese, they should attribute the letters.

But the problem does not concern scholars only. Every reader feels obliged to take part in this debate, and eventually his opinion becomes an article of faith. Why this unusual passion in a discussion of this sort? National pride plays only a small part, and the partisans of the "French" or "Portuguese" position have always had courteous confrontations. *What explains the ardor of the quarrel is that it raises the eternal question of the superiority of art or genius.* To admit that the *Lettres portugaises* were written in a convent, by a nun with virtually no education, and no experience of the world, is to believe that spontaneity, that pure passion inspired a woman to write a work superior to that which the best minds of the greatest period of French literature could offer their public.[2]

This strikes me as a curious, though not surprising way to explain the heat of the debate. To say that the heart of the matter is whether genius is superior to art, whether an untutored heart could produce a text worthy of the best minds of the century, is singularly to disembody the problematics of production. (After all, the genius of this putative heart is located theoretically at least in a woman's body.) An all the more curious translation when what follows in the argument is a series of quotations from male writers who have taken sides over the centuries on precisely the biological or material relations between gender and writing. La Bruyère, Laclos, Stendhal, and Sainte-Beuve are cited on the side of authenticity because women are naturally gifted for love and letter writing;[3] Rousseau on the side of what I will be calling "female impersonation."[4] Rousseau writes in a well-known footnote to the *Letter to d'Alembert:*

> Women in general love no art, are talented in none, and have no genius. They can succeed in minor works which require only a light touch, taste, grace, sometimes even philosophy and reasoning. They can acquire science, erudition, talents, and everything that is acquired by dint of work. But that celestial fire which heats and

enflames the soul, that genius which consumes and devours, that burning eloquence, those sublime transports which carry their ravishments to the depths of hearts, will always be lacking in women's writing: it is all cold and pretty just as they are; it has as much wit as you might wish, never any soul; it is a hundred times more reasonable than passionate. Women know neither how to describe nor how to feel love itself. Only Sappho, as far as I can tell, and another deserve to be excepted. I would bet anything in the world that the *Portuguese Letters* were written by a man. Wherever women dominate, their taste also dominates; and that is what determines the taste of our century.[5]

The logic of Rousseau's proof of authorship here devolves from the truth of castration, in turn guarantor of sexual identity as it can be read in or as textuality: "woman," defined negatively by her relation to what she will always lack, inevitably reproduces and mimes that lack in writing (no "soul"). Conversely, writing capable of bringing "ravishments to the depths of hearts" must have been produced by a subject in full possession of that which is missing in "woman." By virtue then of that sublime attribute periphrastically noted as genius, a man—Rousseau wagers—pens the *Portuguese Letters*. Leaving aside the familiar rhetoric of masculinist cultural theory, one might still ask why a man so endowed should write—as indeed Guilleragues did in this instance—as a woman? Why disguise (superior) phallic identity under the cover of the (inferior) feminine; and then cover the tracks of that impersonation with a second translation (one language into another)?[6]

Although it has become a critical commonplace to claim that the eighteenth-century novel evolved under the sign of "woman"—hypostatized in feminocentric fables consumed by a female reading public[7]—what seems less clear is the ideological content of the masculine investment in such an economy. More specifically, what secondary gains accrue to a male writer who supplies first-person feminine fictions—translations, as it were—within this system of production? My working hypothesis is that female drag allows the male "I" not so much to please the Other—by subscribing or capitulating to women's "taste"—as to become the Other, what Julia Kristeva calls in *Le Texte du roman* the pseudo-Other, the better to be admired by and for himself.[8] By this I mean that the founding contract of the novel as it functions in the phallocentric (heterosexual) economies of representation is homoerotic: "woman" is the legal fiction, the present absence that allows the male bond of privilege and authority to constitute itself within the laws of proper circulation.

Pseudo-feminocentrism as a strategy elaborated to translate this masculine self-affirmation, of course, is not limited to the agency of an "I" in female drag: and I would like to consider very briefly two manifestations of the phenomenon which unveil the workings of this fiction in the eighteenth century with less ambiguity perhaps than the *Portuguese Letters*. In *Manon Lescaut,* for example, Manon is indeed the narrative occasion of male desire for the Other—the Eternal Feminine—but a desire that must be (and ultimately will be) subordinated to the recovery of the same by the same, thus assuring the continuity of the name of the father. From the first line of the novel in which the reader is invited to return to the time in the author's life when he first met the Chevalier Des Grieux, to the last, which ends with the word "arrival" (Des Grieux's return to the world of the fathers), Manon's presence proves to be the privileged pretext of masculine identification: the ties that bind one man of quality to another. Des Grieux's story is literally generated by and deferred in the telling until Manon's death; and his narration justifies the author's investment of six "louis d'or" by providing him with a supplement—the son's adventures—which underwrites the paternal authority at stake in authorship. In *Les Confessions du comte de \*\*\*,* the story of a man's life dissipated through the detour of female sexuality is also told man to man, as a lesson to be understood by the logic of identification: the narrator and the narratee belong to the same family. In Duclos's novel, femininity is plural—twenty-three mistresses, depending on who's counting—rather than unique, and closure includes marriage; but again the precondition of the ideological intelligibility of the fiction is dependent upon a contract of masculine complicity: "I've thought your thoughts, I've found myself in the same situations; therefore don't completely discount the one I find myself in today."[9] In both of these novels the scene of narration is auto-referential: one man defines himself to another like him through the text of his experience of the Other, a text that requires the final neutralization of the Other as object of desire. Thus, the discourse of the Other exists in translation only: her words must pass through the linguistic structures of the dominant discourse as reported or paraphrased. Her words are filtered through the grid of an ideology that understands "woman" as incomprehensible hence admirable (Manon) or knowable hence despicable (the count's conquests: "I was to become disgusted with women by women themselves. . . . The whole sex had become a single woman for whom my taste was jaded"[10]). Curiously, however, perhaps from an unconscious (or self-conscious) need to authenticate for the reader the otherwise disembodied presence of the Other, a brief, "autonomous" text is provided: in both cases a letter. Manon literally signs "faithfully" the document of her infidelity, thus confirming her enigmatic mode in writing. But more interesting for our subsequent argument, Signora Marcella (in a unique, interpolated letter) documents her passion for the Count in a tale of seduction and abandonment translated from the original. The author explains in a note: "We felt obligated to translate this letter for those who might not understand Italian as well as they understand French."[11] In this narrative from one woman to another (which was forwarded to the author) the author/seducer relinquishes the privilege of narrative control to the foreign female text, commenting: "One will see in this letter details that I would have omitted as frivolous, and that are too important for an Italian woman to forget."[12] By temporarily abandoning the "I" of enunciation on his own behalf in favor of an existence in the third person in the amorous discourse of the Other, the count (or "le signor Carle" as he is named in this installment, a unique breach of anonymity) in effect insures the inscription of his irresistibility as a lover. And so we could say that what the masculine "I" of narration might have lost in a more responsible (less frivolous) first-person account, he gains in translation.

The narcissistic gain implicitly achieved by occupying the place of the desired object in the syntax of the Other is perhaps most clearly measured in that text of sexual recollection by a female impersonator, *The Memoirs of Fanny Hill*. In this ostensibly female-centered account of a "woman's" life, the contract of masculine complicity we saw regulating from within the pseudo-feminocentrism of the memorial novel, told from a male perspective, also binds the fathers and the sons, the author and his readers. The assumption of the Other's sexual identity through an "I" in drag constitutes an exemplary, if extreme, model of the erotics of authorship in the eighteenth-century novel: a mode of production calibrated not so much to seduce women readers as to attain recognition from other men. In this sense, it is not true that "Cleland through Fanny is transmuted into the first feminist," that "in Cleland's world of class, it is sexuality that makes all men and women equal."[13] Cleland's cheerful, even comic, pornography in the final analysis supports the prerogatives of both class and masculinity.

Self-consciously commenting on the sense of her ending, Fanny, her readers will recall, draws the moral of the tale for the benefit of her narratee, an anonymous "Madam" who had solicited the story of this remarkable life. Having emerged, as she puts it in her opening salutation, "to the enjoyment of every blessing in the power of love, health, and fortune to bestow, whilst still in the flower of youth,"[14] including marriage with the original ravisher of her innocence—a young man of gentle birth whose family had opposed the couple's conjugal project at the beginning of the novel—and the "legal parentage" of "fine children," Fanny concludes her narrative by paying final and literary homage to virtue:

> If you do me this justice, you will esteem me perfectly consistent in the incense I burn to Virtue. If I have painted Vice in all its gayest colours, if I have decked it with flowers, it has been solely in order to make the worthier, the solemner sacrifice of it to Virtue.
>
> You know Mr. C—— O——, you know his estate, his worth and his good sense: can you, will you pronounce it ill meant, at least of him, when, anxious for his son's morals, with a view to form him to virtue, and inspire him with a fixed, a rational contempt for vice, he condescended to be his master of ceremonies, and led him by the hand through the most noted bawdy-houses in town, where he took care he should be familiarized with all those scenes of debauchery, so fit to nauseate a good taste? The experiment, you will say, is dangerous. True, on a fool: but are fools worth so much attention?
>
> I shall see you soon, and in the meantime think candidly of me, and believe me ever,
>
> Madam,
>
> Your greatly obliged,
>
> and very humble servant,
>
> F******H***[15]

Thus, the novel of candid female experience, whose motto as announced at the start is "Truth! stark, naked truth," swerves in the end away from sexual revelation as it moves toward didactic recontainment. One kind of truth is translated into another; erotic *Bildung* is always philosophical.[16] The novel ends not only with marriage and legitimacy, but more important with the education of the son (and heir), an imperfect replication of the father's own experience. For it was in precisely one of the bawdy houses Fanny describes that his father met his mother. (Indeed, only an accident of "fate" prevented this young scion from having been conceived at a scene of debauchery.) In other words, the sex of female recollection reaches proper closure when it resubmits itself to the gender of paternal authority (Fanny's erotic adventures begin with her departure from the dead father's house), an authority protected by the blanks of anonymity, for we may learn Fanny's "maiden" name but not the family name of her husband, his estate, and his son.

But if in keeping with the prerogatives of the legitimate family, which is to say with the line of descent that determines masculine identity in the world, the generic constraints of memorial representation require the ultimate neutralization of disruptive female desire; this impersonation of female experience betrays the cultural sex of its author throughout—and well before the terms of proper fictional closure—in the play of its signifiers. "Fanny," J. H. Plumb writes in his introduction to the novel, "preoccupied with the climax of love and obsessed by the size and power of the engines"—one of the more common translations of penis in the novel[17]—is "in fact a male dream, with little contact with the reality of feminine passion." And he goes on to comment: "here, perhaps, may be a key to Cleland himself, if not to the cause of the novel's continuing popularity. After all, *Fanny Hill* is written in the first person: Cleland identifies himself, as it were, with Fanny; perhaps this is the reason for what Peter Quenell has called Fanny's preoccupation with the 'longitudinal fallacy' a preoccupation we know from Kinsey is exceptionally rare, almost nonexistent among women."[18] In other words, the "longitudinal fallacy," or the "phallacy" of reference, tells us that the "I" of narration is indeed in drag. The memoir of this woman of pleasure is the celebration of a familiar privileged signifier.

If women, as Virginia Woolf writes in a well-known passage from *A Room of One's Own,* have "served all these centuries as looking-glasses possessing the magic and delicious power of reflecting the figure of man twice its natural size," and if without that aggrandizing support, "the figure in the looking glass shrinks,"[19] it is no great wonder that pornography—the harlot's textuality—has generally been figured by a male "I" in female drag, reinscribing while literalizing the metaphor of feminine reflection. Let us consider the following emblematic passage, this blazon of the desired masculine representation as it is imagined through imaginary female eyes:

> I saw with wonder and surprise, what? not the plaything of a boy, not the weapon of a man, but a maypole of so enormous standard that, had proportions been observed, it must have belonged to a young giant: yet I could not, without pleasure, behold, and even venture to feel such a length, such a breadth of animated ivory! perfectly well-turned and fashioned, the proud stiffness of which distended its skin, whose smooth polish and velvet softness might vie with that of the most delicate of our sex, and whose exquisite whiteness was not a little set off by a sprout of black curling hair round the root, through the jetty sprigs of which the fair skin showed as in a fine evening you may have remarked the clear light ether through the branchwork of distant trees overtopping the summit of a hill: then the broad and bluish-casted incarnate of the head, and blue serpentines of its veins, altogether composed the most striking assemblage of figure and colours in nature. In short, it stood an object of terror and delight.[20]

Fanny's expanded metaphor is structured like the multitiered similes of the *Iliad:* this male member is like a maypole is like an ivory column is like a tree in the forest is like a marble bust. And, as in the epic recollection of heroic excess, the spectator is not so much invited to visualize the signifiers as to grasp their common signified and thus to wonder—like Fanny—in awe, to admire what is larger than life, and to enter into the sublime. The forest matters rather more than any particular tree; and it is a familiar landscape of what used to be called phallic symbols. What is less familiar in this representation is the comparison of masculine impressiveness with female delicacy, as though the feminine were indeed the standard of comparison ("our sex"); the measure of positivity is translated to invoke the breast or perhaps the clitoris ("smooth polish and velvet softness"). Still, though the female is valued in *Fanny Hill,* unlike the violent topographies of Sadian desire, for example, which fundamentally have no place for the biological female, Cleland through Fanny glorifies the phallus no less than will Sade. Fanny practices what Juliette in her first-person narrative is taught by Noirceuil: "This tool is my god, let it be one unto thee, Juliette; extol it, worship it, this despotic engine [*ce vit despote*], show it every reverence, it is a thing proud of its glory, insatiate, a tyrant."[21] Though neither Fanny nor Juliette disregards her own pleasure in the service of the phallus, the economy of representation in both novels is redundantly masculine. Or rather, the erotics erected by female impersonation is a mirroring not of female desire but of a phallic pride of place, a wish-fulfillment that ultimately translates into structures of masculine dominance and authority.

If then, the recollecting masculine "I" disguised in *Fanny Hill* through the memory of sexual history becomes or borrows the body of the Other to better assure the transcendence of the Same—the possibility of difference being lost precisely in translation—if, moreover, "pornography is an expression of *man's desire to have the effect on women that he knows he does not, in reality have,*"[22] is it otherwise when the "I" in drag writes not the pornography of fantasized possession but the romance of fascinating dispossession? Does the tragic female voice, like the comic female voice, conjure up an image that aggrandizes and reassures phallic identity? What might be at stake when a man stages himself as a woman longing for his presence in his absence? Roland Barthes writes in *A Lover's Discourse:*

> Historically, the discourse of absence is carried on by the Woman: Woman is sedentary, Man hunts, journeys; Woman is faithful (she waits), man is fickle (he sails away, he cruises). It is Woman who gives shape to absence, elaborates its fiction, for she has the time to do so; she weaves and she sings; the Spinning Songs express both immobility (by the hum of the Wheel) and absence (far away, the rhythms of travel, sea surges, cavalcades). It follows that in any man who utters the other's absence *something feminine* is declared: this man who waits and suffers from his waiting is miraculously feminized. A man is not feminized because he is inverted but because he is in love. (Myth and utopia: the origins have belonged, the future will belong to those subjects *in whom there is something feminine.*)[23]

Mariana, the Portuguese nun, who waits in vain for the return of her beloved and absent hero, clearly embodies the conditions of this feminine discourse. The model for this prototype of eighteenth-century (epistolary) fiction is the inversion of Greek and Roman epic and myth, Ovid's *Heroides*—twenty-one love letters in verse—which were widely translated in Europe from the thirteenth century on: Penelope writes to Odysseus, Helen to Paris, and most important for the thematic structure of the *Portuguese Letters,* Dido, seduced and abandoned, writes to Aeneas. Although Barthes explicitly invokes the possibility of a male voice of absence, the classical "figure" of absence—its textuality—remains bound to the feminine. Thus, even his privileged and engendering source in the *Lover's Discourse,* *Werther,* does not supply him with the perfect example because according to the rules "amorous absence . . . can only be articulated by the one who remains—not the one who leaves: *I* always present only constitute myself in relation to *you* constantly absent."[24] However, although Werther (like Saint-Preux before him) suffers at a distance from the beloved object, he indeed performs its figures. For "to invoke absence is to posit from the start that the place of the subject and the place of the other cannot be reversed; it is to say: 'I am less loved than I love.'"[25]

Mariana says no more no less than this and, like Echo, withers away in her body by dint of repetition. Rather she writes to the man of her desire, and the writing endlessly reweaves the web of absence, the text of recollection. The fifth and last letter begins: "I am writing to you for the last time, and I hope to make you understand, by the difference in the terms and manner of this letter, that you have finally persuaded me that *you no longer love me and therefore I must no longer love you:* I will send you everything that still remains to me of you as soon as possible. Do not fear that I will write to you; I won't even put your name on the packet."[26] The letter, of course, goes on, rehashing the past, rehearsing her bitterness, asking him not to write and ending with this declaration: "I don't want anything more from you, I am mad to repeat the same things so often, I must leave you and no longer think of you; must I give you an exact account of everything I do?"[27]

Though the text formally ends here, this is the trope of a penultimate masochism, the always renewable figure of feminine suffering. The question clearly requires no reply; in fact it excludes response because Mariana's letters have become self-generating. She has now become one with her pain. The absence of reply, however, in no way evacuates the presence of the addressee. Rather, the love object is eternalized even as it is excoriated. Thus, when Dido imagines the inscription on her marble tomb, she records a figure of immolation beyond its reference and including its authors: "FROM AENEAS CAME THE CAUSE OF HER DEATH, AND FROM HIM THE BLADE; FROM THE HAND OF DIDO HERSELF CAME THE STROKE BY WHICH SHE FELL."[28] Through the wound that comes to the female from the male—Dido writes, she says, the Trojan's blade ready in her lap—Aeneas lives on (like Ovid).

Though Mariana's lover is never named nor the translator of her passion identified, perhaps this model of literary narcissism structures the *Portuguese Letters* as well. We are invited, after all, with the liminal fiction of the "Au lecteur" to remember the addressee of the letters: the gentleman of quality who inspired their production and the man who translated them into French. The "woman" through whose body the text came to exist is thus twice silenced. Mariana's identity, the sex of her "I," is pronominally neutralized: "I don't know the name of the man to whom the letters were written, nor of the one who translated them, but it seemed to me that I wouldn't displease them by making the letters public."[29] Even the fiction of authenticity denies the subject her authorial prerogatives. Her *testimony* as Other, however, remains to insure the continued contemplation and circulation of the same by the same. The letters cannot be returned to the sender, for the sender has been lost in translation.

But the stakes of female impersonation may be more complex, less narcissistic, than I have made them out to be. Perhaps the "extreme solitude" which, Barthes writes in the incipit to his book, is the lot of he who speaks the lover's discourse, is too painful, too threatening to be assumed in a masculine identity. Perhaps the miraculous feminization which attends the man who speaks the suffering of absence resembles inversion too closely in a century preoccupied with the grammar of sexual identity to be spoken with comfort even in fiction. Female impersonation historically has been the protective coloration of the desire to exist in the utopia invoked by Barthes where the anxiety of sexual difference temporarily might be disguised, if not allayed.

# L'HISTOIRE D'UNE GRECQUE MODERNE
## No-Win Hermeneutics

The beloved woman conceals a secret, even if it is known to everyone else. The lover himself conceals the beloved: a powerful jailer.
We must be harsh, cruel, and deceptive with those we love. Indeed,
the lover lies no less than the beloved: he sequesters her, and also is
careful not to avow his love to her, in order to remain a better
guardian, a better jailer.
—Gilles Deleuze, *Proust and Signs*

In *S/Z*—an analysis of Balzac's novella *Sarrasine*—published in 1970
and qualified in its incipit as "the trace of work" that had taken place
in 1968 and 1969, Roland Barthes marks off his distance from the
aesthetic passion of "the first analysts of narrative" (*SZ*, 3) for a single structure capable of accounting for any narrative instance: a desire
indifferent to textual difference. He proposes a more modest pursuit
of structuration and differentiation: a "commentary . . . based on the
affirmation of the plural" (*SZ*, 15).[1] Three years later, in a replay of
the operating procedures which characterized *S/Z*, Barthes, perform-
ing a textual analysis of Edgar Allan Poe's "The Facts in the Case of
M. Valdemar," reiterates and clarifies the stakes of this freer enterprise: "Our goal is neither to find *the* meaning of the text, nor even a

meaning; our work doesn't belong to a hermeneutics of literary criticism which seeks to interpret the text according to the truth thought
to be hidden in it."[2] Barthes would resist hermeneutic hegemony,
abstain from interpretation, unless understood in the "Nietzschean"
sense of the term: "To interpret a text is not to give it . . . a meaning,
but on the contrary to appreciate what *plural* constitutes it."[3] He
would neither dredge up the Truth, nor impose the Gospel from
without, but read—by rewriting—these classic fictions both and
simultaneously in their linearity and in their paradigmatic play: read,
reread of course, for and through polyphony.[4] With characteristic
perversity, moreover, Barthes chooses to read two stories which
themselves are about uncovering the truth and making sense: about
meaning. The challenge implicit in such a choice is obvious: to confront an enigma, to track its inscription step by step, without falling
victim, like Oedipus, to the desire to answer the riddle, to the desire
for the meaning which animates and even organizes the text itself.
But is it possible to traverse such a space—a topography of tempta-
tion—to tie oneself to the mast like Odysseus and not succumb to the
song of the sirens?

Barthes seeks to protect himself against interpretation by not structuring (ranking) the five codes through which he reads: there are no
stars, as it were. The cast of the codes is listed in order of their
appearance. Nevertheless, Barthes acknowledges that two of the
codes—the hermeneutic and the proairetic—block plurality and thus
constitute the limits of the classic text. Although Barthes then proposes a "democratic" (reading) process—one which would not
reinscribe the power of those particular codes in a hierarchy—
because he has chosen to read a fiction structured by an enigma, his
practice, I would argue, necessarily privileges the hermeneutic code,
and its unfolding as/in narrativity. I am suggesting, then, that despite
his precautions, Barthes succumbs to the mimetic fallacy in *S/Z*, and
falls into interpretation—as one falls in love. I am also suggesting
that, despite that surrender, his critical strategy paradoxically exemplifies a modality of reading peculiarly suited to enigmatic texts, of
which *L'Histoire d'une Grecque moderne* is one.[5] In the following
pages I propose to read Prévost's "readerly" text through a move of
mimeticism designed to unveil the novel's resistance to Oedipal
hermeneutics.[6]

Barthes's first step in his reading of *Sarrasine* is a question: "What is Sarrasine?" Or rather, a temporarily rhetorical interrogation, "A noun? A name? A thing? A man? A woman?" that leads him to the definition of the first of the five codes through which he will perform his analysis:

> Let us designate as *hermeneutic* code . . . all the units whose func-
> tion it is to articulate in various ways a question, a response, and
> the variety of chance events which can either formulate the question
> or delay its answer. (*S/Z*, 17)

Within this lexia and this same segment of textual commentary, Barthes identifies his second code.[7] The second code is *semantic,* the code of the signifieds. It is the locus par excellence of connotation(s). And the instance of that code here (the final "e" of Sarrasine) as it happens, is femininity.

> Femininity (connoted) is a signifier which will occur in several
> places in the text; it is a shifting element which can combine with
> other similar elements to create characters, ambiances, shapes, and
> symbols. (*S/Z*, 17)

Thus far, the grid of *S/Z* and Prévost's novel would seem to be made for each other. Moreover, just as Barthes finds the remaining three codes within the title and first sentence of *Sarrasine,* without "forc-ing" as he puts it, by "chance . . . (but what is chance)" (*S/Z*, 18), the same is also true of the *Grecque moderne.*

But as I suggested earlier, the pertinence of *S/Z*'s critical relation with the *Grecque moderne* lies in Barthes's meta-concern with the structuring properties of enigma in/as fiction. Therefore, I would like to suspend the presentation of the codes for a moment to set up the sequence (contained of course in the definition of the hermeneutic code itself) according to which enigma is written. When in *S/Z* Barthes arrives at the epiphany in *Sarrasine,* the moment at which the riddle of narrative desire is solved, he announces: "All the enigmas are now disclosed, the vast hermeneutic sentence is closed" (*S/Z*, 209). What follows is a ten-point outline of the "morphemes" or "hermeneutemes" that make up this standard rhetorical period. It is against this sentential model that I will be reading Prévost's novel.[8]

For reasons of space, I will group the units in clusters, without, however, dissolving their underlying teleology. The first two stages of figuration are: "1. *thematization,* or an emphasizing of the subject which will be the object of the enigma; 2. *proposal,* a metalinguistic index which, by signaling in a thousand different ways that an enigma exists, designates the hermeneutic (or enigmatic) *genus*" (*S/Z,* 210–11). In a parallel operation, I will be focusing specifically on those textual elements that embody most literally and unambiguously the five codes; and having identified them a first time, will leave the pleasure of recognizing them to my readers.

We might well begin with the title, asking as does Barthes confronted with "Sarrasine": *What is* a "Grecque moderne"? The reader familiar with eighteenth-century titles will anticipate correctly a *plot* of love and intrigue—to feature a heroine is to figure an amorous text—the erotic doubled by the exotic, desire inflected by difference: a fiction, in a word, of femininity and otherness. What cannot emerge from an educated guess, however, is the content of "moderne": for to yoke "moderne" to "Grecque" is to bind opposites together (East/West). To the eighteenth-century reader, then, a "Grecque moderne" is an oxymoron in the dictionary of received ideas, a conundrum that requires elucidation. Thus the title at once thematizes the enigma, feminizes its orientation and introduces the symbolic code—concretized first in *Sarrasine* by the rhetorical figure of antithesis.[9] The narrative proper, however, opens with an anxious assessment bearing less upon the object of enigma than on its decryptographer: "Will the confession which will serve as my introduction not cast doubt on me? I am in love with the beautiful Greek whose story I am going to attempt to tell." And a few lines later: "To come straight to the point, what sort of reliability should one expect from a pen guided solely by love?" (*GM,* 3)(59). *What is* a "Grecque moderne"? We are given part of the answer: "a beautiful Greek," an object of love, and more to the point, a textual love object. Indeed, the focus here is upon the narrator's written relationship to the reader via his obscure object of desire: that is, to the reader through her story, which is to say, his text.[10] Will the reader believe him? Is he reliable? The enigma is thus double in its postulation. And its articulation is redoubled yet again by the symbolic code as antithesis: the implicit potential for the truth in confession, threatened explicitly by the equivocality of doubt. The same lexia contains the fourth code as well, the proairetic or action code—"the ability rationally to determine the truth of an action" (*S/Z*, 18)—which in narrative belongs to the purview of discourse: here, the penned confession, *testimony*. Thus the exordium, beginning and ending as it does with a question, and challenging the reader to make sense of "an intentionally obscure statement that depends for full comprehension on the alertness and ingenuity of the reader" (*Webster's Third* definition of enigma), redundantly establishes the hermeneutic mode in which the novel is *meant* to be received.

The fifth code remains to be identified. Although it can be perceived in the title itself as intertextuality, it is perhaps more clearly visible in the first sentence of the narration following the exordium: "I had been appointed to the King's ministry at a court whose customs and intrigues I knew better than anyone else" (*GM*, 4) (61). This fifth code is called the "Gnomic code": "one of the numerous codes of knowledge or wisdom to which the text continually refers; we shall call them in a very general ways *cultural codes* . . . or rather, since they afford the discourse a basis in scientific or moral authority, we shall call them reference codes" (*S/Z*, 18). This code in Prévost's novel takes the form of cultural clichés, maxims, proverbs, all centered as one might expect on the problems of orientalism: of difference doubled by sexual difference, and the vicissitudes of decoding another discourse.

The narrator's eventual plight, therefore, is somewhat surprising. For this outsider, this Frenchman, speaks perfect Turkish. And Constantinople is his home away from home: "I found myself as free and at home in a city where I had lived scarcely two months as I was in *the place where I was born*" (*GM*, 4) (61; emphasis added). This theoretical syncretism of origins, however, which produces such a Turkish Frenchman is in hermeneutic practice undone by an impenetrable epistemological divide: occidental and oriental attitudes toward sexuality. Thus, the narrator's first (and reiterative) interpretive failure—"I could not understand their point of view" (Je pénétrois mal dans leurs vues) (*GM*, 5)(62)—derives from his desire to out-Turk (by his silence) his Turkish connection on the place of women in discourse: "the most delightful subject which could ever enliven a conversation" (*GM*, 5)(62). Although his discretion and

curiosity will soon be rewarded by an initiation into the esoteric mysteries of the seraglio—the origin of his story and introduction to the
object of his enigma—we should perhaps stop here to open a parenthesis on the recurring intersection of certain codes in this novel, and
the relation of that intersection to the narrator's dilemma, his lack of
penetration. As we have seen, the object of the enigma is a woman;
and a woman with whom the narrator is in love. Now in Western
culture and narrative, to write "woman" is *already* to connote enigma. As Naomi Schor has noted in another context: "a character's
femininity institutes from the moment she is named an enigma whose
solution will not necessarily be synchronous with the closure of the
text."[11] If "woman" as linguistic sign is already an inwritten enigma,
a pretext that requires but eludes solution, a foreign woman is twice
enigma. Moreover, in this instance, the key with which the code
might be broken is itself a text, and a text locked (blocked, Barthes
would say) by its own closure: the code of knowledge is auto-referential. By this I mean that the maxims of Western discourse which
constitute the narrator's claim to authority are constantly short-cir-
cuited by ethnocentricity: a linguistic autism which prevents him
from making sense of the very foreignness that intrigues and baffles
him. Finally, the foreignness is coded not merely by difference but by
a radical alterity: the figure of antithesis. As a result, the coding of the
predominant signifieds in this novel—HER: what is a "Grecque moderne"?; SEM: oriental femininity; SYM: antithesis (oxymoron); REF:
Encyclopedia of the West—overdetermine by redundancy the founding undecidability of the narration and the agony of the narrator's
project (ACT: testify). But we should perhaps close the parenthesis
before foreclosing the pleasure of our reading.

The narrator's local Pasha introduces him into the closure of
harem life, singling out one beauty in particular for contemplation:
"'That one is a Greek whom I have owned for only six months. I
have no idea where she came from'" (*GM*, 8)(64). Zara, as she is
then called, puzzles the Pasha: "'However, in view of the breadth and
astuteness of mind that I have recognized in her, I sometimes marvel
at how quickly she was able to adjust to our ways, and I cannot find
any suitable explanation other than the strength of our example and
customs'" (*GM*, 8)(64). The Greek slave, like the French ambassador,
is distinguished by adaptability and an aptitude for flourishing in

translation. Moreover, if the Ambassador is an honorary Turk, the slave is worth a Frenchwoman: "'You may speak with her for a moment if you wish . . . and I will be sorely mistaken if you do not discover in her all those qualities which raise women in your country to the highest positions and which make them destined for great things in life'" (*GM*, 8)(64). The interview thus inevitably dwells on the issue of difference, free Christian women vs. Turkish slave girls. This exchange inspires Zara to action: a letter pleading for freedom and the privileged status of "those women who love virtue" (*GM*, 11)(66). At first blush, the narrator literally does not understand the letter, for it is written in Greek, a language he has yet to master. Therefore, his "language tutor" becomes his translator and go-between until the complicated negotiations involved in Zara's liberation are completed.

Zara marks her new status by changing her name. Abandoning the "Z," the exotic (hence erotic) letter par excellence of the European alphabet, but retaining her Greekness through the linguistic roots *Théo-* and *-phé*, she inscribes her difference from her former self.[12] But if her new Christian name, although italicized in its first appearance in the novel, is passed over in silence, her father's name, her patronymic, though *blank*, is not. Despite Théophé's insistence that in her (parthenogenetic) family tree the narrator is to be all of her fathers—"time and again she called me names like savior, father, god" (*GM*, 22)(77); "she repeated over and over again that it was to me that she really owed her birth" (*GM*, 64)(114)—this rhetoric of nomination leaves intact the question of real origins. Théophé, however, claims not to know the truth of her genealogy: "'My first recollections,' she said, 'are of a town in Morea where my father passed himself off as a foreigner, and it is only because of what he has told me that I think I am Greek, although he never did reveal the place of my birth to me'" (*GM, 23*)(78). This first sentence of her history is riddled with signifiers of doubt: the uncertain civil status of her father; her birth certificate constituted by his word alone; and her birthplace deliberately occulted. Though the veil that hides her origins is not lifted, Théophé's subsequent account of her past life impresses the Ambassador by its intellectual coherence: "Our language differences aside, I found in the young Greek girl all the intelligence that Cheriber had praised" (*GM, 46*)(98). But the very elegance of her narrative raises doubts in his mind: "The more I recognized the way her mind worked, the more suspicious I became of her shrewdness . . . Today, as in ages past, to trust a Greek is an ironical saying" (*GM*, 47)(98). Caught between the maxims of his culture and the vanity of his narcissism, the ambassador undertakes his own research, only to complain to the oriental authorities and potential source of information about Théophé's mother: "And finally, would it not have been an easy matter to retrace the kidnapper's steps and to follow them through in the most minute detail? That is how we proceed in Europe . . . and if we were no more devoted to seeing that justice was done than you, you and I might understand each other better on the subject of how crimes should be investigated" (*GM*, 61)(111). His European methods of detection indeed uncover a plausible, possible, even probable "real" family. The evidence, however, remains circumstantial and the putative father consistently refuses to recognize Théophé as his daughter. But because the narrator/detective is determined to solve the problem of Théophé's origins, in the absence of incontrovertible facts he is reduced to wish-fulfillment: taking his desires for realities.

Now, the ambassador's urgency in legitimizing Théophé—having left the seraglio and being without a family she would be vulnerable to the laws of circulation—is both Christian and "French." And the ambiguity inherent in this double agenda—his stated desire to be the father and liberator Théophé wishes him to be and his unstated desire to possess her—is inextricably bound up with his ambivalent assessment of Théophé's "true" nature. Despite her experience, could she still be innocent? Was her desire to be released from the constraints of the seraglio moral and disinterested, a "natural," instinctive yearning for a better life, triggered and concretized by her high-toned exchange with the ambassador? Or, weary of harem life "and perhaps encouraged by the hope of a more independent life for herself, she had considered leaving Cheriber in order to change her environment . . . hoping to inspire some feelings of compassion in me for her, she had taken advantage of the little speech I had made in order to win me over where I was most vulnerable" (*GM*, 47)(99). Convert or opportunist? Pure or soiled? Exception or the rule? This undecidability constitutes point three of the hermeneutic sentence: the formulation of the enigma.

What does it mean to be a "Grecque moderne"? What's her story? Faced with competing claims on Théophé's destination—from her "family" and from the Sélictar, a local rival—the ambassador chooses to act on a shred of plausibility: "Moreover, what I had found to be most believable in her story was how ignorant she still was about love" (*GM,* 49–50)(101). The ambassador would rewrite the truth of her past; eradicate the stain and the stigma of his predecessor's caresses. Thus convincing himself that Théophé is both untouched *and* available to him, the ambassador, following a less than impeccable logic, makes Théophé an offer he cannot imagine she might refuse: to live with him *à la française*. This proposition corresponds to the fourth point of the hermeneutic sentence, *"request for an answer"* (*S/Z,* 210), and as such initiates the fundamental question/answer sequence at the heart of this and every enigmatic fiction. The proposition is of course a declaration of love disguised as an offer of political asylum:

> You will be free and respected there. Put aside all these ideas you have of life in a seraglio . . . I do not intend to bring other people out to see you, with the exception of a few French friends of mine who can give you some background information about the customs of my country. . . . In the end you will come to understand the difference between having to share an old man's heart with other women in a seraglio and living with a man my age who would do everything possible to please you and who would make a conscientious effort to make you happy. (*GM,* 81)(128–29)

Since every declaration of love is in fact a question—do you love me?—only a reply of reciprocity can supply a satisfactory answer:

> Consequently more concerned with my own feelings than with a plan that I had formulated with such elation, I waited most impatiently for her to explain how she felt about me and what she thought about the tranquillity and security I was trying to emphasize in the offer I was making. *Her hesitation to answer was already causing me some concern.* (*GM,* 81)(129; emphasis added)

Théophé's delay in answering and the narrator's resultant anxiety are built into the structure of the hermeneutic quest:[13] "Narratively, an enigma leads from a question to an answer, *through a certain number of delays.* Of these delays, the main one is unquestionably the feint, the misleading answer, the lie, what we will call the *snare*" (*S/Z*, 32). This dilatory movement toward and away from the truth (a straight answer) corresponds to points five and six of the rhetorical period. Thus, Théophé answers without answering: she expresses her gratitude for the generosity extended, but circumvents the erotic thrust of the proposition. (We might also say that the slave refuses to play the master's game, refuses the trap of magisterial discourse, a discourse constructed around the power of the *double entendre*.)

The ambassador does not ask again. Instead, "too happy to see her agree to be taken to my country estate, I did not even go to the trouble of pondering whether she had understood my intentions or even whether her answer was a consent or a refusal, and I hastened to leave with her immediately" (*GM,* 82)(129). This failure to analyze a response so equivocal as to be qualified as either assent or refusal is the blind spot, the figure really of what I referred to earlier as the vanity of narcissism. And I might well borrow here again from Barbara Johnson's analysis of Sarrasine's symptom: "What is at stake is not the union between two people, but the narcissistic awakening of one"; like Sarrasine, the diplomat "cannot listen to the other as other,"[14] assumes he will get the answer he wants by subsuming Théophé's feelings to his. On the point of entering Théophé's room to reap the fruits of his generous protection, the narrator retroactively comments upon the status of his confidence: "Up until then, it had seemed to me that Théophé had concurred quite willingly with my plans, and I thought her so well disposed to the logical conclusion of this evening that it never crossed my mind to veil my hopes for what was to follow" (*GM,* 92–93)(139). But if what he takes to be unveiled language stems in part from his confusion of identities, it proceeds too from his code of reference. This Frenchman rescued Théophé from a harem, after all: "I hardly considered it necessary to take those roundabout ways one sometimes must use in order to overcome a young, inexperienced girl's modesty in light of the fact that here was a woman who had spoken to me so frankly about her adventures . . . in the seraglio" (*GM,* 93)(139). Launched from the trajectory of his desire, he forgets Théophé's original appeal to his esteem for "those women who love virtue" (*GM,* 11)(66), cancels the maxims of "Christianity" he himself just put into circulation, reinscribing instead—and justifies after the fact—the reputation of "the galant gentlemen of our nation" (*GM*, 6) (63): chauvinist *avant la lettre*.

As the scene plays itself out, Théophé has recourse to the well-stocked arsenal of modern, i.e., French and novelistic, feminine delaying tactics: she expresses pained surprise at the frank (at last) articulation of masculine desire, and weeps. And then, abjectly, begs for pity: "'Oh, best of all men,' she said, using an expression common to the Turks, 'be a better judge of what your poor slave feels" (*GM*, 96)(142). The ambassador is discountenanced and Théophé asks for time to answer. Before she has a chance to explain herself, however, the ambassador redeclares himself. Théophé replies by citing his blindness: "I am dying of shame because ever since the time I have been trying to make you understand what is in my heart of hearts, I have succeeded so wretchedly in making you comprehend what I really feel there" (*GM*, 101)(146). The narrator then acknowledges his perplexity: "I tried to make her comprehend . . . that everything that had been in any way connected with her since I had first seen her was a *perpetual enigma* to me and that even the way she was speaking to me then made her more difficult to understand [*pénétrer*]. 'Speak in a straightforward manner [*naturellement*],' I said to her. 'Why do you hesitate? To whom could you speak more confidently than to me?'" (*GM*, 102) (146; emphasis added). The narrator thus arrives at point seven of the hermeneutic sentence: *jamming*, acknowledgment of the insolubility of the enigma" (*S/Z*, 210).

Théophé of course can neither perform "naturally" (enter into the lie of his scenario), nor speak "naturally" because by definition she is unscriptable and dispossessed of a natural, maternal language. Instead, she returns the enigma to the eye of the beholder (the narrative "I") by repeating her story. Her answer to the implicit question—but what *is* a "Grecque moderne"?—is a reiteration of her history coded by the founding opposition of vice to virtue, East to West. This time, the ambassador, confronted by the language of his own official discourse, submits to Théophé's voice, and to being a Pygmalion who will not seek to make his statue flesh: "I promised Théophé all the attention I could possibly give to completing the work which I had had the pleasure of starting, and I pledged to her unequivocally that I would give her the freedom . . . to hate and despise me if she ever saw me fail to meet the conditions that she herself would wish to impose upon me" (*GM,* 106)(150). The enig-matic sentence would seem to be on the point of foreclosure, of dissolution. The narrator embraces the terms of Théophé's truth—a "Grecque moderne" is a freed slave in love with virtue—even to the point of eliminating future linguistic interference (the "jamming" produced by translation) by initiating Théophé into the finer points of his culture (the text of her modernity) through language and litera-ture: "She received her very first lessons in our language right from me. She made surprising progress. . . . Nothing that had to do with the way I really felt about her escaped" (*GM,* 114)(157). But if Book I of the novel ends on a suspension of interrogation (and desire), Book II reinscribes it.

The return of the quest for the truth hidden in the object of desire is inevitable, at least predictable. The preceptorial arrangement described above is based upon the containment of desire on the nar-rator's part. But the frustrated lover, as he styles himself in the exordium, has not renounced all hope of one day possessing his "beautiful Greek"; he has merely postponed and attempted to subli-mate his erotic impulses. Nor can the rustic sanctuary in which the couple resides protect Théophé from the laws of circulation to which a "Grecque moderne" is subject: Synese is or is not Théophé's broth-er; Paniota Condoidi is or is not her father; Théophé is or is not forever bound to her "mentor in the ways of virtue" (*GM,* 173)(209). Because of these ambiguous alliances—by definition neither truth nor falsehood—Théophé's hermeneutic status is dependent upon her social inscription. And within the closing phase of Book I, renewed doubts about that inscription guarantee that the interrogation will resume.[15] Moreover from the beginning the question of Théophé's "essence" was linked to a problematics of *destination.* Before the ambassador had acknowledged any conscious pretensions to possess-ing Théophé, he had wondered what was to become of her: "I was curious to find out exactly what her plans might be. She must have understood that by setting her free I had no right to exact anything from her and that, on the contrary, I was waiting for her to tell me what she wanted to do next" (*GM,* 48)(100). Even and already at that time Théophé did not answer, but instead encouraged the ambassador to talk about "our European ladies and of those princi-ples by which they were reared" (*GM,* 48)(100). And when it becomes repeatedly clear that Théophé's status cannot remain quo, the ambassador finds himself caught in a trap of his own making: the maxims of his code of reference.

Indeed, in the maxims that construct the bar separating East from West lies the obstacle to the satisfaction of his desire: "I came to realize that my major blunder had been to put into Théophé's hands several books on morality in which the basic principles . . . which could have been too trenchantly interpreted by a young girl who had been confronted by them for the first time" (*GM*, 174–75)(211). Frustrated by the blockage produced by the direction modernization has taken, Théophé's instructor has fleeting thoughts of insinuating his counter-text within a racier curriculum that might include stories of "*Cléopatre, La Princesse de Clèves*, etc."; but he thinks again: "I know Théophé. She would fall back on her Nicole, on his *Art de penser*" (*GM*, 176)(213). What is he to do with a woman who will not be seduced by fiction? Who will not move from philosophy to the bedroom? Marry her, substituting one topos for another. But Théophé is no Pamela secretly in love with her master. And she deflects the new declaration by reinscribing the text she has now learned by heart: "She reminded me what I owed to those obligations imposed upon me by the circumstances of my birth, what I owed to my station, to my own self-respect and to reason, and she recalled that I had been the very one from whom she had had her first lessons about these things and that I, so fortunately for her, had first taught her their guiding principles" (*GM*, 206)(240). By turning the code of reference against the narrator, and by substituting maxims for an expression of desire (or lack of desire), Théophé prevents the hermeneutic sentence from reaching its final punctuation. Thus the narrator is returned to reifying the enigma:

> I remained convinced that Théophé's heart was unaffected by any effort that any man might make to win her over, and either because she was so instinctively disposed or because she had acquired such a sense of virtue through her studies and her reflections, Théophé was in my eyes *a unique woman* whose conduct and principles ought to be suggested for individuals of her sex and of ours to emulate. The confusion I had experienced because of her refusal became easy for me to dispel once I had resolutely stopped myself at this thought. (*GM*, 298) (241; emphasis added)

By now it should be obvious that the enigma posed by Théophé is only one side, and the less interesting one, of the hermeneutic coin in this novel. Rather, the reader is led slowly but surely to relocate the problem of truth. As Barthes says of Balzac's tale: "the sculptor's blindness becomes a new message, object of a new system henceforth destined solely for the reader" (S/Z, 85). Like Sarrasine's, the ambassador's blindness, all the more insistent because of his diplomatic savvy, is an inability to see into the other's heart peculiar only to him. What he cannot see is that Théophé refuses his offers not so much (but partly of course) because her heart is closed to all masculine desire, but because it is closed to *his*. In this sense, the person who might have benefited from (re)reading *La Princesse de Clèves* is not Théophé, but the narrator himself. And the final phrase of the novel suggests that the structuring intertext is not Prévost's biography and Racine, but Lafayette.[16]

Thus to return to the network of destination linking narrator and reader, if in the linear space of narration which is our time of reading, the rejected lover momentarily substitutes the enthusiasm of sublimation (Théophé as exemplar and beyond sex) for the agony of aporia, retroactively as *narrator* he is plagued with doubts and reminds the reader that the meaning of the text (Théophé's *story*) is no less our problem than his: "after I have impartially reported those facts which threw me into this last state of consternation, I wish to leave the final judgment up to my reader" (GM, 209)(242). And this reminder cuts the novel as it builds toward conclusion. Diplomatic difficulties oblige the couple to head for France. The problematic of origins and destination is rearticulated.[17] The hermeneutic syntax is recharged: what will a "Grecque moderne" do in Europe?

More of the same, but in an accelerated, Western tempo. Indeed, when the narrator's jealous quest for the truth becomes, as has been noted, thoroughly and obsessively modern, Théophé's equivocation attains the contrapuntal insistence of a fugue in an echo chamber: "You have told me a thousand times . . . and I learn every day from the books that you place in my hands the necessity to accommodate oneself to the weaknesses of others . . . I am merely carrying out your principles and those maxims that I constantly derive from my reading of those books" (GM, 257)(283). To Narcissus's desire to be loved, Théophé is an irrelevant Echo. There are no straight, that is, complete answers forthcoming. Only the penultimate quid pro quo of the hermeneutic sentence: the partial response.[18] For although Théophé does admit, like her virtuous predecessor, Mme de Clèves, to "a change she could scarcely understand" which resulted in an "irresistible passion" for another, she also maintains her titles of innocence (*GM*, 234–35)(264). And all the narrator's efforts to discover whether "a girl who was so steadfastly virtuous could have lost something of that same discretion that I have delighted in portraying in such positive terms until now" (*GM*, 208)(242) are a *no-win operation*. His final attempt at espionage ends with a replay of Théophé's original response: "Then, suddenly bursting into tears again and being reduced to Greek expressions of humiliation which she should have lost the habit of using in France, she dropped to her knees" and begs for permission to end her days, like a modern heroine, in a convent (*GM*, 270)(286).

Permission is not granted. And the truth: "*disclosure, decipherment, which is, in the pure enigma . . . a final nomination, the discovery and uttering of the irreversible word*" (*S/Z*, 210). Now in *Sarrasine* we (the reader and the sculptor) do find out whether the object of love and fascination is "ce ou cette Zambinella": "*But this Zambinella— he or she?*" (*S/Z*, 209). There is proof, revelation and finality. In Prévost's novel, the narrator falls ill, and while still under his roof, Théophé exits from his life and our text, victim of an unexplained "dreadful mishap" (*GM*, 272)(66). The very last sentence of the novel returns us to the exordium, and to our status as reader/judge. The narrative, we are told, was generated by the news of the death of "this charming foreigner" and was written in order to "put the public in a position to judge if I had mistakenly entrusted in her my esteem and my love" (*GM*, 272)(288). How to conclude, then? The last sentence of *Sarrasine*, "*And the Marquise remained pensive*" (*S/Z*, 216) leads Barthes to conclude that "the (classic) text inscribes within its system of signs the signature of its plenitude" (*S/Z*, 216). This interrogative closure is like a gesture, a finger pointing to the ultimate fulfillment of meaning. It is not difficult to see that Prévost's novel signs off with a textual flourish of this sort as well. With this crucial difference, however. In *Sarrasine* there is penultimate closure, and an answer to the enigma that has structured Balzac's "story": that period is complete. At the end of *L'Histoire d'une Grecque moderne* we are still without the answer to the riddle.

Denied the answer, we are obliged to retrace our steps. But rereading will not change the fact, as Mauzi puts it in his introduction to the novel: "the work is closed upon itself, it contains all of its meaning (at least in Théophé's case) which is not to have any" (*GM*, xxxiii). Théophé, of course, makes sense to herself and from the beginning. But from the beginning, it is not *her* story. As for the other side of the enigma, then, an interpretation of the narrator's interpretation (his "overabundance of meaning"), Mauzi is less categorical and less convincing, finding, as he does, in that story, "our modern psychology which is much older than we think, already in search of its language" (*GM*, xxxviii). It seems to me that the modernity at stake is not psychological but literary. The anti-climax of the novel is a deliberate dead end, as calculated as the paradox of the title and its incarnation in Théophé. We have a displaced Greek, a problem of origins, intimations of incest, a quest for the truth, suffering, and no answer. Like Théophé's name that looks Greek (as in Psyché) but doesn't scan, it all *almost* means. Prévost is perhaps more modern than we had imagined. And his novel, not a classic text after all, for its hermeneutics are non-Oedipal.

At the end of his analysis of Poe's tale, Barthes suggests that one ought not "exaggerate the distance that separates the modern text from the classical narrative."[19] The facts in the case of a "Grecque moderne" suggest that the opposition between the readerly and the writerly is not so easily determined. What Barbara Johnson says of *Sarrasine*—"Balzac's text already 'knows' the limits and blindnesses of the readerly, which it personifies in Sarrasine"[20]—can also be said of Prévost and his narrator. Moreover, to follow Johnson's insights once more, if in *Sarrasine*, "castration is the way in which the enigma's answer is withheld" (*S/Z*, 8), by the same token, in *L'Histoire d'une Grecque moderne*, femininity (as the bar of difference), even doubled by orientalism, is not the answer to the enigma of desire but the way in which the possibility of truth is forever evaded.[21] To judge, as we are asked to do, whether the narrator makes a good or bad "investment" is to disregard all the writerly warnings of the novel, and to remain within the economy, as Derrida puts it, in which "woman . . . is twice castration: once as truth and once as nontruth."[22] To pass judgment is a losing strategy, and it spells victory for the *déjà lu*.

# *JUSTINE,* OR,
# THE VICIOUS CIRCLE

I don't know whether we must burn Sade; I do know that it is difficult to approach his work without getting burned: any literary
analysis runs the risk of betraying Sadian *écriture,* of neutralizing
what is meant to be violation, of bridging the gap where there is
meant to be rupture. The difficulty, of course, lies in the coincidence
of sex and text: inevitably turned on or off, analysts generally tend
to treat the one at the expense of the other.[1] Aware of the danger,
and without seeking to put out the fire, I would like to propose a
reading of one of Sade's novels, confronting simultaneously sexuality
and textuality.

I have chosen *Justine, ou les malheurs de la vertu,*[2] neither the original nor the ultimate version, but the second variant which has
provoked both extreme distaste—"It is a kind of philosophical tale in
which the heroine is frankly caricatured and frankly implausible;"[3]
"Sade wrote his worst and only vulgar work"[4]—and boundless admiration—"This is undoubtedly the most complete and most perfect
work of Sade, because in following his conviction and his genius
through to the end, the philosopher-poet remains master of his imagination, of his heart, but primarily of his art."[5] This polarized reaction
(a perfect homology to Sade's own *esprit de contradiction*) is symptomatic of the double and very literary bind in which the second
version of *Justine* places her readers. Leaving to one side the problem

of esthetic value, however, but respecting both the protocol of consumption encoded in the text and its status as the product of a genre, I shall try to expose the text of the dilemma, the reader's—and the critic's—trap.

*Justine* apparently obeys the conventions of fictional organization as they prevail in the eighteenth-century novel: a first-person account of suffering virtue. And not any virtue, but that eminently popular and vulnerable commodity, exemplary femininity via the metonymy of virginity. From the beginning, however, the reader can anticipate not only *Perversion* with a capital "P," defined by Phillipe Sollers as "theoretical thought itself,"[6] but a concretization of this phenomenon by a conversion of establishment values, where positivity is marked with a negative sign, and negativity with a positive one.[7]

The title itself serves as the first signpost directing the calvary to come; and the English translation, *Justine, or Good Conduct Well Chastised,* points even more clearly to the reversal of canonical and positive itineraries, the sagas of virtue well rewarded. The dedication explicitly states the author's preference for literary revalorization: "The scheme of this novel (yet, 'tis less a novel than one might suppose) is doubtless new; the victory gained by Virtue over Vice, the rewarding of good, the punishment of evil, such is the usual scheme in every other work of this species: ah! the lesson cannot be too often dinned in our ears!" (*JGC,* 455)(7).

However, if the byway down which the reader is then invited to travel is characterized as "a road not much traveled heretofore" (*JGC,* 456)(10), there is familiar and comforting compensation promised for any hardships incurred along the way: "one of the sublimest parables ever penned for human edification" (*JGC,* 456)(10). The dedication thus officially salutes the reigning ideology while preparing the reader for a renewal of its dominant cliché. This double stance, which involves co-opting a structure designed to support other values, is the key to this version of *Justine.* As *Shamela* mocks *Pamela, Justine* subverts every quest for happiness undertaken by a virginal heroine in the fictional universe of the eighteenth-century novel, although it is a parody that elicits no laughter.

The novel opens with the all-purpose eighteenth-century celebration of the truth as guiding light, and the reader's indulgence is requested for the exposure of the "sometimes rather painful situa-

tions" (*JGC,* 458)(14), that love for truth requires. Yet it is not difficult to predict that verisimilitude, as Genette has defined it, "the
formal principle of respect for the norm, that is, the existence of an
implied relationship between the particular behavior attributed to the
character, and the implicit and accepted general maxim,"[8] will suffer
in the process of illumination. It is a rule of thumb that authenticity
serves as license to mutilate the maxim, to promulgate the implausible and/or unacceptable. In the eighteenth-century novel, "fact" is
often stranger than fiction.

The opposition of Vice to Virtue is first concretized in the characters of Justine and Juliette; as the title of the novel indicates, it is
Justine's destiny that has been granted primacy. Nonetheless,
Juliette's function is crucial to the structure of the novel; not merely
as the dark-haired vicious foil to Justine's blond virtue, but as a
point of narrative suture: Juliette solicits Justine's tale of woe.
Juliette's dizzying rise, the author informs us, begins with the succes-
sive and successful exchange of her "pristine fruits" (*JGC,* 464)(20).
Hyperbolic courtesan, she sleeps her way to the top. Justine, on the
other hand, like the virtuous heroine of the sentimental novel, is
mortified by and rejects the prospect of such prosperity attained at
the cost of purity. It is her misfortune that poverty does not guarantee integrity: it is difficult to remain poor and honest, Pamela
notwithstanding.

It has been said that in eighteenth-century fiction, chastity attracts
rape as the sacred invites sacrilege.[9] And what figure is more vulnerable to sexual catastrophe than a destitute, friendless, virginal and
virtuous orphan? Justine is indeed marked for disaster: "she was
ruled by an ingenuousness, a candor that were to cause her to tumble
into not a few pitfalls" (*JGC,* 459)(15). Like Candide, that other
innocent abroad, Justine's physiognomy matches her soul. She looks
the part she is to play: "a virginal air" (*JGC,* 459)(16), corroborated
by the appropriate material complements—the most beautiful blond
hair, big blue eyes, and the loveliest complexion. Every detail of the
portrait is a cliché, which means that Justine is introduced to the
reader as a type of feminine perfection. Moreover, if the accumula-
tion of superlative attributes is a sure sign of type-casting, the
presence of an extra-textual model is confirmed by the pictorial code
that concludes the portrait: "there you have a sketch of this charming

creature whose naive graces and delicate traits are beyond our artistic power to portray" (*JGC*, 459)(16).[10] Justine defies depiction and the completion of the sketch is left to the reader's imagination.

Similarly, Voltaire, in a more blatant acknowledgment of the titillating powers of the artist's brush, withdraws at the last moment in his portrait of Agnès Sorel, the maid, in *La Pucelle*, "The Maid of Orleans": "But virtue, which the world good manners calls, / Stops short my hand—And lo! the pencil fails."[11] But Voltaire's heroines belong to another type of femininity; they have attributes of availability corresponding to what we might call the code of woman as fruit. Candide's beloved Cunégonde is "rosy-complexioned, fresh, plump, appetizing,"[12] the "Maid" herself, equally healthy, shares those tasty qualities, although they are metonymically assigned to her mouth: "High in color / Appetizing and amazingly fresh."[13]

Justine's source of attraction comes, on the contrary, not from her ripeness (after all she is only twelve years old at the start) but from her greenness. Or to choose a less gustatory metaphor from the catalogue of descriptive clichés of femininity, she is the bud and not the rose. Her fragility, her delicacy, the essence of positive femininity in the eighteenth-century novel, provide the measure of her potential for suffering: she is not robust enough for comedy. The occasion of Justine's first trial, the one with which *her* narrative opens, clearly establishes the pathetic-erotic pattern of her trials to come. Confronted with the sexual imperative, Justine adopts the position of victim and pleads for mercy on her knees, seeking generosity from her tormentor: "be so generous as to relieve me without requiring what would be so costly I should rather offer you my life than submit to it . . ." (*JGC*, 473)(30). Like the sentimental heroine, Justine prefers death to dishonor. Such is not her destiny, however; consistently she is condemned to that fate worse than death.

In this first round, Justine is saved from the fatal sacrifice and is left technically pure, but the significance of the initiation is not lost on her: "It seemed that the Supreme Being wished, in that first of my encounters, to imprint forever in me all the horror I was to have for a crime whence there was to be born the torrent of evils that have beset me since" (*JGC*, 473–74)(31). Within the first scene of sexual confrontation, the fundamental paradigm is established: as a victim, Justine's unique means of self-defense consists of a posture of supplication; the supervising agent of her destiny is in heaven, and all is not right with the world.

From the beginning, Justine is concerned with assuring the reader as to the authenticity of her suffering and alienation: "I was far from wishing to participate in the thing, to lend myself to it was as much as I could do, my remorse remained lively" (*JGC*, 474)(31). Thus, in conformity with the role of victim, Justine submits, protests and regrets. Yet there are those who find complicity, or at least an index of ambiguity in her claims to pure disgust. Another case of the lady protesting too much. While this may be true of Cunégonde, who, it has been noted, admires the skintone of her very own Bulgarian captain, thus casting some doubt on the resonance of her lamentations, Justine is less oblique.[14] She in fact admits, early in her history, to an overwhelming attraction for the Count de Bressac: "nothing in the world was able to extinguish this nascent passion, and had the Count called upon me to lay down my life, I would have sacrificed it for him a thousand times over" (*JGC*, 511)(71). These irresistible feelings constitute the one and only error in her accounting: "the one deliberate fault with which I have to reproach myself" (*JGC*, 511)(71). But Justine's love remains unrequited; her sex, for once, is a deterrent.

The problem posed by Justine's version of the facts, however, is less a function of psychological reliability than narrational liability. As subject and object of a scatological destiny, Justine must account for the repertory of sexual experiments and experiences in which she is a reluctant participant. Moreover, since the Sadian erotic involves at least as much sexual discourse as sexual intercourse, Justine's role as narrator compels her to relay and relate to the reader the text of her oppression—the libertine's credo. This results in what some consider an insurmountable implausibility: "the philosophical arguments of sadism, more amply developed than in the first version, are not plausible in the mouth of the victim who retranscribes them."[15]

Adopting an intertextual perspective, I would suggest that this aspect of verisimilitude is part of a larger problem, and one that afflicts the first-person narrators of what are essentially briefs designed to elicit both sympathy and salvation. A case in point is that victim with credentials, Diderot's *Nun*, Suzanne Simonin. Condemned to a scene fundamentally abhorrent to her sense of self, in order to authenticate her victim status, to reinscribe her martyrdom, Suzanne relates in glowing detail both the words and deeds responsible for her misery. On any page taken at random, the reader finds the "I" representing her voice at the service of the oppressive "they" ("on").

Moreover, in order for the reader's compassion to be sustained in the face of what is essentially the same old story, pathos-producing devices must be varied. Therefore, to balance self-pity, self-congratulatory remarks, tinged with complacency, sporadically punctuate these texts. They serve to revalorize the victim in the reader's eye ("I was meant for better things") and should not be interpreted necessarily as a sign of complicity. For example, while Justine is working as Gernande's medical assistant, she boasts about her tactics: "But I had discovered the secret of winning this man's very highest esteem: he frankly avowed to me that few women had pleased him so much; and thereby I acquired the right to his confidence, which I only exploited in order to serve my mistress" (*JGC*, 644)(213). The rationale for ingratiation is assigned to the laudable motive of rescuing a fellow victim; and through the use of indirect discourse the burden of self-aggrandizement is displaced onto another.

Still, Justine does admit to knowledge of the dynamics of feminine wiles which she generally claims to ignore or despise: indeed, the very confident "frankly" is a dead giveaway that she understands the dialectic of seduction. Yet does that make her less of a victim and more to the point, does it undermine her credibility as reporter at the scene of the crime? We might consider Suzanne's last words as she wonders whether *her* Monsieur de Corville will think that she has addressed herself to his vice rather than to his charity: "This thought worries me. In reality he would be quite mistaken if he ascribed to me in particular an instinct common to all my sex. I am a woman, and perhaps a bit coquettish, who can tell? But it is a result of our nature, and not of artifice on my part."[16] A measure of ambiguity is always encoded in the discourse of a virtuous and female narrator; it's a standard feature in the representation of femininity.

The sexual reliability of narrative voice, however, is only one area of critical attack on Justine's believability as a character. Justine has often been accused of mental and physical retardation: "Whatever befalls her, Justine is unprepared for it, experience teaches her nothing, her soul remains ignorant, her body more ignorant still."[17] But this sort of criticism proceeds from the assumption that Justine is a character with the potential for development associated with the traditional psychological novel, where according to the famous Jamesian formulation, character determines incident and incident illustrates character in an interlocking system of exchange. Justine above all must carry the weight of the author's counter-demonstration as articulated in the dedication. From the title she is presented as suffering virtue itself. Like Candide whose name is given as an equivalent to optimism, and whose trials and tribulations serve to deliver a message, rather than to motivate a "rounded" character, Justine's suffering is designed not to enhance her, but to support the system in which she circulates. However, even Candide as character and tale is narrated by a voice that can comfortably arrange the events of the narrative to support his case. In Sade's text a situation must be created from which the victim's self-narrative could plausibly be generated. Thus for Justine to speak for herself, and at length, a captive is granted an audience. Motivated by the extraordinary posture in which she finds herself, Justine, like Scheherazade, is given one night to tell her story.

Sade's novel belongs to that form of literary production defined by Todorov in his essay "Narrative-Men."[18] In this kind of literature (exemplified by *A Thousand and One Nights*), action is privileged at the expense of character, what counts is the verb and not the subject (or in our case, the object) of the verb. In such an apsychological mode, a character is no more than his own story, a "narrative-man," he is what happens. As a result, tautology replaces causality[19]: thus, Justine is a victim because she is victimized; she is victimized because she is a victim. If to understand a character one adopts Genette's formulation: "to understand the behavior of a character is to be able to refer to an accepted maxim,"[20] then there is only one maxim possible that can account for Justine in etiological terms, and it is a uniquely Sadian one: "the victim's duty is to consent."[21]

But the added dimension to Justine's suffering as the exemplary victim in a universe where eros is inseparable from logos, is that she must also record and play back. In this sense, more like Scheherazade than Suzanne, Justine's life is defined and measured solely by what she tells—as a "narrative-woman;" her life ends when there is nothing more to tell. Nevertheless, despite the potential for the infinite prolongation of the process of narration that characterizes a mode of production where "story equals life; the absence of story death,"[22] at some point there is an ending.

Indeed, although Justine is denied the satisfaction of even a superficial linear progression—she goes in circles despite her desire to reach the south of France, and at the end of practically every adventure finds herself back where she started, except that time has passed and things are worse—the fiction of her wanderings is at last brought to a close. The final installment of the trials of suffering virtue crystallizes the problems of narrativity and credibility in the text as I have sketched them out until this point; at the end of the novel, the disparity between the code and the message, the mimesis of the quest and its subversion, is unequivocally confirmed.

It is Saint-Florent, Justine's first violator, who orchestrates Justine's last torture, her final incarnation as hyperbolic victim. Justine warns her listeners that this experience represents the summit in the hierarchy of horror: "Oh Madame! never had anything similar soiled my gaze, and whatever may have been my previous representations, what now I beheld surpassed everything I have been able to describe until the present: 'tis like unto the ascendancy the imperious eagle enjoys over the dove" (*JGC*, 728)(302). The neoclassical comparison and the cliché of narration as depiction mark the discrepancy between Justine, subject of discourse, and Thérèse, object of violation. Moreover, the temporary pause in transmission, serves as a signal to the reader to be on the alert, and creates a sense of progress in Justine's unhappy pilgrimage.

The scene begins with the familiar permutations of postures available to four libertine men and one female victim; nothing unusual for Justine. What is new is the preparation for immolation that she must undergo to satisfy Saint-Florent, whose specialty consists in deflowering virgins. He requires that Justine be altered to reproduce the measurements of her virginal dimensions. She is to be sewn up. Despite her vast experience, Justine is puzzled, confused by the obscurity of the message: "I am not familiar with the expression: a cruel experiment soon reveals its meaning" (*JGC*, 730)(305).

This particular variant of torture has elicited critical attention: for Roland Barthes, sewing represents a secondary castration and a desexualization[23]; for Michael Riffaterre, reading Sade with Barthes, sewing, in this context, is a "purely verbal scandal."[24] It seems to me, beyond the merits of either analysis, that this extraordinary needlework confirms the fundamental circularity of the text. The fact of Justine's being sewn up, restored to her virginal space, just as previously her wounds were healed to leave no traces, means that her story as victim is potentially endless, despite the conclusion of the novel, beyond the terminus of the printed page. Curiously, this also means that in the final analysis, Justine's virginity can be reproduced as artificially as Juliette's was at the beginning of her career—which undermines, once again, the sanctity of virginity—and to return to another point of departure, the reader may recall that Justine's first venture on the job-market was to approach her mother's seamstress.

After the relation of this final torture, Justine is recognized and rescued by Juliette and Monsieur de Corville. In the comfort of home, through tender loving care, Justine is nursed back to health and restored to her Edenic before. All traces of former misery are erased. Justine, however, is not made for happiness; though more fortunate than Cunégonde in that her suffering is not engraved on her face, she lacks the strength to cultivate a garden. But before she has time to pine away, lightning strikes, in a final impalement. Horror-stricken, Juliette interprets Justine's death as a divine warning, and promptly embarks on a career of compensatory piety. Like Cécile at the end of the *Liaisons dangereuses,* she enters a Carmelite order, and like the Princess of Clèves, she becomes a legend in her own time. Finally, the very last paragraph of the novel takes up the terms of the dedication, evoking the tears shed over the misfortunes of virtue, apologizing again for the "heavy brushstrokes" (*JGC,* 743)(318), and praising the mysteries of divine providence and its ultimate rewards. The novel stops, having come full circle. But what kind of circle has been described, if not a vicious one?

The three definitions of a vicious circle in *Webster's Third New International* pertain to different aspects of the novel. The first, "a chain of circumstances constituting a situation in which the process of solving one difficulty creates a new problem involving increased difficulty in the original situation," describes the automatic conversion process that controls Justine's interaction: she asks for help and is betrayed by her protector, she extends a helping hand and is victimized by her beneficiary—whatever she does, she makes matters worse. The third, "a chain of abnormal processes in which a primary disorder leads to a second which in turn aggravates the first one," characterizes the chain reaction of disasters set in motion by her first sexual encounter (we might recall here Justine's evaluation of abnormality: "a kind of crime *whence there was to be born* the torrent of evils that have beset me since" (*JGC*, 473–474; emphasis added)(31)). The second, "an argument or definition that is valueless because it overtly or covertly assumes as true something which is to be proved or defined," describes the author's discourse as demonstrated by the identity of his assumptions and conclusions.

Indeed, when as readers we arrive at the end of the road, and measure the distance traveled, we realize that like Justine we have gone around in circles.[25] The narrative has ended; there seems to have been a story with a beginning, a middle, and an end, an innocent heroine, villains, an unfortunate destiny and a moral—in other words structural conformity with the eighteenth century's house of fiction. The end of the novel is a model of literary construction: just as the beginning of Justine's suffering is marked by the separation of the two sisters, an end to suffering is brought about by their reunion. Moreover, the apparent reversal of the relation of their trajectories, in which Justine's descent had been opposed to Juliette's rise, provides the novel with the moral ending as promised: Justine's death engenders Juliette's conversion.

However, if a disfiguring death blow dealt by a divine hand, or the nunnery, as the consequences of contact with illicit sexuality, are narrative clichés perfectly consistent with the plausibility of the eighteenth-century novel, mimesis is subverted by conversion: Justine is given the punishment the ideology of the period would have visited on Juliette, and Juliette is given the privilege of a retreat from the world that would have suited Justine. Thus if it is true, as Todorov points out, that we weep when we read *Manon Lescaut,* but not *A Thousand and One Nights,* by the same token, despite the author's confidence that we have shed tears upon hearing of virtue's miseries, we have not.[26] And of course, we are not meant to. Despite the intertextual connections between Justine and related victims of suffering virtue cited earlier, there is a founding difference at work. As a result, one cannot take Justine's response to the extended rape that constitutes her life span with the seriousness, say, of Clarissa's. On the other hand, if the reader smiles when Agnès Sorel sighs, "In vain we strive to shun those ills we know, / We can't be virtuous, though we'd fain be so,"[27] or smirks when Cunégonde repeats her leitmotif of violation, Justine's lamentations do not provoke laughter. Unlike Cunégonde and Agnès Sorel, sisters in serial violation, Justine is resolutely closed to humor. Ultimately, Justine is neither a comic nor a tragic heroine; she is the object of a verb use to trap the reader and lure him into Sade's world.

Under the Sadian sign of perversion, the linear logic of before/after, now/then, why/because, the logic of memoir as history, proves to be vicious. What Justine registered as chronology was in fact stasis; progression, repetition. Justine's text is but a pretext for a sexual combinatory whose permutations are infinite.[28] It is not surprising, then, that Justine and Juliette should be revived for a final version a few years later. Vicious circle where circle of virtue spirals into circle of vice, there is no way or reason to stop until the author or his reader is exhausted.

# *JULIETTE* AND THE POSTERITY
# OF PROSPERITY

The prosperities of *Juliette* are still more solitary—and endless.
—Foucault, *Les mots et les choses*

Within the critical canon on *Juliette* it is generally acknowledged that
the heroine's trajectory demonstrates the characteristics of a
*Bildungsroman.* And Juliette's passage from innocence to sophistica-
tion, ignorance to knowledge, apprenticeship to mastery, can indeed
be classified as the story of an education—even a spiritual one, for the
eschatological intersects the scatological at every point of the graph.[1]
It has also been observed, however, that the *Bildungsroman* is a
"male affair," "a male form because women have tended to be
viewed traditionally as static, rather than dynamic, as instances of
femaleness considered essential rather than existential."[2] The typical
subject of the genre is a sensitive young man, who upon moving from
a sheltered environment to the challenges of the world, loses an original innocence as he achieves a measure of social integration and
*savoir-vivre.* Although radically transformed by her exposure to life
as experience, Juliette represents a double exception to that formula:
she does not perform in the world as the reader is likely to know it,
and she is a *female* apprentice. Thus, reading Juliette's apprenticeship
as intertext, say, to Wilhelm Meister's, reveals, on one level, a text
whose specificity lies in a relation of variance with an ideal (generic)

model.[3] But there is a further methodological consideration: How is the semiosis of apprenticeship generated when the feminine sign must be articulated within a system of signification in which it has no place? The answer lies in a characteristic trait of Sadian *écriture:* reversal. Juliette's *Bildung*—her self-development—is achieved by a reversal of the valorization assigned to the cultural and literary conventions encoding femaleness, the positively marked status of daughter, wife, mother. The novel builds upon the stages of emancipation from the familial, on the denegation of bourgeois femininity.

Beautiful, wealthy, and convent-educated, Juliette is an ideal daughter perfectly equipped to circulate in society as an object of legitimate and sanctioned exchange. The untimely loss of both parents puts an end to such expectations: a life of leisure and procreation under the aegis of a prosperous husband. (Orphans have no title to privilege.) Undaunted, Juliette determines to pursue her interrupted schooling: "To be sure, I had a rigorous apprenticeship to undergo; these often painful first steps were to complete the corruption of my morals" (*J*, 103)(VIII, 107).[4] The educative principle of Juliette's text entails the un-learning of official scholastic values; and her training program is designed to eradicate any lingering traces of moral prejudice by completion of the requirements as established in the catalogue of sexual offerings. A university of perversity, perhaps, but academe prevails—at the very least in the form of hierarchy—until the end.

Juliette learns quickly, for she is highly motivated from the start:

> Endowed with the most energetic temperament, I had, starting at the age of nine, accustomed my fingers to respond to whatever desires arose in my mind, and from that period onward I aspired to nothing but the happiness of finding the occasion for instruction and to launch myself into a career the gates unto which my native forwardness had already flung wide, and with such agreeable effects. (*J*, 4)(VIII, 16)

She performs the permutations of sexual exercises with astonishing skill, and advances so rapidly, in fact, that after her first indoctrination the reader might well wonder how the remaining volumes can be structured convincingly upon a developmental premise. But as Barthes has pointed out, "For the libertines, the educative project has another dimension. . . . The mastery sought here is not that of philosophy: the education is not of this or that character, but of the *reader* [du lecteur]."[5] The reader of *Juliette*—or to be more precise, the *narratee* (the reader as inscribed)—is reminded constantly by the pervasive educational code and by footnotes that a lesson is to be learned.[6]

> Hot-blooded and lewdly disposed ladies, these are words to the wise, hark attentively to them: *they are addressed not only to Juliette but to yourselves also;* if your intelligence is in any sense comparable to hers, you'll not fail to extract great benefit from them. (*J,* fn., 340; emphasis added)(fn., VIII, 328)

> So offer us your thanks, mesdames, and *imitate our heroines,* we ask no more of you; for *your instruction,* your sensations, and your happiness are in the verity *the sole objects* for whose sake some wearisome efforts are undertaken; and if you damned us in *Justine,* our hope is that *Juliette* will earn us your blessings. (*J,* fn., 489; emphasis added) (fn., VIII, 468)

The exhortation to emulate, to imitate the process as set forth, creates the impression of development, both ongoing and potential, even if, in a cooler moment, the measurement of changes proves to be a rhetorical device: hyperbole. (The paradox is only apparent; persuasion being the *telos* of rhetoric.) In addition to these formal indices, moreover, the sense of progression that is indeed decipherable in an otherwise heterogeneous mass of sexual exploits, derives, as I said earlier, from the particularly valorized program which is the enfranchisement of the individual from the family: all the more striking because undertaken by a woman. In both cases, it is a case of generic *topoi.*[7]

That liberation should pass through the family to go beyond it, is not itself surprising within the Sadian system, where in order for libertines to "prove themselves" they must break the bonds of "natural" kinship. Since the family, as a matrix formed by the ties of blood, and sanctified by society rules, is a mediating term between nature and culture, it provides an ideal arena in which to do battle. But Juliette is an orphan, and thus, one would expect, exempt by definition from the family principle. Her text, nevertheless, is opened, closed, and punctuated by references to the family, as though absence could be assured only by the reiterated denial of presence. Juliette's sister Justine, for example, is named and dismissed in the first paragraph, and the reader is invited to remember her presumably only as a point of reference, contrapuntal reminder of another kind of destiny. And yet Justine will reappear at crucial moments in the narrative with a good deal more impact than a simple index of polarity.

In the same way, Juliette's original and desultory account of her parents' demise will be recapitulated with new significance when she gives her history to Noirceuil. For she will learn in the course of the first "scholarly lecture" pronounced for her benefit that Noirceuil is nothing less than "the murderer of [her] parents" (*J*, 149) (VIII, 148). The revelation leads to a declaration of love from Juliette: "Monster . . . thou art an abomination, I love thee" (*J*, 149) (VIII, 148). Such admiration wins Juliette admission to Noirceuil's school of crime, and guided by a mentor and lover, Juliette blossoms; the apprentice dedicates herself to pleasing the master, seeking to model her soul upon his: "As for the submission you request of me, it shall be entire; dispose of me, I am yours; a woman, I know my place and that dependence is mine" (*J*, 207)(VIII, 201). Noirceuil, however, clarifies their relationship: "I would have you a woman and a slave unto me and my friends; a despot unto everyone else . . . and I here and now swear that I shall avail you of the means" (*J*, 207) (VIII, 201). Juliette is thus granted freedom to perform—sexually and criminally—but that freedom is mediated by a higher authority. The supremacy of the couple is maintained, and within that couple, the male prerogative supported by power in the world.

Despite the mutual fondness at the heart of their union, it is deemed expedient for Juliette to take up residence with Noirceuil's friend, the Minister Saint-Fond. Because of the latter's extraordinary fortune, Juliette find herself (at age seventeen) mistress of the interior, the ultimate "maîtresse de maison." Juliette is given "all France" to devast with crime and a premium for domestic originality. But again there is a restriction: "while you are here, your condition will be that of a *common whore;* and *everywhere else* you will be one of the *greatest ladies* in the kingdom" (*J*, 236; emphasis added)(VIII, 227). Two sets of oppositional criteria are relevant: spatio-social: inside/outside (the message, moreover, is delivered in a "cabinet secret"); and gender determined mastery: female slave/male master:

"wherever I am, my Lord, I shall be your slave, your admirer eternal-ly, and the very soul of your most exquisite pleasures" (*J,* 236) (VIII, 227). That this relationship of authority is fundamental to the apprenticeship model can be clearly shown by adopting a Greimasian perspective according to which Noirceuil's role—and Saint-Fond's to a lesser degree—is that of the Donor (*Destinateur*):

> In a narrative of exemplary apprenticeship, this role is played by the father—or by someone who acts 'like a father'—of the subject-hero. . . . The father also has a tendency to add on the role of helper, since one of his functions is to facilitate the hero's appren-ticeship; either by communicating essential knowledge, or simply by encouraging him in his quest.[8]

The importance of this father-figure status as exemplified by Noirceuil will be elaborated upon at the end of our analysis. At this point, what is pertinent is the articulation of the significant and for-mative power role in masculine terms.

In the world of *Bildung,* hyperbolized by a Sadian dynamic, the *status* is never *quo.* Juliette requests a role model to emulate, and at the same time a tutee of her own: "I'd like to share my knowledge with another; I keenly sense my need of instruction, I no less keenly desire to educate someone: I must have a teacher, yes, and I must have a pupil too" (*J,* 263) (VIII, 252). The educational principle is thus reinscribed, but with a critical nuance: Juliette attains the rank of instructor within a female hierarchy; again, within the egalitarian atmosphere of sexual utopia, difference pertains. Clairwil, hand-picked by Noirceuil for the position, refines Juliette's techniques, and introduces her to "the Sodality of the Friends of Crime." Noirceuil, for his part, no longer maintains membership:

> In the days when men were in the majority there . . . I never missed a single one; but I have given up going *since everything has fallen into the hands of a sex whose authority I dislike.* Saint-Fond felt the same way and dropped out shortly after I did. But that is not partic-ularly relevant, if those orgies amuse you, and since Clairwil enjoys them, there is no reason why you shouldn't join in. (*J,* 298; empha-sis added) (VIII, 287)

So with Clairwil as her model (and Noirceuil's fiancée as her experimental subject), Juliette continues to progress, although total approval is withheld for what Clairwil considers Juliette's inability to act in cold blood.

Juliette is soon given a perfect opportunity to demonstrate her improvement. Her biological father, Bernole, unexpectedly appears, seeking to enlist his daughter as a mediator vis-à-vis Saint-Fond. The canonical recognition scene, complete with documents and identifying birthmark, motivates an exclamation from Justine, who, we are reminded, is present at the gathering in which Juliette is holding forth. Justine is censured for her filial piety and returned to a silence that she maintains until the very end of the novel where she reappears, only to be condemned to death. The familial component of this sequence is thus reinforced; and the pause created by Justine's intervention functions as a marker, a juncture in the text, isolating this particular trial as a narrative unit. Unlike her sister, Juliette is indifferent to the discovery of her real father and the difficulty of his situation: "the proof was there, but to it Nature incited in me no response at all, none. It was with sheer indifference I stared at the person standing in front of me" (J, 466) (VIII, 447). After consultation with Noirceuil and Saint-Fond, Juliette revises her initial impulse to dismiss the importunate progenitor and determines instead to seduce and kill him—to prove that the efforts to reform her soul have not been fruitless. The plot is carried out with the father caught *in flagrante delicto,* in a posture of unambiguous compromise. Juliette shoots her father, while participating fully in the concomitant orgy. If the subversion of the family were not clear enough, a pregnancy (Juliette's first) results from these incestuous relations, followed by a remarkable, painless, and cosmetic abortion. Thus the family is truncated, as it were, at both ends of the tree. The convergence of taboos redundantly confirms the symbolic nature of Juliette's progress in liberation.[9]

Clairwil, however, is not satisfied with Juliette's evolution and in particular chides Juliette for not seeing that every man "belongs to an enemy sex, a sex bitterly at war with your own;" and that consequently she must never miss "an opportunity for avenging the insults women have endured at its hands" (J, 527) (VIII, 505). Curiously like Rousseau's Claire D'Orbe, Clairwil is a female-identified woman, while Juliette like Julie consistently embraces male identification—

hence the Father.[10] But I am anticipating. At this stage of her adventures, Juliette is introduced by Clairwil to yet another (female) mentor, Durand, through whom Juliette becomes a sorceress's apprentice. Durand initiates Juliette into the art of poison; since Medea, the archetypal female art. Equally important, she foretells the conditions of Juliette's fall from favor: "when vice doth cease woe shall betide" (*J,* 531) (VIII, 509). Indeed, immediately following this exchange, and at the very center of the novel, Juliette reveals, by an involuntary shudder, a moral compunction that Saint-Fond deems to be fatal. His power turns against her. By violating the terms of their contract she has abrogated her right to (paternal) protection and is forced to fend for herself. Within six months, however, married to the Count de Lorsange, Juliette has a new domestic arrangement and can start making plans again. Notably, despite the anti-procreative stance maintained by Juliette and her fellow libertines throughout the novel, Juliette decides to have a child: "The measure was essential: I had to consolidate my claims to the fortune of the man who had given me his name. I could not do this without a child—but was it fathered by my virtuous husband?" (*J,* 561)(VIII, 539). As one might expect, for Juliette conjugality is no more compelling than filiality. Indeed, when she learns that Saint-Fond is searching for her, she rapidly disposes of her "tender spouse" (with Durand's poison), leaves her daughter Marianne with a curate friend and lover, and sets out to seek fortune and pleasure on her own, made possible only by her new status as a rich widow.

Thus travels follow apprenticeship; Juliette develops her own style and is vastly successful as a practitioner of the crimes of love. But she at last decides to return home, seven years later, and towards the novel's close, to rejoin Noirceuil and her daughter in Paris.[11] Upon seeing Marianne, she finds her pretty, but explains (in terms identical to those used in describing her reaction to the discovery of her true father) that Nature—in this case the maternal function—was mute: "I am obliged to say that in embracing Marianne I felt absolutely nothing stir in me but the pulsations of lubricity" (*J,* 1152) (IX, 547). Juliette looks forward only to guiding Marianne's nubility—to apprenticeship: "There's a pretty subject for educating" (*J,* 1152) (IX, 547). We would seem to have here a Sadian premise for a familial continuum, but any vestiges of the nuclear family are destroyed in the last orgy recounted by Juliette. Noirceuil is determined to "have" Marianne. Juliette's reaction reveals the traces of motherly distress. But pity for the victim, albeit her own child, is short-lived. Seeing Noirceuil demolish his two sons, Juliette concurs with his desire; and after a momentary reluctance, gets caught up in the activity: when Noirceuil throws Marianne into a roaring fire, Juliette helps him with a poker. The murder of Juliette's daughter is the last fully described episode; by its position in the text, and its obvious symbolic connotations, it marks the culmination of Juliette's progress, her emancipation from the role structure of the family. Noirceuil and Juliette spend the night following this crime together in mutual congratulation and harmony. Noirceuil, confirming his earlier assertion, "you are indispensable to my existence; I like committing crimes with nobody but you" (J, 1153)(IX, 547), pays Juliette the ultimate compliment, inviting her to spend the rest of her life with him: "Then let us live in crime forever; and may nothing in all Nature ever succeed in converting us to different principles" (J, 1153) (IX, 581).

But the novel is not yet purged of the familial. And it is the author who intervenes to tie up the threads of the narrative. In an inevitable repetition of her previous history, Justine's tears, stimulated by the "scandalous details" of Juliette's text, cause her to be cast out of the comfort of the chateau into the elements. Conveniently, Justine, perennial orphan in the storm, is struck down by a thunder bolt. Interpreting the disaster as divine collaboration, the libertines abuse the corpse with Juliette's excited encouragement: "Truly . . . this most recent episode more than ever confirms me in the career I have pursued up until now" (J, 1191)(IX, 584). And precisely, this episode reconfirms the desecration of the familial as the thematic component structuring the text of Juliette's quest for emancipation. Ungrateful daughter, unnatural mother, unloving wife, unsisterly sister, Juliette defies all semantic expectations: she chooses to orphan herself, thus creating a neologism, making a normally passive verb active. And by widowing herself, she further subverts linguistic patterns, flaunting the need for protection proverbially ascribed to "the widow and the orphan."

The extent to which the semantic investment of normative structures is subverted here can easily be summarized by a model of socio-sexual relations adapted from Lévi-Strauss and elaborated by Greimas and Rastier:

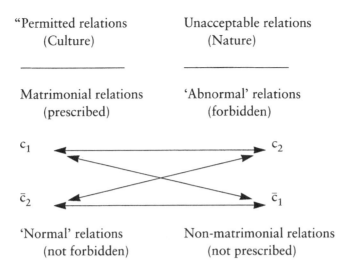

"Permitted relations      Unacceptable relations
     (Culture)                        (Nature)

Matrimonial relations      'Abnormal' relations
     (prescribed)                      (forbidden)

$c_1$ $\qquad\qquad\qquad\qquad$ $c_2$

$\bar{c}_2$ $\qquad\qquad\qquad\qquad$ $\bar{c}_1$

'Normal' relations      Non-matrimonial relations
     (not forbidden)                (not prescribed)

Note: In traditional French society, for example, we
     have the following equivalences:

$c_1$ conjugal love;
$c_2$ incest, homosexuality;
$\bar{c}_2$ adultery by the man (over and above conjugal love);
$\bar{c}_1$ adultery by the woman (over and above homosexual-
     ity, etc.).

Whatever the investment of the model, it is a question,
in the case of nature as in that of culture, of social values
(and not of the rejection of nature outside meaning)."[12]

In this perspective, the permitted and matrimonial relations of
Culture are prescribed and opposed to the forbidden, abnormal relations of Nature. In traditional French society, the first category is
exemplified by conjugal love, the second, incest and homosexuality.
Obviously, in such a society, the first set of roles ($C1$, $\bar{C}2$) is privileged and positively valorized, the second, ($\bar{C}1$, $C2$) marked with the
negative sign of transgression. In the fictional universe of the eighteenth-century novel, these relations of positivity to negativity are
respected, that is to say, transgression is punished. But to measure
fully the distance separating the Sadian universe from the most libertine of bourgeois fiction, it must be noted that the "normal"

non-forbidden relation of male adultery lies within the category of "permitted" relations, whereas female adultery belongs to the category of "unacceptable" relations. Thus if we were to compare *Les Liaisons dangereuses,* for example, with *Les Prospérités du vice* (texts often compared because of the similarities between the two major female figures, Madame de Merteuil and Juliette), Merteuil ($\overline{C}1$) and Juliette (C2) would both be labeled as "unacceptable." For they defy the founding cultural constraints of both pater and familias: Merteuil, by usurping male prerogatives[13]; Juliette, by incest and homosexuality. Despite the fact that Merteuil does not occupy the place of supreme violation, however, the maximum of abhorrent activity (as does Juliette), she is nonetheless the character most severely punished in a scenario of sexual promiscuity. Prévan and Valmont, for example, her homologues in adultery, are in the case of the former applauded, and in the latter, allowed to die—gallantly— by the sword; whereas Merteuil is stripped of prestige, fortune, family, servants, friends and allies. And that is not all: she is given the punishment befitting a monster: an eye is destroyed, symbolic sexual mutilation. Juliette, on the contrary, is consistently rewarded for her progress in transgression. Every crime affords her new respect—particularly in the eyes of the supreme arbiter of value, Noirceuil. The further she goes in her daring, the further she is integrated into the universe within which she functions. The novel concludes with her ascension. Society cannot eject Juliette as it can Merteuil because Juliette is beyond its reach; once Juliette has delivered herself of internalized oppression, she is free of opposition.[14]

Thus, Juliette realizes the full potential of the apprenticeship program. On the one hand, she fulfills the criterion of the genre that at the end the "hero . . . has ripened via a series of amorous exploits ranging from the sensual to the sublime."[15] On the other hand, her *Bildung* culminates with the assimilation of Sadian philosophy in the microcosm of the Sadian world, as defined early in her formation by Noirceuil:

> Nor ought you to view familial ties as more sacred than these others, they are all equally fictitious. It is not true that you owe anything to the being out of whom you emerged; still less true that you are obliged to have any feeling whatever for a being that were

to emerge from you . . . upon what rational basis can consanguinity establish duties? (*J*, 193) (VIII, 180).

Indeed, in her particular praxis, she has achieved—or so it would seem—personal liberation from the constraints of a role that would bind her to the bourgeois family.

But as the story draws to a close, a messenger arrives to deliver a letter announcing Noirceuil's summons to the Court, where he is to assume the reins of government: the outside world merges with the inner sanctum. Noirceuil then invites Juliette and her old friend Durand—unexpectedly arrived in the midst of these happy few—to accompany him to the Capital, while naming his male friends to high and official positions. Once again, the inside/outside differentiation pertains; Juliette will reassume her role as super-mistress to Noirceuil's supreme administration: "As soon as Ulysses appears, Circe becomes a woman again, and the daughter of the Sun submits to the Hero."[16] It is in this sense that the ending recreates a familial situation: power roles based on gender distinctions. When the last blood relation is eliminated, a socially homologous relationship is substituted: the (extended) Sadian family reproducing the Freudian triangle.

Juliette, an orphan who chose to orphan herself, returns to the rule of the Father—of Noirceuil, but finally of the Author who has the last word.[17] Her text is not autonomous; however subversive, it remains sub-text. Juliette has wished the story of her life to be entitled *Les Prospérités du vice*. That is, of course, the narrative we have. But the author tells us that our heroine, "unique in her kind," lived for another ten glorious years, and died "without having left any record of the events." Continuing the fiction of his status as scribe, he adds "no writer will be able to chronicle it for the public" (*J*, 1193)(IX, 587). However, since "genuine *Bildung* involves a restructuring of recollections often analogous to the creative process itself,"[18] this deprivation, surely, is Juliette's and not the author's. Ultimately, her *Bildung* proves to be as volatile as her word; oral history is not art; a voice is not a signature.

There is nothing fundamentally inconsistent here; it is in the logic of the idiolect. Noirceuil had celebrated the symbol of his power in the following manner: "this tool is my god, let it be one unto thee, Juliette: extol it, worship it, this despotic engine [*ce vit despote*], show it every reverence, it is a thing proud of its glory, insatiate, a tyrant" (*J*, 185)(VIII, 170). From the phallus to the pen and the word, culture transcodes for us. In the Sadian hierarchy, "The master is he who speaks, *who disposes of the entirety of language.*"[19] In the final pages of the novel, it is precisely this problematics of mastery in language that is at stake. Juliette does not contest her restricted status, as will, for example, Emma Bovary: "What she envies in a man is not so much the possibility of traveling, but the possibility of writing; what she lacks in order to write are neither words nor pen, but the phallus."[20] Nonetheless, in the final analysis, the feminine sign, "the sign without voice in the world of the Law,"[21] the world of the Father and culture, even in Sade's text is mediated by masculine discourse.[22] So that if, in the posterity of prosperity, in the euphoria of "happily ever after," Juliette bypassed the binary rule of the Father, we will never know. Her sign is silence; she is written.

# PART FOUR

# EXQUISITE CADAVERS

# THE EXQUISITE CADAVERS
## *Women in Eighteenth-Century Fiction*

> When lovely woman stoops to folly,
> And finds too late that men betray;
> What charm can soothe her
>     melancholy?
> What art can wash her tears away?
>
> The only art her guilt to cover,
> To hide her shame from every eye,
> To give repentance to her lover,
> And wring his bosom is—to die.
>
>           —Goldsmith, *Songs*

"What can you say about a twenty-five-year-old girl who died?"

That poignant question has been answered recently in two different modes; in 1970 as fiction: Erich Segal's slender (130 pages) best-seller *Love Story;* in 1972 as mythologizing about fiction: Pierre Fauchery's massive (895 pages) *doctorat d'état.*[1] As so often is the case, the answers are less interesting than the question. Or rather, what is interesting is the ideological matrix out of which the question arises: why *should* the death of a beautiful and brilliant girl (the etiquette as well as the epithets are Segal's; Fauchery calls married girls women) be the hallmark of eighteenth-century fiction and the herald of popular literature/culture in the 1970s? What is the appeal of the feminine death: if it is a literary strategy, what is its objective; if it is a code, what message does it transmit?

Fauchery begins his autopsy (and eulogy) of the exquisite cadavers by positing what Georges May established in a chapter of his fundamental book *Le Dilemme du roman au XVIIIe siècle,* the feminocentrism of French eighteenth-century fiction: "No novel without a lover [*amoureuse*] or beloved [*bien-aimée*]."[2] Fauchery is emphatic—if chronically overblown—in underscoring this productive meeting/mating of gender and genre:[3]

> Thus to us the decisive factor in the history of the novel seems to be the encounter between a genre still in the making—although intensely active and anxious to establish its prerogatives—and a feminine principle unfolding, bringing its graces and powers into play, appearing to extend its conquests without end. The eighteenth-century novel extols the oneiric reign of woman; in solemnizing the great moments of her career, it seems to liberate her from the constraints of her condition; it tears her away from the weight of the everyday in order to launch her into the sky of myth, on the orbit of her *destiny.* (*DF,* 11)

Unlike Georges May (and the Goncourt brothers before him), Fauchery distinguishes between feminocentrism ("the valorization of every kind of reality of which the feminine image is the magnet" [*DF,* 11]) and feminism. Indeed, he goes further than Laurent Versini who already commented on May's vision of this distinction: "To observe, even to celebrate the reign of women over the society of this period is one thing; to give women the means to be themselves is another. . . . It is not because the heroines of a novelist are touching, true and authentically feminine, that the author is a feminist; it's just that he's a real novelist."[4] "Authentically" feminine? Fauchery, to his credit, recognizes that to place women and their destiny at the center of a fictional universe is not to renounce androcentric privilege in the world.

By destiny, Fauchery means the concept of life as organizable process, life charted: linearity under the sign of *fatum.* But the literary transcription of an essence—a being—is less a mimetic function than a semiological one: recorded destiny is a *system* of signification. Destiny as experienced by the representatives of literary femininity in the novel—*la femme romanesque*—is a trajectory given pertinence only at specific points of intersection: the encounter with love, the encounter with death. Eros engendering with fatal, textual logic: *thanatos*. (Unless of course, there should be sublimation of the instincts via marriage, à la Pamela.) Unlike the archetypal nineteenth-century "novel of destiny" whose hero—traditionally, an ambitious young man—journeys into a world of things and forces to be mastered, the eighteenth-century novel's hero is a heroine who stays home. The formative process/progress under the feminine sign takes place in the gyneceum; focus is restricted to women's "fertile career" (*DF,* 14). Destiny is inflected by gender, not to say declined.

The eighteenth-century novel (of which there are more than five hundred listed in the bibliography, favored-nation status being granted to the French, English and German), its heroines and secondary female characters, is Fauchery's text. Or is it? "Doesn't the novel reveal the dreams of the century that it flattered itself not to dream? To grasp the modes according to which the eighteenth century dreams [of] Woman, and dreams through her, this then will be the basic objective of our study" (*DF,* 15). But can we separate the dreamer from the dream? His first sentence gives us the genesis of his book: "born of a reverie about a few touching and beautiful women" (*DF,* 5); his last, the traces remaining of his contact with them: "something of their incorruptible matter still inhabits the most intimate cells of our dreams" (*DF,* 859). Daydream to night dream, his sequence is impressive but disquieting.

Faced with a monumental corpus, like Diderot and d'Alembert before Falconet's marble statue, Fauchery pulverizes[5]: abandoning the chronology of influence and generation in favor of a synchronic perspective; rejecting the hierarchy preserved by literary history; deconstructing the masterpiece to form a homogeneous matter from which in turn he can reconstruct. Recreate the Woman of fantasy whose being/body is scattered through the novel: *the* woman of the novel. For, neologizing without a qualm, Fauchery would account for a *gynécomythie:* woman as myth, the myth of woman; geno-text, gyno-text.[6] Is he the intrepid explorer he sets out to be, or merely another victim of the Eternal Feminine? Mythography or mythogenesis? In the course of his quest he looks to the "fable," the story told over and over again; the story of a ritual sacrifice.

The fabulous creature he seeks is hypostatized in a binary mode: Girl and Woman, generally discrete incarnations of the feminine principle. (Rousseau's Julie being one of the rare heroines to pass from one to the other via marriage.) The table of contents (containing at least sixty separate entries) organizes the scenario of the "girl" (whom I will call the adolescent heroine) under the following major headings: "Prelude"—"Offertory"—"Sacrifice." The Women's division is organized as a typology of roles. In the first case, then, we might say, the emphasis is syntagmatic, a grammar of contiguity. What emerges are basic narrative sequences. Crudely, the story of a fall or the story of an ascent. The Clarissa story vs. the Pamela story. In the second case, the emphasis is paradigmatic: a lexicon, or repertory of stereotypes: wife, mother, libertine, whore, etc. Of course no novel taken as a narrative entity can be deemed exclusively paradigmatic or exclusively syntagmatic. Indeed, Clarissa's virginal status is as significant as her trajectory of martyrdom; Mme de Tourvel's trajectory of seduction and betrayal is as relevant as her type—the fallen woman. What is true, however, is that the sacrificial scenario is established hyperbolically in the novel of the adolescent heroine; and that there is a greater variety of roles in the novel of the "older" woman.

The ideal adolescent heroine must be both representative and exceptional to be literarily efficient. This apparent contradiction depends upon assumptions common to the thinking about women in the period: (1) Every woman equals every other woman as a being defined in terms of her sex, both as gender, member of the fair/opposite sex, and her sexuality as symbolic function: "bearer of a 'treasure' which is not hers to dispose of" (DF, 181); and (2) Extraordinariness (in the areas assigned women characters as pertinent: beauty, virtue, sensibility) is the norm. From Pamela on, "perfection becomes canonical" (DF, 217). The life story of the adolescent heroine does not begin at a random point in time. Nor does it begin at the beginning, at least not literally. Fictional memoir or epistolary novel, the chronology of the feminine destiny is rooted in sexuality.[7] In a universe ruled by the prerogatives of gender, it is logical and economical to have the movement of plot triggered by the "polarizing conjuncture" (DF, 222): the erotic confrontation. The memoir—whose author is often an orphan—usually opens with an exposition/exposure of the heroine's vulnerability, coded as a lack of experience, protection, money. Think of Fanny Hill, fifteen-year-old orphan on her way to seek her fortune in London; or Justine, twelve-year-old orphan seeking work in Paris. Young, beautiful, ignorant, poverty-stricken, and of course virginal, the combination is irresistible. The advent of the seducer, inevitable. In the epistolary novel where the heroine is often a daughter well-protected by parents determined to guard their offspring's innocence, the challenge to security generally results from the transformation of a masculine figure already in place: from neutral to sexual. Thus, Saint-Preux preceptor becomes Saint-Preux lover, Lovelace sister Arabella's suitor becomes Lovelace Clarissa's seducer. Curiously then, circumstances do not so much motivate as camouflage a necessity independent of "reality." A young woman is vulnerable (and etymology is relevant here) by nature, by virtue of her gender. Absent parents or omnipresent parents simply overload a circuit, overcode a system already set up to transmit only one kind of information. Once the seducer is on the scene, the phallus on the horizon, reader interest, not to say suspense, is quickly oriented towards a conflict whose outcome is articulated in a simple binary opposition: acceptance or rejection of the sexual and implicitly territorial imperative. To be sure, there are refinements: reluctance, temporizing, self-delusion, and rape. Nevertheless, regardless of attitude, the heroine's ultimate fate correlates directly with her performance in the sexual arena. Illicit sex (and the exceptions to this rule such as Fanny Hill and Moll Flanders would involve both a discussion of their redemptive powers of marriage specific to the English novel, and the implications of serial sexuality in what might properly be called a mythic mode) must be punished; preferably by death. Since virginity is the essence of femininity, which in turn is the essence of any (positive) female character ("According to the ontology of fiction, to be, is to be a virgin" [DF, 307]), it is not surprising that the archetypal eighteenth-century novel of the feminine destiny should focus on defloration. (The advantage of the strategy is obvious: it highlights directly or indirectly the primacy of the phallus.) Virtue would be neither interesting nor credible if untested. Virtue cannot be rewarded if untried: it is tried by metonymy. No novel structured by the sacrificial scenario demonstrates more clearly than *Clarissa* to what extent a loss of "honor" is a fate worse than death. Richardson sets in place what Sade will exploit reiteratively: the esthetic power (bourgeois or anti-bourgeois) of rape. "Rape, in the imaginary society of the century, is presented as the potential destiny of every woman; but it maintains with virginity one of those antithetical relations in which contradiction becomes attraction. Chastity attracts rape as the sacred invites defilement" (*DF,* 317). In fiction, the exercise of female sexuality is rarely perceived as anything but degradation: having given herself to Saint-Preux, Julie sees herself as worthless. By resisting Mr. B., Pamela proves her worth. Even Moll Flanders, that "essentially masculine" character, participates in the system when she comments on the implications of her initiation: "I had nothing left of value to recommend me, either to God's blessing or man's assistance."[8] And one might remember that it is Moll herself who puts into circulation the word "whore" as self-description. In *Clarissa* the sense of degradation is so powerful that only death can restore value and meaning. What can you say about a nineteen-year-old girl who wants to die because she is no longer a virgin? That she is fulfilling her destiny; paying the appropriate price for her crime. What is her crime but her femininity? Fauchery states, "It is indeed the original vice of *being a woman* that we see pursued assiduously in the fictional universe, whether in novels of virtue or novels of gallantry" (*DF,* 653). Death is the highest calling of the fictional woman; marriage and a glimpse of the "happily ever after," the tepid alternative—a traveled but less captivating route. In both cases, however, the disruptive potential of female sexuality is neutralized, removed from general circulation.

If it is easy to see *how* the mechanics of the feminine destiny operate in the eighteenth-century text, it is less easy to say *why*. Fauchery is briefly tempted by the "sociological" grid: "The feminine destiny would be, in the final analysis, no more than a hypostatized projection of the collective will (fundamentally male)—mystifying or protective according to the perspective—in agreement to confine the female sex to a flatteringly inferior position" (*DF,* 834). The defeat of the feminine would be a fantasmatic displacement, a vicarious victory in the transposed battle between the emerging bourgeois novelist and his class enemy. An interesting idea, but Fauchery abandons this line of reasoning and scraps the argument with a footnote from Marx to support his own contention that "by according privileged status to the sexual, the novel goes back to the beginning, to a situation of a battle between sexes that predates the class struggle" (*DF*, 835).

What then? Citing the antithetical nature of femininity as represented in the novel—angel/devil, virgin/whore—Fauchery hypothesizes a metaphysical solution: "All this leads us to think that [fictional woman's] fundamental mandate could well be to dramatize [*mettre en spectacle*] contradiction" (*DF*, 835). Here he might have turned to Simone de Beauvoir (listed in his bibliography): "There is no figurative image of woman which does not call up at once its opposite: she is Life and Death, Nature and Artifice, Daylight and Night. Under whatever aspect we consider her, we always find the same shifting back and forth, for the nonessential returns necessarily to the essential. In the figures of the Virgin Mary and Beatrice, Eve and Circe still exist."[9] In this sense, there is nothing specifically literary—at least novelistic—about woman's role. Woman as contradiction is a general, *cultural* phenomenon. The novel simply exploits that figment of the masculine imagination. What Fauchery seems to be delineating here is the role of fictional woman as catch-all—a device to absorb the overflow of reality; an "ideological magnet" (*DF*, 651, 837); the ideal scapegoat. Like the white man's burden, woman discharges imperialistic guilt. Once again we have text as displacement, one anxiety disguised as another. There is more. Woman is a means to man's self-fulfillment, for she permits "the writer to have access to the zones of his self normally forbidden to him by his masculinity"; and through her, this "accommodating medium" [*filtre complaisant*], (*DF*, 837) the world.

Finally, however, Fauchery characterizes the sexual dimension of the literary project as an androgynous enterprise, a matter of gender transference: "'muliebrity,' the mimetic operation by which in the universe of so many writers, man 'becomes woman'" (*DF*, 855). In his perspective, what subsequently distinguishes the nineteenth-century novel from the eighteenth, is the assimilation of the feminine: "Romanticism completes the integration of the feminine half of the psychic function of the fictional hero. And by natural compensation, as the 'hero' becomes devirilized, the fictional woman becomes blurred and faded" (*DF*, 855). Polarization is mediated, difference muted. The novelist need no longer operate "in drag" to experience and communicate what is "feminine" in his self. Perhaps. But in this erotic game of hide and seek that we discuss as literature, Kristeva seems closer to the mark: "The place of concealment or valorization, woman will be a pseudocenter, a latent or explicit center, that is exposed openly or else camouflaged with modest precautions, the present or absent center of modern fictional [romanesque] discourse in which *man seeks man and becomes godlike,* or else women try to become men."[10] Woman as *agora,* as marketplace where man meets man (himself, his self); this functional role seems less specific to the eighteenth-century novel than to fiction itself. And the encounter, if not homoerotic, is fundamentally narcissistic. As Simone de Beauvoir remarks in the course of a commentary on *Man's Fate:* "Woman is the supreme recompense for [man] since, under a shape foreign to him which he can possess in her flesh, she is his own apotheosis."[11] Woman permits man to celebrate himself; feminocentrism underwrites androcentrism. Thus, when we look to the literature of the twentieth century with Fauchery, gender opposition has returned to the service of masculine values. (If indeed it ever disappeared.) While he discounts the *nouveau roman* as a relevant testing ground by virtue of its limited "sector of consumption" (*DF,* 856) (although I wonder if the rich mine of sexual polarization is not exploited in novels such as *Project for a Revolution in New York,* or *The Modification*), Fauchery finds the sediment of feminine mythos in popular culture: best-sellers, songs, magazines, movies still perpetuate a vision of the Eternal Feminine. Irresistible, pathetic essence cementing the foundations of the male bond.

In the end, with a parting and rare gesture of anxiety, Fauchery wonders about mythmaking: "and it may be that we have only added our own and unworthy myth to those that women raise everywhere on their footsteps" (*DF,* 859). And beyond myth, about phallocentric/cratic pretension: "But these definitions, they will say, are masculine in origin. What guarantees do we have that the 'real' woman is present in them?" (*DF,* 838). None, of course. Fauchery's self-consoling solution and ultimately good conscience result from a final twist of the art imitating life, life imitating art cliché. Art, via the novel, *teaches* life, teaches women how to live (and die); and the novel as "night school" (*DF,* 838) undermines the pertinence of the opposition fictional/historical woman. Moreover, not only do real women adapt themselves to the literary model, women writers reduplicate it. They collaborate in the politics of oppression. Citing

Germaine de Staël as the epitome of the feminine consciousness in the novel—and chronologically its last incarnation in this slice of time—Fauchery concludes: "Thus we would say quite readily of this superior woman that she represents the last word in feminine masochism by her sinful adoption of virile values" (DF, 847). And bidding a reluctant farewell to "our divine evanescences" (DF, 859), Fauchery goes back to dreaming.

Nevertheless, he cannot resist spending a titillating moment with Mme de Merteuil; and ponder her fate. Although there is critical controversy over the sense of the ending of the Liaisons dangereuses, and hence, the meaning of Merteuil's destiny, Fauchery's determination to read her rout as triumph is to me the best example of his failure to understand the implications of his own knowledge, and for all his feminocentrism, a clear demonstration of the lack of a feminist hermeneutic.

By a feminist hermeneutic I do not mean a simplistic act of interpretation that imprints its own prefabricated shape, reducing "these mimetic fragments of life to their lowest common denominator."[12] Although this condemnation comes from the pen of a feminist, it is difficult to think of any theory or practice that is not accused of reductionism in those very terms—by non-partisans. The issue belongs on another level, for it is a question, ultimately, of the values and assumptions operative in the processing and re-writing of information, textual data gathered according to the idiosyncrasies of one's critical preference.[13] It may also be premature, not to say inappropriate, to speak of a feminist hermeneutic in the absence of a clearly articulated theory about the text and its cultural inscription: "On the whole," Elaine Showalter writes, "feminist literary criticism and scholarship have been stubbornly empirical; they have generated relatively little theory and abstraction. . . . It seems unlikely that any theoretical manifesto could be both intellectually and politically adequate to describe the extreme diversity of the current approaches to literature which involve women, sex roles, the family, or sexual politics in any of their permutations and combinations."[14] Nevertheless, in this interim period, it is possible and, I think, imperative to expose an interpretive strategy along a feminist/non-feminist axis by analyzing the critic's stance toward his/her findings: does he/she identify with the narrator/narratee? "buy" the message? project into the text?

The key lies not so much in the critic's gender (although that often is the case) but in his or her attitude towards gender; and in the final analysis, this is a matter of ideology, of cultural complicity.

Thus, to the extent that Fauchery reads the ending of the *Liaisons* as punishment for Merteuil, in his eyes her crime is the arrogance of individualism: "A heavy sin is attached to the enterprise of creating one's own values oneself, except when it is paid for by total renunciation" (*DF, 675*). It seems to me that the sin in question, however, constitutes a rebellion of the individual spirit against a collective will only insofar as the rebellion challenges the strictures of sexual politics. Fauchery's reading turns on an issue of gendered complicity, here between reader/super reader and fictional text: "*As a man*, the reader forgets that it is with men that Merteuil has a score to settle. Because we *temporarily reject* the virile constraint imposed on women, we approve the stratagems by which this woman succeeds in *outwitting* it. . . . It is Merteuil who in the novel represents *us*, the intelligent reader" (*DF, 672*; only the italics marking "*us*" are Fauchery's). So then. We the reader are men, intelligent men who temporarily forget—and enjoy the fact—that this clever and powerful woman is out to get us (castrate us?). But as a woman, the reader doesn't forget the score; neither does the author. Why else the uniqueness of Merteuil's fate? The oxymoron of a living death. The grammatical rules of the universe of eighteenth-century fiction are rigorous and do not tolerate exceptions. If woman is object of desire, the subject is masculine. Merteuil's attempt to reverse the laws of grammaticality, to become desiring subject, is the clearest example of the gravity of solecism. Merteuil refuses the rules of a universe which would define and constrain her in a binary opposition according to which the feminine term is always generated and never original. Her evident linguistic prowess, however, is a threat too serious to be tolerated. As Kristeva has said in another context: "To tamper with the taboos of grammar . . . is to tamper with the veiled recommendation of identificatory sexuality: the revolution of language is an intersection of sexuality and all the social coagulations (families, sects, etc.) that are attached to it."[15] Disfigured, dispossessed, and displaced, the punishment fits the enormity of the crime: alienation is complete. Merteuil is ejected/rejected outside the community of value, hence meaning.

If Merteuil is victorious, the victory, surely, is pyrrhic: she is "unmanned."[16] And one senses Fauchery's determination to deny the evidence by his waffling: "Merteuil finally wins (to what end is another problem) her definitive independence" (*DF,* 675). But that is precisely the problem. Independence requires a context; winning is meaningless when no one else is playing. Thus, it is not in the least surprising that the last word on Merteuil's singular destiny should come from the "publisher" of the novel. It is addressed to the reader: "For the moment we cannot . . . inform him of the sinister event which completed the misfortunes or the punishment of Madame de Merteuil." The rest, if not silence, is extra-textual. The terms of the fiction are saturated. Yet Fauchery is dissatisfied: "No ending of a novel is in this sense more valorizing, no imaginary woman of the XVIIIth century disappears in a more irritating 'majesty'" (*DF,* 675). His use of inverted commas confirms the hedging of the parenthesis until he finds his solution at the end of the royal road of the expanded metaphor: "Queen in exile, exiled even of her charms but still queen" (*DF,* 675). French nostalgia for a lost monarchy? Or rhetoric in the face of a conundrum? It is, perhaps, his fascination at finding *himself* represented by so extraordinary a woman that blinds him to the scene of her final humiliation: humiliation that he so clearly sees in the obviously sacrificial scenarios: "From all these observations there emerges the idea of a profound unity, in apparently contradictory forms, of virile sexuality—and also of a connivance of the reader with the authors and their characters in the humiliation of woman, in her sacrifice as flesh" (*DF,* 521). Ultimately, is Mme de Merteuil any less sacrificed to a masculine idea(l) than Mme de Tourvel? The most sophisticated woman "writer" of eighteenth-century letters "tried to become a man" and ended like Polyphemous: outwitted; a mutilated monster.

But we are talking about the problem of complicity. It is to be remembered that within the *Liaisons* it is Valmont's definitive realignment with the male bond that causes Merteuil's downfall, and leads to the publication of her letters, and then the text, or rather the founding fiction of the reader's text. After all, male solidarity exists to protect masculine prerogatives. The very exercise of desire depends upon a gender-related balance of power: "In sexual enjoyment [*jouissance*] man frees himself from the power woman held over him: by the desire [man] had of her, she fettered and dominated him."[17] By this formulation, masculine desire functions as calculated and violent revenge; resentment, if we are to believe Mailer, based on envy. I cite him here—in his defense, in *The Prisoner of Sex,* of Henry Miller under attack by Kate Millett—at length and for reasons that should become obvious:

> For he captured something in the sexuality of men as it had never been seen before, precisely that it was man's sense of awe before woman, his dread of her position one step closer to eternity (for in that step were her powers) which made men detest women, revile them, humiliate them, defecate symbolically upon them, do everything to reduce them so one might dare to enter them and take pleasure of them. . . . *Men look to destroy every quality in a woman which will give her the powers of a male,* for she is in their eyes already armed with the power that she brought them forth, and that is a power beyond measure—the earliest etchings of memory go back to that woman between whose legs they were conceived, nurtured, and near strangled in the hours of birth.[18]

Merteuil would refuse that destruction and execute a counter-revenge. But that involves a usurpation, an arrogation of masculine power. The ending of the *Liaisons,* however "conventional," makes clear that such a reversal of "identificatory sexuality" is unacceptable and unforgivable. Merteuil, and not the men, is castrated; *l'oeil crevé* is the ultimate symbolic wounding. She will no longer be able to call herself the "new Dalilah." It may be true that despite her loss, "her great mind [remains] untouched," but there will be no more Samson to seduce, the better to destroy with scissors.[19] Merteuil's power depends upon the *packaging* of her mental energy; denied the power of attraction, Merteuil becomes sexually dysfunctional.[20]

It is inevitable that generalizations about the nature of literary femininity in the eighteenth-century novel should end with its *hapax.* More than Juliette, whose author defined her as "unique in her kind," Merteuil deserves the accolade of unicity, for she finally refused the hegemony of a male partner. It follows too, then, that unlike Juliette, she does not enjoy a "happy end": "female heteroclites [are] inevitably sacrificed to purge threatening symptoms of disease and pollution from society."[21] In the imaginary universe of the novel, there is no room for the exceptional woman who calls into question the ground rules of the oldest game in the world.[22] That may well be the message of the medium.

The death of the Other restores men to each other. Thus, *Love Story* ends ostensibly with a feminine death but actually with the glorification of the paternal and the filial: the son weeping for the first time in his life in the embrace of the father. The heroine remains by metonymy only, through her aphorism of forgiveness: eucharist in a communion from man to man.

# TENDER ECONOMIES
## Mme de Villedieu and
## the Costs of Indifference

While civil war tore France apart during the reign of Charles IX,
Love still found its place amid so many disorders and caused many
in its own Empire.
                              —Mme de Lafayette, *La Princesse de Monpensier*

I look for myself in everything I write.
                              —Mme de Villedieu, *Galanteries Galantines*

In the preface to a feminist edition of Mme de Lafayette's *Histoire de
Madame Henriette d'Angleterre,* Claudine Herrmann, seeking to
explain her author's desire for anonymity, contrasts her position on
the signature with that of a contemporary woman writer: "Madame
de Villedieu didn't hesitate to sign her novels . . . But what could anyone do to her? She was nothing and had nothing to lose."[1] I invoke
this pairing of the two writers, the woman of privilege close to the
scene of (virile) power, and the one who "was nothing," for several
reasons, but first of all to review its inevitability. The work of Mme
de Villedieu is never cited—though here the order of reference is
reversed—without the obligatory comparison (generally invidious, as
becomes the binary mode) to the *oeuvre* of the other.[2] In particular,

the second story in Mme de Villedieu's "novel," *Les Désordres de l'amour* (1675),[3] which comes to illustrate the maxim, "that one cannot allow love so little power that love doesn't take advantage of it," has been retained by the construction of literary history—beginning with Valincour—because of a troubling predecession to *La Princesse de Clèves* (1678).[4] The story figures an *aveu*, an avowal made by an unhappy young wife to a husband passionately in love and solicitous of her well being, that she desires—against her will and chastely— another man. In the earlier work, the avowal leads not to a subsequent (and heroic) refusal of love, but to banal possession and, ultimately, as Bruce Morrissette describes this "favorite theme" of Mme de Villedieu's, to "the degeneration of a great passion as a lover's ardour cools and his mistress struggles desperately to hold him."[5] Rather than dwell again on this obvious point of convergence and disparity, however, let us look elsewhere and otherwise in the *Désordres* for the predecessor's specificity.

Henri Coulet, in his magistral account of the evolution of the French novel, offers a socio-critical reading of the differences separating the two women (writers) and of the grounds of their identity. Noting that the experience of Mme de Villedieu—by her own account—is that of an "adventuress," and not "a lady of the court," he argues that the same period of history—the reign of Henri III— portrayed in their works emerges in two rather different lights: Mme de Lafayette shows "the collapse of heroism," Mme de Villedieu, "people without heroism." Coulet concludes that, "Within the classical formula of the genre she helped elaborate, Mme de Villedieu prefigured the novel of the next century much more than did Mme de Lafayette."[6] How then does the woman who was nothing write herself into history?

At stake in this collection of stories is the proper relation between the spheres of love and state. If by virtue of the logic of the maxim that underwrites the whole work—"*that love is the moving force behind all the other passions*"—love rules all human relations, what in their representations can distinguish, for example, the state of love from affairs of state, private life from public life, women from men?

By way of conclusion to the second story, the narrator speaks in her own voice to point out the moral; she begins her summary by connecting the fallout of love's miseries with the mapping of national borders: "Thus the same love that in the first part of this work sowed the seeds of the League, presents, in this part, a secret obstacle to the general peace of kingdom and costs us a tract of land that would be regained only at the price of much blood and work" (*LD*, 117). This formulation, by locating the costs of love as impropriety in property ("a tract of land"), reiterates the founding contiguity linking sexual relations and social relations also at the heart of the universe evoked in the opening lines of *La Princesse de Clèves* where *la galanterie* is inseparable from the definition of a reign: "Opulence and gallantry were never so brilliantly displayed in France as they were in the last years of Henri II's reign."[7] But perhaps what is equally important here, beyond the syllepsis implicit in the affairs of state, is the status of the "we"—the French kingdom—which binds the woman writer to her readers nationally and narrationally (this sense of national identity is essential to the definition of the *nouvelle*'s generic specificity).

Villedieu then looks to the continuation of her narrative through another modulation of the *we* and *I*:

> I hope to report more than the least proof that not only does [love] stir up our passions, but it often deserves all the blame that these passions attract; it brings us to despair, and the most perfect works of nature and of art sometimes depend on a moment of its capriciousness and furor. (*LD*, 118)

This penultimate gesture of provisional closure announces the slight shift in emphasis from the first part to the second; from the paradigms of love's power—"that one cannot allow love so little power that love doesn't take advantage of it," "that love is the moving force behind all the other passions"—to love's privileged signifier in the third maxim (and story): "that there is no limit to the despair to which love can lead a man who is very much in love" (*LD*, 119). Let us consider these theorems and speculate about the sentence that both concludes the second story and frames the third. "I do not doubt that at this point more than one reader will say with an ironic tone that I have not always spoken this way, but it is even because of this that I am justified in speaking so badly of [love], and it's because I have had a perfect experience of it that I find myself authorized to paint it with such black colors" (*LD*, 118). Micheline Cuénin sees in this intervention a break with convention—a familiarity associated more with an oral tradition—and, at the same time, Villedieu's acknowledgment of her moral responsibility to her female reading public. Cuénin observes that she thus communicates "to her women readers, like an advice columnist, her own conception of love," and goes on to claim that the commentary assigned to the Princesse de Guise (author of the *Maximes* in the third story) is "the expression of her personal convictions" (*LD*, lv). Whether or not one wishes to conclude a perfect coincidence between the voice of experience and the experience behind the voice, it is the case that the stories of unrequited love are bleak: the woman in love—or the man in love *like a woman* (in love)—is always the example of a trajectory that leads to suffering and (or) death. I would like to propose, taking Cuénin's projection a bit further, that the author in fact doubles herself in the narrative: figuring both as the phallic woman—the narcissistic princess whose poetry has repercussions in affairs of state—and the classic woman in love—Mme de Maugiron, the ambiguous woman with a past whose prose ultimately leaves her on the margins of history.[8]

The third story announces itself as the story of a man madly in love. A hero of historical reference, Givry, at the beginning of the tale, is in love with the fictional Mme de Maugiron. Mme de Maugiron is a widow, young and beautiful—the incarnation of feminine freedom in the seventeenth century. Her (female) plot is given briefly: "she pleased Givry and wasn't indifferent to the charms of this young lord" (*LD*, 122). Despite his youth (he is younger than she), he is both naturally gifted for love, brilliant, and at the age of twenty-two put in charge of light cavalry in France: "So perfect a lover couldn't help but make much headway with a lady who was predisposed to have a violent inclination for him" (*LD*, 123).

What is the fate of exclusive possession outside the marriage contract? It is an idyll as perfect as the lover: "She was impolite to all his rivals in public; they spent entire days in sweet conversation and when they were interrupted by some of Givry's duties, the beautiful widow wrote him letters so tender that they consoled him in some measure for not seeing her" (*LD*, 123). In this model, Givry's ambition—his function in the state (his duty)—is confined to the status of an interruption and an effect rather than an origin, as though the erotic continuum were the scene and the source of identity in the world.

The letters not only supply the absent woman, they fill the leisure moments that punctuate his martial activity. They also operate a metonymic displacement of the proper virile identity: "he took more care for the safety of his casket than for his own." Despite his obsessive and displaced care, the letters are captured along with "all the rest of his baggage" (*LD*, 123). But letters are lost, we know, the better to be found. A messenger from the enemy camp returns the "casket," explaining that the Holy League, "didn't want to enter into any intrigue of gallantry" (*LD*, 124). Moreover, since love letters were neither "of use to religion and the public," nor "proper for this use" (*LD*, 125), they will not be recirculated (whereas pieces of his "baggage" will). To this distinction between the public and private, Givry replies that a heroic heart, "was big enough to satisfy the duties of love and war." Are these duties compatible? Should the male sphere of "the public good" remain separate from the zone of the female? Can a man of state afford to behave like a woman in love? Can the state?

When Givry opens the box to reread the letters, he finds verses "in an unknown hand" folded in the first letter he scans. The verses, which are called *Maximes,* are commentary on the prose of Mme de Maugiron. As Givry rereads the texts of one woman's love in the light of what will turn out to be another woman's scrutiny, he fantasizes about the person of the exegete: "a woman in love who made a *profit* from all the innocent pleasures of love and who *made for herself a law out of this tender economy*" (*LD*, 128; emphasis added). As he represents to himself the happiness of the man who would be loved by such a woman, he succumbs to the powers of idealization, to the perfect because imaginary woman. Against that model, Mme de Maugiron's bodily claims necessarily pale.

When it emerges that the maxims were authored by the Princesse de Guise, daughter of the enemy, Givry evokes, against the warnings of his intimate friend Bellegarde, the rules and privileges of *galanterie:* "I am young, I'm ambitious, and Mademoiselle de Guise is one of the most beautiful princesses in the world. I would be treated like a madman if I could have a love intrigue with her but passed up the occasion" (*LD*, 131). Givry here again—this is a standard male plot—articulates the parataxic order governing his ambitious and erotic wishes, dismissing not only any loyalty to the current beloved, but disregarding as well his loyalty to the king, evacuating the political connotations of the signifer *intrigue,* as though love stories could be preserved from the historical demands of the state.[9]

Once Givry actually sees the woman whose hand author[iz]ed his fantasy, the "remains" of his established passion vanishes (*LD,* 156): he forgets to read Mme de Maugiron's letters; he goes further and proclaims this new indifference to the poet(ess), "that the verses she had sent him had dispelled his heart's blindness" (*LD,* 159). But his progress—"Mademoiselle de Guise took pleasure in having his protestation repeated to her"—is interrupted by the renewal of the war and the princess's enigmatic and abrupt retreat from further contact. When after months of rigor, Givry finally obtains a meeting with Mademoiselle de Guise, the cause of her coldness is revealed to be textual. More specifically—the plot again turns on the axis of communication—Givry's *lèse-majesté* is located in a letter Mademoiselle de Guise has received, a declaration of love signed in his name, and that Givry denies having written. The symmetry is not trivial: Givry's passion crystallized on discovering that the princess's name was attached to her verse. The direction of the princess's "inclination" will depend as well on the origin and authenticity of the signature. The mystery intrigues her: "Mademoiselle de Guise found this adventure *so bizarre* that she wanted to pursue it" (*LD,* 176; emphasis added). When Givry reads the letter, he discovers the handwriting in his name to be that of his friend Bellegarde.[10] The question, the mystery to penetrate, thus returns again to origins and intentions: "Who could compel you," the princess wonders, "with such reckless and extravagant feelings?" (*LD,* 177).[11] The erotic effects of this hermeneutics of uncertainty on the princess are immediately identified by the narrator:

> Love is full of capriciousness, one cannot imagine any whim so extravagant that love wouldn't be capable of it . . . through a quirk seen only in examples of love, [Mademoiselle de Guise] found the Grand Squire's actions singular and felt an extraordinary curiosity to discover the motive behind them. (*LD,* 177)

Though logically the princess should be as outraged by a declaration from Bellegarde as by one from Givry (who in fact surpasses the former in "élévation"), through the paradoxes (also the *doxa*) of love, she softens.

The truth of her feelings—she favors the "author"—will be revealed only among women. In an episode both more straightforward (conventionally) and more complicated (communicationally) than Nemour's overhearing of the Princesse de Clèves's avowal to her husband, Mme de Maugiron, "sliding behind the fence," eavesdrops on a conversation between Mademoiselle de Guise and her confidante. Then, in the logic of her tender economy (LD, 186), Mme de Maugiron reveals Bellegarde's betrayal and "happiness" to Givry.

At this point in the narrative, the love plot again comes up against the affairs of state: the rivals' quarrel between Givry and Bellegarde must be covered over for His Majesty's sake, so that it "wouldn't be an example of division between the leaders of his party" (LD, 189). Givry, leaving to accompany the King, arranges for Mme de Maugiron to have a place with the Queen and a pension. These arrangements are designed to function within an erotics of circulation and ambition: "if she could have been content with simple friendship and much care for her fortune, she would have been satisfied with Givry; *but she counted as nothing all that was not love*" (LD, 190; emphasis added). What is the fate of such a tender economy, of such excessive accounting? In the face of Givry's assertion that his indifferences are so powerful that he would rather love "a third person" than return to requite her love, Mme de Maugiron replies with the logic of the Portuguese nun: "I will love you no less because of that: my fatal passion doesn't need any hope to survive, and for a long time it has seemed to take on new strength without it" (LD, 191). And as she finishes her declaration (these are her last recorded words), in "conversations that show too well the extravagance of love not to be recounted" (LD, 190), she reinscribes in prose, of course without suspecting her belatedness, the poetic truth penned by the princess—"it is the star that decides, / And discernment has no part in it" (LD, 127): "You don't owe me any recognition; this is not a voluntary love; but you owe me some pity, for the stars treat me so harshly" (LD, 191).

Mme de Maugiron loves Givry who loves the Princesse de Guise who (might) love Bellegarde (who loves her) (though surely she could never do more than allow him to "please" her—the King sees this). What can come of these sub-Racinian arrangements of the flow of desire?

The King appeals to a more public economy and tries to encourage Givry by promising him services to render Mademoiselle de Guise, his hope being that "recognition would win out over her caution." Returning to the realm of *duty,* Givry determines to repress his hostility to Bellegarde, his jealousy, valorizing instead and submitting to the "will of so familiar and obliging a master" (*LD,* 194). The love plot submits to the higher public good, peace is declared; the King converts, and enters Paris. Concomitantly, however, the rivalry between the two men explodes; they forget the orders of the King and draw their swords against each other (*LD,* 197). The aftermath of the duel seals Givry's disfavor in the eyes of the princess.

The King himself pleads Givry's cause but to no avail; Mme de Maugiron returns and tries again, but the narrator underlines the symmetry of failure linking the two unhappy fates: "But the destiny of this woman in love and of the unfortunate Givry was to love without being loved" (*LD,* 200). More poignantly (and predictably), unrequited love is only half the story; there is also the requisite motor of masochism: "the disdain with which they were treated was far from awakening their courage, it seemed that their love increased through such vexation" (*LD,* 201).

*What is the ultimate fate of the man in love like a woman?*
The King sends Givry on a last mission, a political "commission" that will permit a legitimate meeting between Givry and Mademoiselle de Guise. In the name of the King's interests, he gains admission to the bedroom: transported by the sight of her beauty, Givry forgets himself; the princess—pulling rank—banishes him from her presence. Outside in the garden, her confidante rebukes Givry for blurring other distinctions beyond rank and hierarchy, for confusing again, through the sociolect's metaphors of love as war, nothing less than *love* and *state:* "Is this the way one obtains the favors of a virtuous and courageous princess? Were you looking at her like a rebel city that you resolved to besiege?" (*LD,* 204). On leaving her chamber, Givry has promised the princess his death as a mark of his obedience and renunciation. He dies taking "the city of Laon": the City gives him what the Woman refused. His death underwrites his sincerity, and history, it would seem, has preserved the letter his historical double wrote announcing his death. In fiction as in life, the letter did not arrive at

its proper destination; it was seized by the enemy—like Mme de Maugiron's letters—and preserved in the Bibliothèque de l'Arsenal.[12] The King himself communicates the text of Givry's despair, and of his own anger, to the princess: "You've killed Givry" (*LD*, 207). But the princess is unmoved. The one who will grieve, for whom the personal loss equals and surpasses the King's loss (of state), is of course Mme de Maugiron: "she fell into a languor that ended only with her life" (*LD*, 207).

Mme de Maugiron is "too constant" in the pair she forms, not so much with her female rival, but with her fickle lover: the "too lovable and too inconstant Givry." But in the end does love erase all differences? The final verses, like the earlier maxims would seem to make this point:

> Love, cruel love, enchantment of souls
> Alas! shall we never see
> The deadly effect of your flames
> Respect the wisdom and peace in our hearts. (*LD*, 209)

The prose has already answered the rhetorical question. The final paragraph begins with the narrator's assumption of her own intentionality: "The examples I have chosen to persuade [you] of love's malice could not end with a story more able to inspire all the horror love deserves" (*LD*, 208). And it concludes, equally emphatically:

> This is how almost all persons end up who abandon themselves unreservedly to this fatal madness. If one feels it slightly, it is an inexhaustible source of perfidy and ingratitude; and if one submits to it in good faith, it leads to excessive disturbance and despair. (*LD*, 209)

Is there anything to be learned beyond the power of repetition? Or what have we learned from these examples?

The story of Givry is identified by the narrator as being the most apt to inspire the degree of horror proper to understanding the cancer of love. Although she is explicit about that choice, the logic of her ranking is left implicit. It is not, however, impossible to uncover, and I think if we return to the ending of the first story in *Les Désordres*, we can begin to assess the values of Mme de Villedieu's balance sheet.

In summarizing the events of her narration, and in drawing the moral, Mme de Villedieu's "I," unlike, for example, the veiled narrator of *La Princesse de Clèves*, explains and justifies her project in writing. She relates her didactic concerns to the annals of history, in this instance allying herself to, and aligning herself with, the evidence in "the Memoirs on which I base this commentary" (*LD*, 65). Her specific point of convergence with what has already been written is her demonstrated conviction that the origins of the League are to be located in "the love intrigues I have just written" (*LD*, 65). The male bond that ought to have held Le Roi de Navarre and the Duc de Guise together was fractured by a "fatal passion" (inspired by the dangerous coquette Mme de Sauve). So too would one find love "guilty or complicitous" in all the "revolutions that happen in monarchies" (*LD*, 66). But if this ubiquity of love is only "too sufficiently proven by the diverse intrigues that make up this example," then what justifies the redundancy of more examples? Put another way, if the truth already exists in history, what is to be gained by writing fiction?

There would seem to be something to be learned about love itself: "I am going to try to prove similarly that if it is deadly in these excesses, it is no less to be feared in its beginnings . . ." (*LD*, 66). In this move from the disastrous end results of love to its equally dangerous beginnings, the narrator invokes the actors of the second story; their "story," she claims, "comes to my memory to provide this second proof" (*LD*, 66). But if the story properly carries her point about the overlap of sexual and national intrigues—their founding *conjunction*—it is surely disingenuous of her to cite her "memory" as the origin of her material.

Indeed the logic of these concluding paragraphs is not overpowering. One feels instead the self-conscious construction of a discourse which might bridge the gap separating one *nouvelle* from the next, and, at the same time, the woman writer's auctorial anxiety about her right to address her "real" subject in writing. As she will finally say, the story of the Maréchal de Bellegarde "is a great lesson of the care one must take to fight the first impressions of love, but it allows me *to join the important truths of general history with the gallantries of my subject*" (*LD*, 66; emphasis added). The national scale of history comes to legitimate the attention in fiction to the local maneuvers between the sexes. What Givry's, like Bellegarde's, story shows, however, is not merely the intimacy that coordinates the concerns of state and love and conjoins their metaphors. More important, perhaps, for Villedieu, this parataxis results in our being led, instructed really—such is the logic of the troping—to reconsider the dominant definitions and valorizations of masculinity as the privileged source of social value and the proper measure of historicity. Kibédi-Varga has argued that "in an aristocratic society with masculine predominance, war is man's distinctive trait, a value that lets him be idealized. War is what tears man away from love, it appears to be the opposite of love; but it fascinates woman too."[13] This is the truth of the sociolect and can be read, I think, in Mme de Lafayette's placing of her heroine in front of a painting of the siege of Metz, of "those who had distinguished themselves there," which is but one of a collection of virile events: "All the remarkable actions that had happened in the king's reign were in these paintings."[14] Female eroticism here is charged by the controlled contemplation of distinguished masculine activity after the fact and fixed in representation. But in *Les Désordres de l'amour*, the war is at hand and the effects of fascination—the historical re-presentation—are undercut by the plots of love, the false other of heroism.

Villedieu's feminism, by which I mean her coded self-consciousness about writing as a woman about the costs of love, leads her to question the grounds of impeccable masculinity (Givry's)—through the invention of a woman born to live an entirely fictional female plot (Mme de Maugiron). Thus in the final paragraph of the novel, bracketed by the moral discourse of rhetorical closure, we have this portrait of Givry: "Givry was the most accomplished of all the men of his century; at twenty-six, he was showered with honors, favored by the good grace of his King, and in a position to obtain all the dignities to which gentlemen can aspire" (*LD*, 208). But the perfect male plot of ambition to be fulfilled in the world of the polis is foiled from the sphere of love. The next sentence continues: "A loving despair aborted all these hopes and deprived the kingdom of one of its most beautiful ornaments." The aborted hopes that come from the female establish an odd feminization of Givry: earlier, the portrait of Mme de Maugiron had described *her* as "one of the Court's greatest ornaments" (*LD*, 122). And here she is again joined to Givry in a single trope of fatal love: "this same passion threw into disorder and brought finally to death a woman whose constancy and sincerity deserved a better fate" (*LD*, 208–209). But the parallel is deceptive: The Court is not the Kingdom, and a "better fate" does not figure the hyperbole of desolation reserved for Givry. When a man loves like a woman, the boundaries separating the zones of love from affairs of state become confused, and the founding authority of social arrangements is threatened: "You have killed my Givry, Mademoiselle" ("Vous m'avez tué Givry, Mademoiselle") (*LD*, 207), the King laments after the fact. This is not an acceptable breakdown of difference. Despite the conjunction of the spheres encouraged by the generalizations about love, the plots of gender are not so easily undermined; just as, in the final analysis, *galanterie* will be ranked below general truth, love below the state, fiction below history. Givry is "too inconstant," Mme de Maugiron, "too constant," and these symmetrical (asymmetrical) excesses are the generative paradigms of the social relations between the sexes in seventeenth-century fiction, even if women in other cited instances may prove perfectly capable of inconstancy themselves, and men willing to die of disappointment. (This opposition continues through the eighteenth century).[15]

In the end, however, if it is true that both sexes lose in love and that the reader is left to feel that the real (perhaps the only) justification of this story called love ("this fatal madness") for women is its capacity to produce textuality: "the most perfect works of nature and of art sometimes depend on a moment of its capriciousness and furor" (*LD*, 118). It is also some consolation to know that these aristocratic disorders of love permitted a woman born to love and to die, as she in fact did, undistinguished, in the provinces, to have written herself however marginally into the history she could not by definition make.

In 1699 Mme de Villedieu was granted a royal pension.[16] This distinction was shared by only one other woman writer, Mademoiselle de Scudéry.

After 1675 she stopped publishing. *Les Désordres de l'amour* was probably her last novel.[17]

# "TRISTES TRIANGLES"
## Le Lys dans la vallée *and Its Intertext*

It is impossible for me to admit—I'd sooner admit to the existence
of God—that she wants to be possessed, that she dreams of it.
—J. Laforgue, *Carnet,* 1884–1885

Apocrypha has it that Balzac, having been panned by Sainte-Beuve in
the *Revue des deux mondes,* exclaimed to Jules Sandeau: "He will
pay for this; I will pass my pen through his body . . . I will rewrite
*Volupté.*"[1] Whether or not Balzac articulated exactly those "machis-
tic" desires, evidence exists that he was stimulated enough by
Sainte-Beuve's "puritanical book"[2] for us to include it as an important page—at least on the level of (rivalrous) intentionality—in the
intertext of *Le Lys dans la vallée.* Balzac's primary conscious objective in redoing *Volupté* appears to stem from his objection to the
character of its heroine; more specifically, to the dosage of her femininity: "Mme de Couaën isn't woman enough and so there's no
danger."[3] The challenge, as it can be read here, was to rewrite what
has been rather elegantly described as "the chaste [*blanche*] adventure of a hopeless love,"[4] intensifying the excitement implicit in such
a drama, without, however, changing the outcome of the script; to
rewrite, then, making his heroine more of a woman, but without
changing the color of her destiny.

The creation of Mme de Mortsauf, the (white) flower announced in the novel's title, proves to have challenged the critics as much as it apparently challenged Balzac; the question for them was, curiously, despite (or perhaps because of) the ostensible intertext, one of origins: was there a model (other than Mme de Couaën), and if so, who was she?[5] Although source hunting is a commonplace pursuit in traditional Balzacian scholarship, in the case of Mme de Mortsauf, the mystery to be solved is complicated by a peculiarly insistent enigma: "from whom could Mme de Mortsauf have received the *taste for pleasure,* innocent or not, that Balzac has given to his heroine?"[6] The earliest textual model of feminization pointed to is Marguerite de Navarre's lady of Pamplona,[7] for whom, like Mme de Mortsauf, the double bind created by the conflicting demands of virtue and illicit desire is resolved by and in death. The intratextual commentary on that resolution in *The Heptameron* provides the following analysis: "But just consider, here we have a wise woman, who, for the sake of showing herself outwardly more virtuous than she was in her heart and for the sake of covering up a passion which the logic of Nature demanded she should conceive for this most noble lord, goes and allows herself to die just because she denies herself the pleasures that she covertly desires!" (*H,* 302)(218).[8] The verdict is clear enough: having repressed her natural desire, the lady falls victim to nature's revenge. Her death, however, is only half the story; as she exits from this world, our "wise woman" tells all. The trajectory of the story, therefore, links death with an end to denegation: telos emerges as topos: the revelation of truth *in articulo mortis.* Thus, "the hour has come when all dissimulation must cease, and I must confess the truth that till now I have striven so hard to hide from you. Know then that if you have felt deeply for me, I have felt none the less deeply for you. . . . For God and my honour forbade me ever to declare it to you . . . Yet, though so often I said *no* to you, I confess that it hurt so much to pronounce the word that it is now the cause of my death" (*H,* 302)(218). Her denial, her "no," is italicized in the text and designates (by hypotyposis) the specifically linguistic forum of repression.

The lady of Pamplona, however, dies happy: "for it is by God's grace that I die before the violence of my love should strain my conscience and my name" (*H,* 302)(218). The conviction of her victory is such—and this is the topical twist that interests us here—that it permits her to ask her lover (as secular confessor) to share the good news with her husband, "so that he will know how truly I have loved God and loved him" (*H*, 303)(218). This gesture of sublime confidence is Julie de Wolmar's too; with the latter, however, it is the husband who delivers the message to the lover, and in writing. In both cases, by putting a term to all future intercourse, death brings freedom of sexual expression, permits enunciation of desire, for which—on balance—death seems a small enough price to pay: "too happy," Julie concludes, "to purchase at the price of my life the right of loving you forever without crime and of telling you so one more time" (*NH*, 407)(731).[9] Death reactivates a silenced discourse, giving the lie to a politics of neutrality, to what Mme de Mortsauf will call "this negative happiness" (*LV*, 246)(199).[10]

But if Mme de Mortsauf's last words in the linearity of the novel, that is, in her farewell letter (also communicated to the beloved with the sanction of the husband) reflect (as do those of her predecessors) a measure of optimism about God's mercy and her own righteousness—"God will know better than I if I practiced His holy laws in their true spirit. I stumbled no doubt, often, but I did not fall" (*LV*, 246)(322)—those last words must be read in counterpoint to her own earlier vocal confession. Julie can write peacefully from her deathbed: "I have for a long time deluded myself. This delusion was advantageous to me; it vanishes the moment I no longer need it. You had thought me cured of my love for you, and I thought I was too. Let us give thanks to the One who made that delusion last as long as it was useful" (*NH*, 405)(728). She embraces death because it prevents her from acting out, from acting on what she now knows to be true. Mme de Mortsauf, disillusioned and enlightened, yearns at death's door for a reprieve: "Everything in my life has been a lie; I have been adding them up these last few days—all those impostures! Can I be dying—I who have never lived, I who never went to meet my sweetheart on a heath?" (*LV*, 230)(301). Whereas Julie feels that heaven can deprive her of nothing, since life has nothing left to offer—"What advantage was left for me to deprive from life? By depriving me of it, Heaven no longer deprives me of anything regrettable and instead protects my honor" (*NH*, 405)(729)—Mme de Mortsauf wants her heaven on earth: "An hour with Lady Dudley is worth an eternity" (*LV*, 513).

That last equation, however, does not appear in the final version of the novel. It was excised, we are told, to placate Balzac's superegoistic reader Mme de Berny. As Wurmser describes the operation in his *Comédie inhumaine:* "It's more than the model can support, and the docile Balzac will silence Mme de Mortsauf and falsify the story of her agony."[11] Mme de Mortsauf is not completely silenced, but her bitterness at dying without having known sexual pleasure is attenuated by the deletions; the violence of her desire muted by a periphrastic retreat from the explicit; her feminization euphemized. For what is eliminated in the final version—one hundred or so lines available to the reader in the variants reprinted in the Garnier edition—is nothing less than the heroine's rejection of the underlying assumptions that support and justify the sublimation of female desire. A refutation of the *doxa* is accomplished by the simple assertion of female sexuality as an operative reality. (I should mention here that even without the actual suppression of the "offensive" material, its potentially subversive content is undercut by the context of enunciation: namely, the act of enunciation itself is placed under the sign of madness. Thus, the abbot in attendance, horrified at Mme de Mortsauf's passionate outburst, exclaims, "Let us hope she is not conscious of these fits of insane frenzy!" Félix reassures him: "No . . . she is no longer herself" [*LV*, 231; 302].)

To return to eu-feminization, following the periphrasis cited earlier—"to meet my sweetheart on a heath"—Mme de Mortsauf in the unexpurgated edition asks: "whom would my happiness have harmed?" (*LV*, 513). And she answers, reversing the nineteenth-century novelistic cliché that sexual mothers kill their children, or at least are bad for their health:[12] "If you had been less dutiful Félix, I would live, I would be able to see my children's happiness" (*LV*, 513). The reversal is radical (even if subsequently repressed) in terms of her own, which is to say Félix's, previous discourse and narrative. Thus before Félix set out for Paris, he had exclaimed: "I would give all eternity for one day of happiness—while you . . ." "While I?" Mme de Mortsauf had then replied to such a sacrilegious trade-off, "I? . . . Which of the many I's do you mean? I am conscious of so many selves in *me*. Those children . . . are two of my selves" (*LV*, 164)(219). In that (domestic) economy, to give herself over to love for "one day of happiness" would be to kill her children: "It would mean certain death for them" (*LV*, 165; 220). And she concludes, melodramatically, "Get married do, and let me die!" (*LV*, 165)(220).

In the "dedoxatized" variants, however, where another economy is at work, Mme de Mortsauf refutes this notion that a mother and a sexual woman cannot coexist in the same body; she refutes too the notion that spiritual love is superior to, and more complete than, sensual fulfillment: "The heavens do not come down for us, it is our feelings that take us to heaven. We have only partially loved. The union of souls does not precede a great love, it is the consequence" (*LV*, 513). The potential for scandal in such a transvaluation is easily measured by contrasting this passage with Julie's "feminine" invitation to Saint-Preux: "Come to swear, even in the midst of pleasures, that from the union of hearts they draw their greatest charm" (*NH*, 122)(121); or with Julie's nostalgia for heavenly bliss: "A passion more terrible than fever and delirium sweeps me away to my ruin" (*NH*, 76). Mme de Mortsauf's disinvestment of the platonic and the vertical, moreover, though a significant departure from the canon, is not presented as idiopathic dissent. In her "sensual delirium"[13] she diagnoses *all* women: "Every woman is veiled and every veil begs to be lifted; you lacked daring, daring would have made me live!" (*LV*, 513). These assertions, however, have a curious ring to them; they sound both false and familiar. Indeed, Mme de Mortsauf would seem to be mouthing standard, fictional masculine discourse, adopting the language of the "vile seducer." It is in this sense (and in this sense only) that one might agree with M. Le Yaouanc when he claims: "and one can barely accept as *plausible* the regrets, the sensual cries,—against which Mme de Berny has protested, but above all for the moral and esthetic reasons,—given by a woman in agony, exhausted from hunger, and tortured by suffering."[14] What is not "plausible" is neither the content nor the context of her regret but its language, its intertext. For in making Mme de Mortsauf "more of a woman," Balzac attributes to his heroine the phallocratic discourse of an eighteenth-century roué. It is as though in tampering with the perfect model—Mme de Couaën, for example, who says nothing but whose silence is eloquent—Balzac, at a loss for a countermodel, puts a man in her place. Feminization spirals into virilization.

Mme de Mortsauf's revelation of desire and of the claims of the body is not entirely buried in the variants; it survives in the final edition, primarily in the tempered, less subversive written testament that is her deathbed letter. (This letter is less subversive because of its intertextual resonance: Mme de Mortsauf's final words, like Julie's, are to be read through the reassuring grid of an older (Ovidian) rhetoric—the art of persuasion *a posteriori*. Mme de Mortsauf, "that Christian Dido!" (*LV*, 179)(237), whose husband's name cannot save her, writes with consummate control, the pyre in sight.) The thematic parallels linking Henriette de Mortsauf's letter to Julie de Wolmar's have not been ignored by the critics. And we shall not rehearse them here except to signal an important dissymmetry. Julie touches but briefly upon the past; she has already rewritten history, that is, the etiology of their passion, for Saint-Preux, in other letters.[15] Her farewell, therefore, is bearer of revelation only in its account of continuing desire. Thus, to the extent that Rousseau's fiction functions as intertext to Balzac's, the letter itself will serve us as an emblematic counterpoint.

Mme de Mortsauf frames her final analysis within the parental strategy that had characterized her relationship with Félix: "the woman in me is dead; only the mother lives on" (*LV*, 241)(316). This assertion, though confirmed in part by the preceptorial program set forth in the letter, remains open to scrutiny; for the reader will remember that when the letter literally is transmitted to Félix, Mme de Mortsauf says to her husband: "He is my adopted son now, that is all . . . I am still a woman" (*LV*, 237)(310). The structure of the letter reflects the strain of the screen scenario, the family romance in which she and Félix negotiate their subtextual desires. How do you love me, she had asked in an earlier catechism: "Like a mother?" (*LV*, 141)(189). To which Félix had replied: "Like a mother secretly desired" (*LV*, 141)(189). The letter, then, articulates the split in Mme de Mortsauf's self-concept—mother and woman—and the history of that split as it played itself out between Henriette and her "adopted" son: Félix, addressed in the beginning of the letter as "friend whom I loved too well" (*LV*, 241)(315), and at the end, as "dear child of my heart" (*LV*, 246)(321)—problematic object of desire, illicit and legitimized.

Saint-Preux's status as addressee is less ambiguous: he remains "l'ami" throughout; a shift in intensity is marked, however, by the passage from the initial "vous" over whom Julie exercises control to the final "tu," the dangerous relation from whom death alone protects her. By their allocutionary strategies, then, the two letters stand in chiastic relation to each other: Julie's is metaphoric and overdetermined by the jubilation of desire sublimated (at last) in death: "When you see this letter, the worms will be preying upon your lover's features" (*NH*, 407)(731); Mme de Mortsauf's is metonymic and structured by the resignation of substitution: "As I could not be yours, I bequeath you my thoughts and my duties!" (*LV*, 246)(321).

Mme de Mortsauf writes as a mother in order to persuade Félix to replace her in that function: "so I must make use of the last glimmers of my intelligence to beg you once again to replace the heart you took away from my children" (*LV*, 241)(316). For this politics of guilt to work, Mme de Mortsauf must demonstrate Félix's responsibility: "You will see, dear one, how you have been the prime cause of my ills" (*LV*, 241)(316). There follows her "novel," which as readers we receive as the deconstruction of the text we have just assimilated: Félix's fiction. In this sense we might go so far as to suggest that Félix's story is Mme de Mortsauf's intertext; or, as Peter Brooks comments in his elegant and illuminating Freudian reading of *Le Lys*, "Mme de Mortsauf's ultimate letter which, read only after her death, in fact presents another perspective on the whole story from its beginning, thus creating a true effect of palimpsest."[16]

## Chapter 1: The Awakening

Until that ball given for the Duc d'Angoulême, the only one I ever attended [and during which Félix, having been mistaken for a child, responds with equal misprision, embracing Mme de Mortsauf, as he puts it, "like a child throwing itself on to its mother's bosom" (*LV*, 16)(25)], marriage had kept me in that ignorance which gives an angel's beauty to a maiden's soul. True, I was a mother, but love had crowned me with none of its lawful joys. How had I stayed like this? I do not know: nor do I know by what law everything in me changed in the space of a second . . . your kisses? . . . have dominated my life . . . I was experiencing a sensation for which I know no terms in any language . . . I realised that there existed in the world something unknown to me . . . I no longer felt more than half a mother. . . . If you have forgotten those terrible kisses, I myself have never been able to wipe them from my memory: I am dying of

them! . . . Neither time nor my firm will could master that imperious delight. (*LV*, 242–43)(316–18)

This description of passion at first kiss is not without echoes, since it
is a conventional concretization of love at first sight.[17] Julie, for example, remembering her first kiss in the grove, underlines the same
instantaneity and indelibility: "a moment, only a moment inflamed
my senses with a fire that nothing could extinguish; and even if my
will resisted still, from then on my heart was corrupted" (*NH*,
341)(321). And in her farewell letter, where the sensual is spiritual-
ized after the fact: "Yes, I tried in vain to stifle the first sentiment
which inspired me; it is concentrated in my heart" (*NH*, 405)(728).
For both heroines, passion is an irreversible narrative.

## Chapter 2: Combating Passion

For Julie, giving in to passion is to be a "bad" daughter; for Mme de
Mortsauf, a "bad" mother. And for both, the encounter with the
imperatives of sexuality threatens the fundamental equilibrium of the
female self, setting in motion a life-and-death struggle. Thus, Julie,
reviewing the past, recollects: "I wished to be released from life . . .
but cruel death spared me only to betray me. I saw you, I was cured,
and I was ruined" (*NH*, 322). She succumbs where Mme de
Mortsauf cannot. Although Julie survives this moment of weakness
to make a voluntaristic sacrifice of her "bad" self in her marriage to
Wolmar, and as Mme de Wolmar—wife and mother—(re)lives, at
Clarens, a struggle roughly parallel to Mme de Mortsauf's martyrdom at Clochegourde, the fact that she has experienced those feelings
that are not permitted—to use Mme de Mortsauf's code—constitutes
a fundamental discriminant of difference between the two texts. For
although in tribute to Félix's "generosity of soul" (*LV*, 245)(320)
during her husband's nearly fatal illness, Henriette contemplates the
total gift—"I wanted to give myself to you as a reward for so much
heroism" (*LV*, 245)(320) (a notion to be paired with Julie's famous
"pity" for Saint-Preux)—she dismisses, in retrospect, this courtly
notion as madness—"that fit of madness was shortlived" (*LV*,
245)(320)—and gives herself over to God instead. Félix is to enjoy

her sexuality by synecdoche only; he is made a gift of her hair, the price of her resistance: "There was a moment when the struggle was so terrible, that I would weep all night long. My hair fell out. That very hair I gave to you!" (*LV*, 245)(320).[18]

## Chapter 3: Virtue Rewarded

The trial of Julie's virtue as Mme de Wolmar differs from that of Mme de Mortsauf in several important ways. As we have seen, Julie knows what she is resisting for having experienced it; moreover, Julie and Saint-Preux are partners in innocence, or rather, in sublimation; then too, Julie is spared jealousy, for Saint-Preux is committed to total chastity: "I have nothing left of an ordinary man" (*NH*, 666). Unlike Saint-Preux (and unlike Amaury), Félix believes in an invincible masculine condition: "We have a potency from which we cannot abdicate, on pain of ceasing to be men . . . Nature cannot be thwarted for long" (*LV*, 188)(249). And he gives in to that nature.

Mme de Mortsauf, for her part, not only does not know what she is missing, so to speak, but she only discovers the depth and violence of her own erotic desire when she learns that Félix has made love to another woman: "Then your quite natural love for this Englishwoman revealed to me secrets of which I was myself unaware" (*LV*, 245)(320). In a strangely hysterical process, Mme de Mortsauf becomes sexualized vicariously through the pleasures experienced by Félix with Arabelle. The variants make clear the ideological implications of such an illumination: "My gift of second sight revealed to me these pleasures which made you betray me, you were right to abandon me in order to taste them, that's what life is, and I was wrong, because my sacrifices were made to this world and not to God! Those around me console me by talking about the other life, but is there another life?" (*LV*, 513). But this worldly epiphany, this newly found understanding of her own erotic potential, has no place for expression; it takes her on a death trip. Instead of going to Paris and killing the other woman—"I wanted to go to Paris, I was athirst for murder, I wanted that woman to die" (*LV*, 245)(320)—she allows herself to die of hunger and thirst; instead of acting on her fantasmatic impulses, she passively acts out; as a self-inflicted punishment for not having given in, she gives up. And like the lady of Pamplona, that renunciation is written in the body.

In both cases the symptoms mime the contradiction that generated them: the heroine of *The Heptameron,* we are told, suffers from an unabated fever and melancholia: "her extremities became quite cold and internally she burned incessantly" (*H,* 302)(217); the heroine of *Le Lys,* as Brooks writes, "the representative of humidity and tenderness, is burning hot, and the water of Indre . . . only increases her thirst."[19] Feverish and apathetic, hot and cold, the body language of the two patients is characterized by their double bind. Thus, Mme de Mortsauf's physician explains: "This state is brought about by the inactivity of an organ whose function is as necessary to life as that of the heart. Grief has done the dagger's work" (*LV,* 220)(288). Medicine cannot cure so fundamental a dysfunction. Upon Félix's reappearance, however, Mme de Mortsauf's appetence miraculously returns: "They think that thirst is my greatest torment" (*LV,* 229)(301), she explains to him, "I was thirsty for you" (*LV,* 230)(301). Her illness, then, which dates from the day she learned of Félix's affair with Lady Dudley, might be diagnosed more interestingly as a form of conversion hysteria,[20] specifically as anorexia nervosa, than as generally interpreted: cancer of the pylorus.[21] Mme de Mortsauf's auto-punishment is a violence of privation, a refusal of sustenance engendered by the undeniable proof of her own sexuality.

But if what Henriette learns about herself "kills" her, ultimately it makes her want to live because it revises the scenario, abolishing the distinctions, the dichotomies, upon which the logic of the novel (her text) is founded. On the one hand, as Mme de Mortsauf explains in her letter: "I was not without feeling" (*LV,* 244)(320) and as a result, "our love pangs were indeed cruelly equal" (*LV,* 245)(320)—which is to say that desire's challenge to the body existed on both sides, female as well as male. And here the counterpoint to *La Nouvelle Héloïse* is particularly pertinent: "Without a doubt," Julie writes to Saint-Preux, "I felt for myself the fears that I thought I was feeling for you" (*NH,* 405)(729). In her hysterically "feminine" innocence, she had been blind by virtue of what we might call denegation by projection. On the other hand, Mme de Mortsauf abolishes the difference, removes the cordon sanitaire separating Henriette, "wife of the spirit" (*LV,* 175)(232), and Arabelle, "mistress of the flesh" (*LV,* 175)(232). At the end of her life Mme de Mortsauf asserts the identity of contraries: "Arabelle was in no way superior to me. I too was one of the daughters of that fallen race whom men love so" (*LV*, 245)(320). To measure the reversal at work here, one has only to look back to the "official" narrative: "The Marchioness of Dudley has saved me. Let her love be soiled, I do not envy it. Mine is the glorious love of angels!" (*LV*, 196)(259).[22] In the end, then, Mme de Mortsauf asserts not only equality in infelicity between her and Félix, but equipollence between the pure and the impure. She would be a fallen angel. Indeed, in her "delirium," in the stage of her acting out that was not corrected for the final edition, Mme de Mortsauf made it quite clear that what she wanted was to be just like Arabelle: "I want to be loved. I shall run wild, like Lady Dudley! I'll learn English, so I can call you 'My Dee'" (*LV*, 230)(302). Those are the last words of her outburst: she would learn another language, the other woman's maternal language, the better to name the object of desire; to name, and hence make hers, that feeling for which, as she says in her letter, "I know no terms in any language" (*LV*, 242)(317). Having at last given voice to her desire, she adds calmly: "We will dine together" (*LV*, 230)(302).

## Epilogue

Félix refuses this collapsing of polarities and imagines for himself castration, death, and the monastery—in that order. If Henriette were no different from Arabelle, then he was "like all men" (*LV*, 231)(303) and barred from the sublime. So at the end of his narrative, his love letter to yet another woman, he attempts to reinscribe ideal femininity and define its function: "For stricken and ailing spirits, the superior woman has a sublime role to play—the role of a Sister of Mercy who staunches wounds, that of a mother who forgives the child" (*LV*, 252)(329). His addressee rejects the script: "Your project is unrealisable . . . Do you know anything about women at all?" (*LV*, 255)(332). She thus condemns the necrophilic impulse of Félix's fantasy.

The epigraph to *La Nouvelle Héloïse* consists of two lines from Petrarch, translated by Rousseau himself: "The world possessed her without knowing her, / And I, I knew her, I stay here below and lament her."[23] Félix, who before Henriette's death had wished she had been more like Dante's Francesca than Petrarch's Laura, concludes in mourning: "I alone was to know the whole life story of this great, unknown woman, I alone held the secret of her feeling, I alone had explored the far reaches of her soul; neither mother, father, husband nor children had known her" (*LV*, 250)(325–26). Both novels, then, are presented to the reader as acts of revelation, of the lifting of the veil: "This is human life in all its truth" (*LV*, 250)(326), Félix exclaims upon reading Mme de Mortsauf's parting words. And both novelists choose, as vehicles of that truth, deathbed confessions; specifically, articulations of female desire simultaneously hyperbolized and euphemized. The mourner's consolation is to have unlocked that private door; the artist's, to have created fictions of what was hidden.

If the ending of *Le Lys* (in exposing as truth the "secret" that merely the fine line of denegation makes "the difference between a wanton woman and a wise one" [*H*, 304]) not only rewrites the Renaissance tale and the Rousseauian fiction, but by evoking, to use René Girard's terms, "vertical transcendence," conforms in a wider perspective to the rules of closure proper to "novelistic truth" (the inevitability, as he describes it, of "the absolute banality of what is essential in Western civilization"), then what transposition has Balzac wrought upon his intertext?[24] And has he in fact redone (outdone) *Volupté*? I would suggest that Balzac's repenning can be deciphered in an intensity, in an ambivalent impulse (as attested to genetically by the variants) to deconstruct, as Peter Brooks reads it, "the intoxication of virtue" and "much of the Romantic structure of self,"[25] but perhaps more insistently, to interrogate the geometry of desire, the ideology of representation that reposes upon the assumption that positive femininity (since Rousseau, inseparable from the maternal function) and female sexual desire are incompatible in one and the same body. In this sense, both of the novel's triangles, the courtly love triangle (married woman, older husband, young lover) and its double (chaste woman, fallen woman, divided-heart lover), prove to be cover triangles: obviously fragile but no less persistent constructs dependent upon a cultural logic of contraries that might be transcended or superseded. This might be, were it not for the power of the matrix in which they are inscribed, a "doctored" theology in the service of the teleology of fiction; a ritualization of (male) textual desire.

Not surprisingly, Mme de Lafayette came up with another angle on the triangle. Her heroine does not have to die in order to reveal the truth of her desire; she survives her confession to go on at a healthy distance from the court, far from what Girard diagnosed as "metaphysical contagion."[26]

# NOVELS OF INNOCENCE
## *Fictions of Loss*

Galeotto fu il libro e chi lo scrisse:
Quel giorno più non vi leggemmo avante.
—Dante, *Inferno*

The story of Eden has long been a nostalgic intertext for the secular literature of the West, and it is not surprising that the modes of the novel should be bound up with fictions of innocence and loss:

> Most novels, because they so wholly enlist our sympathies, seem to tend toward the subjective, the passive, the feminine. The subtitle of the Marquis de Sade's *Justine, the Misfortunes of Virtue,* might no less pertinently be attached to Henry James's *Portrait of a Lady* or *Wings of the Dove.* Such a loss, from a more detached, more dynamic, more masculine point of view, may be envisaged as a gain of experience.[1]

Harry Levin thus poses "loss of innocence" as a thematic continuum linking Sade's late-eighteenth-century version of the novel to the Jamesian text. R.F. Brissenden, in a parallel reflection, both narrows and expands Levin's postulation, isolating the privileged status of the feminine in fiction as the keystone in that historical arch:

For whatever reason, the entrance of a young lady into the world . . .
became an established and enduring theme in eighteenth-century fiction, and one which was to exercise the imagination of the novelist
until at least the beginning of this century. We see the fullest development of the theme probably in some of the novels of Henry
James—*Portrait of a Lady* and *The Wings of the Dove* particularly.[2]

That entrance into the world is plotted at the intersections of gender
and knowledge is not a notion with which readers of eighteenth-century novels (and James) are likely to quarrel.[3] What's crucial is
learning how to read the signs of the world in which human identity
takes on social meaning.

Peter Brooks reads the major eighteenth-century French novels
through the constraints of a grid he calls "worldliness":

By "worldliness," I mean an ethos and personal manner which indicate that one attaches primary or even exclusive importance to
ordered social existence, to life within a public system of values and
gestures, to the social techniques that further this life and one's
position in it, and hence to knowledge about society and its forms
of comportment.[4]

To delineate structures of signification in the eighteenth-century
novel, therefore, is to operate within the closure of a coded socio-
text. Worldliness might then be redefined as a form of discourse, a
metalanguage articulating and reflecting the valorized possession of a
certain *savoir:* the knowledge pertinent to a circumscribed, hierar-
chized existence. And innocence, in this sense, can be seen as
imperfect linguistic competence, demonstrated in performance by an
absence of *savoir-vivre,* of *savoir-faire.*

Unlike the worldly, the innocent do not know how to interpret the
very signals regulating their circuit; worse yet, they fail even to "consider a substance, an object, a being as if they emitted signs to be
deciphered, interpreted."[5] As a result of this disparity in perception,
the innocent and the worldly exist in unequal and dangerous relations of power, where the worldly are in a position to manipulate and
sometimes destroy by the simple exercise of their semiological practice and prowess. The worldly, however, *need* the innocent: the
inevitable misapprehensions of innocence validate the effectiveness of

the system, and confer meaning upon it. Novels of worldliness are no less novels of innocence, for both depend upon a single fiction: the power of knowledge to shape and transform human experience.

In the novels that concern us here, the epistemology in question is not a static one. To know is first to find out, and the process of finding out is characterized by a particular and irreversible momentum. The "before" can never be retrieved; one does not return to Eden. Nevertheless, the innocence of before is not completely erased by the worldly knowledge of after; it remains as trace, as nostalgia, a faded mark against which both present and future are measured—with a sigh. Hence Kate Croy's melancholy words at the end of *The Wings of the Dove*: "We shall never be again as we were!"[6] Something happened, something was lost, and the simple fact of knowing that is to be changed. In James, this understanding is all the action,[7] the thematic constant that subsumes every event; but this is not to suggest that we are dealing with an empty structure. There are, of course, figures in the carpet, and those figures are innocents, posed and poised in opposition to sophisticates: experienced men and women of the world.

The loss of innocence in James is structured by finding out; and the modalities of this structuration provide a useful grammar for the eighteenth-century novel. We might take as our point of departure Ruth Yeazell's analysis of the dynamics of discovery in *The Wings of the Dove*:

> On the face of it, then, Kate exerts no power; she simply *helps* Densher to *understand* their *situation*. Yet a strange *coercion* operates beneath the surface of this dialogue, for what Kate *asserts* will happen is also, we suspect, precisely what she wishes to happen: she very much wants Milly to feel just this consolatory love for Densher . . .

> And the *deception* apparently kills: When Lord Mark *reveals* the true relation between Densher and Kate, Milly Theale turns her face to the wall and chooses to die.[8]

Disillusionment, or enlightenment, brought about by the communication of information, and with such violent consequences, is of course not a phenomenon restricted to James. One has only to think of the lethal quality of the famous "it's not my fault" letter that Valmont sends Mme de Tourvel; and of the fatal repercussions of that cruel *envoi*. But the Jamesian text, as we have suggested, by virtue of its so clearly thematized structure, lends itself to generalization. Indeed, the pattern identified by Yeazell corresponds very closely to the definition of information and its possible roles in narrative strategy articulated by Claude Bremond in his *Logique du Récit:*

> In agreeing to name information all influence that tends to communicate to a patient the awareness of an aspect in the situation in which he is located, we have made an abstraction of the truthful or deceptive nature of this information. The narrative, moreover, can refrain from clarifying whether the information is true or false. Most often, however, the narrative takes a side in this issue: if it specifies that the information is true, then it is called *revelation;* and its opposite is *deception*. The agent responsible for true information takes on the role of the revealer; the agent responsible for what's false, the deceiver.[9]

Despite the obvious differences in critical vocabulary and stance, both Yeazell and Bremond are concerned with models of communication; in both instances, the relationship isolated is one of power based on the characters' access to the information that in fact defines their situation.[10] Yeazell is describing a social exchange, a verbal operation; the action involved is limited to the communication of information. But messages can be deadly, and this holds, whether or not the information transmitted is strictly and entirely true; whether or not it is the *whole* truth. In this instance, for example, the fact that the superseding relation between Densher and Kate is ultimately infirmed by the no less potent truth of Densher's posthumous love for Milly does not alter the structure of the sequence: Milly Theale cannot survive what she is told; knowledge spells the end of illusion, the destruction of her insufficiently informed version of social realities.

Thus, in the novels of innocence lost, the tree of knowledge is more than a tree of sexual difference, the original locus of dissemination. Man-made gardens are more sophisticated than Eden, and innocence is not lost by carnal knowledge alone. The innocents are stripped of their illusions when they learn that they are not desired as they thought they were. And what they learn constitutes a wound to their definition of self, a social definition largely dependent on sexual integrity.[11] Milly Theale and Isabel Archer, for example, discover that they were desirable only to a point: that as objects of desire they had been circulating in a system both synchronic and anterior to them. The revelation bears too on the powerlessness of the victims to make their private understanding prevail in the face of a metadiscourse that subsumes all such understanding. In both instances, unbeknownst to them, the poles of their private relation involved not two, but three points of contact; in other words, they had been part of a triangle, part of the world. The obvious comparable structure in the eighteenth-century novel is of course the relationship linking Mme de Tourvel, Valmont, and Mme de Merteuil. Mme de Tourvel is informed by Valmont's letter that she is, after all, just like the "multitude of women" from whom she thought she had been distinguished. Mme de Tourvel, like Milly Theale, cannot overcome such a misapprehension, nor does she desire to. Isabel Archer alone survives the destruction of illusion, the loss of innocence, to continue, to begin again.

In these examples, the "patient" is a woman, lacking in worldly knowledge; her mode of experience "passive and subjective," to return to the language of Levin's paradigm. The reader fully expects, by virtue of superior information (that information systematically withheld from the innocent victims), the degradation that finally takes place: suspense is nothing more than a matter of time. But the logic of the sequence is neither overdetermined by gender, nor necessarily a function of insufficient exposure to the world. For if we can think of innocence in these novels as a set of illusions,[12] a prefabricated scenario imposed upon the world, a fantasy grid, innocence can be seen to coexist with worldliness, experience, and masculinity. Let us turn to the exemplary novel of worldliness and innocence that is *La Princesse de Clèves* for an instance of this paradox. While Lafayette's novel is often read as the Princess's *éducation sentimentale,* it is equally possible to read the novel as the Prince's disillusionment.

The Prince of Clèves is a man of the world, in every sense of the word. He knows how to interpret signs of desire, in particular, his wife's gestures and involuntary reactions; he knows that he is not loved as he loves:

Monsieur de Clèves saw only too well that she was a stranger to him, that her genuine feelings—really not understood by herself—were anything but satisfactory to him. *(PC, 19–20)(51)*[13]

However, when the Princess, in her extraordinary innocence, confesses her vulnerability to those very feelings she indeed had not originally experienced, his consolation is destroyed; and the jealousy that previously had had neither place nor function explodes like Phèdre's:

Who is he, Madame, this lucky man who inspires your fear? Since when has he attracted you? What has he done to win your heart? What road did he discover to find your love? I consoled myself in some fashion thinking that, since I was incapable of touching your heart, no one could. Now another has done what I have been unable to do. *(PC, 98)(123)*

Again, the end of illusion is brought about by the revelation of the triangular structure of desire.

The Princess wounds her husband with her own wound, and the irony is not lost on him: "You have made me unhappy only by the greatest proof of fidelity that a woman could ever give to her husband" *(PC, 99)(123)*. The Princess, patient, harmed by the revelations, the information, the marks given her by Nemours, becomes agent to her husband: by revealing the measure of her innocence she becomes responsible for her husband's death.[14] But her status is doubly contradictory: she is not only patient and agent, she is also informant and dissimulator; and here rejoins the Jamesian schema. She does not tell all (just as Kate does not tell Densher all until it is too late). When the Prince seeks the rest of the information (the name of his rival), is denied that piece of information and falsely concludes that his wife is therefore guilty, her sole defense is to reiterate, redundantly, the signifiers of innocence: "So listen to me, please, for your own sake. Is it possible, with so much truth on my side, that I can't convince you of my innocence?" *(PC, 143)(163)*. But the truth is irrelevant to the *mechanism* of the deadly message, and the Prince will not recover from his lost illusions.

Now, if the innocent can harm the worldly, what does this do to our original opposition which was based on the advantages that accrue to superior knowledge of the world? If we continue to restrict our perspective to the transmission of information which voluntarily or involuntarily "degrades" the status of the patient in a social and sexual context, then it would seem that innocence, or rather, the agent's assumptions about his or her own innocence, harm as much as the unambiguously marked evil actions of the worldly. I would like to read an episode from *Manon Lescaut* in this framework, superimposing it on the dialogue between the Prince and Princess of Clèves. The episode in question is Manon's third, final, and ostensibly worldliest betrayal of Des Grieux.

Manon and Des Grieux, the *fille de joie* and the seminarian, are generally posed in opposition to each other on the worldly/innocent axis. Without oversentimentalizing Manon, however, without subscribing to Des Grieux's persistently exculpatory interpretation of the enigmatic text that Manon weaves, and recognizing her often brutal and quite conscious manipulation of her lover, it is possible, nevertheless to read her literally, to believe in her version of history, her good intentions: her innocence. Manon, like the Princess, expects to be taken at her word. When she explains why she sent Des Grieux a double of herself to console him, he comments:

> I listened to this speech with much patience. I certainly found in it a quantity of points that were cruel and mortifying for me; for the deliberateness of her infidelity was so clear that she had not even taken the trouble to disguise it to me.[15]

Realizing that Manon nevertheless would have spent the night with his rival, Des Grieux is no less mortified than the Prince:

> What an admission, for a lover! . . . Besides, by a natural trait of my particular make-up, I was touched by the ingenuousness of her story. (*PL*, 143)(147)

Manon, like the Princess, makes an avowal: candor and innocence based on a system, a concept of self that defies the logic of the other ("the fidelity I wish from you is that of the heart,"[16] Manon explained), and, in fact, of the entire social context in which they operate. Faithful in their manner, Manon and the Princess expect neither to be challenged, nor to be thought disingenuous. Their narratives are fictions only to the other, to the receiver of the information. In both cases, the interlocutors, paralyzed by the signifiers of innocence, reluctantly accept the extraordinary quality of the discourse with which they are confronted and are silenced.

That innocence has powers of its own can be seen more clearly in the less ambiguous examples of the phenomenon: Milly Theale, Mme de Tourvel, and Clarissa. Innocence threatened and lost seems to have a built-in, counterpower mechanism which I will call the "ricochet" effect: the aftermath of supplemental information; the unexpected backlash of a displaced signifier. In these three cases, the innocent victim is understood and read properly, posthumously. Although Milly turns her face to the wall and dies, Mme de Tourvel immures herself in a convent where she expires, and Clarissa shuts out the world, making her rented room a mortuary, the innocents of the world end by making victims of the worldly: Densher, Valmont, and Lovelace learn that they have been betrayed by their own failure to decode, to recognize a level of feeling, a notion of self that goes beyond the overvalued, inflexible strategies of social discourse. The clichés of social relations that had allowed them to play with innocence—if the kind of game playing that includes rape can still be called a game—are finally found wanting.[17] Thus Lovelace finds himself revising his thinking: "I admire her more than ever; and my love for her is less *personal*, as I may say, more *intellectual* than ever I thought it could be to a woman."[18] But this reevaluation of the rules of the game, of the underlying assumptions regulating the strategies of desire that link the worldly to the innocent, comes too late for all players. Clarissa's death engenders Lovelace's; Mme de Tourvel's agony, Valmont's death and her own as a result of his; Densher survives in a posture of perpetual nostalgia: he has fallen in love with a memory of innocence sacrificed to calculation and worldly ambition.

Clarissa's admirers, like Mme de Tourvel's and Milly's, are left to mourn the loss; for the sense of waste engages more than the lovers: it contaminates the social circle in which the lovers operated. The realities of worldliness are shown to be shallow and dysfunctional; subverted by the "stupendous" gestures of the passion of innocence. As Percy Lubbock comments:

> With Kate's last word the story is finished; the first fineness of their association is lost, nothing will restore it. Milly has made the change

by being what she was, too rare an essence for vulgar uses. Those who wanted the intelligence to understand her must pay their penalty.[19]

Thus, however this-worldly the novels of James, and the secular the novels of the eighteenth century, the final gestures of the innocents at their death are curiously Christian in style. Milly's bequest, after all, is one of forgiveness, and not without dove-like resonance:

> She saves Densher *from* this world, not within it, and thus her destruction of his worldly comfort may be seen as the practical form of her love. This is a Christian idea: to be thrown off the wheel of Fortune, however painfully, is to receive the merciful action of divine Providence.[20]

Clarissa too would save Lovelace by forgiveness, and destroy his "worldly comfort": "And may God Almighty, clasping her fingers and lifting up her eyes, forgive him too; and perfect his repentance, and sanctify it to him!"[21] And, in the same way, Mme de Tourvel's last words are *for* Valmont: "Almighty God, I submit myself to your justice; but pardon Valmont."[22]

However, if as Brooks points out, in that novel Baudelaire famously called "terribly sociable," "through the breakdown of the system [of worldliness] and through the story of Valmont's experience with the Présidente, Laclos suggests that there are things on earth undreamt of in the philosophy of worldliness,"[23] we should not overvalue such sophisticated regret for paradise lost: Mme de Tourvel's "other reality"[24] may reveal the tomb beneath the couch, but there is no hope in these novels of returning to what Baudelaire named "that verdant paradise of childhood loves." Everyone knows too much for that. So while the sacrifice of innocence may revive momentarily the possibility of moral choice, the fact remains that innocents have no place in this world. Their death, moreover, reinforces that "self conscious 'being together' of an élite" which constitutes the necessary condition of worldliness and of its novels.[25]

I would argue further that the sacrifice of innocence is a ritual of loss that tends to structure the fictional matrix of the eighteenth-century novel itself (particularly in France); and that the ritual in question is nothing less than a sexualized rite of passage. As R.F. Brissenden has seen:

> In its basic form, [entrance into the world] is an act of sexual initia-
> tion . . . and the act of initiation can itself be violent and painful.
> The rape of Clarissa by Lovelace is one of the most significant
> actions in the whole of eighteenth-century fiction.[26]

Rape is the hyperbolic index of a society so turned in upon itself, so
enamored of its own rigidity and fascinated by its own rules, that it is
unable to imagine and hence integrate a self that is not coded.[27]
Anomaly may be admirable (Clarissa is angelic, Mme de Tourvel rare
and astonishing, Milly Theale a dove), but survival in the world
requires an aptitude for the ordinary language of reality, a feeling for
the sociolect. Thus Frederick Crews writes of Milly Theale:

> She has never had the capacity for genuine social contact. Somewhat
> like the Lady of Shalott, she is destroyed by her first direct meeting
> with reality. She had hoped to fasten her notions of the ideal on
> Densher, thereby connecting her own spiritual world with Densher's
> practical one. Her death is the measure of her failure.[28]

Milly's reaction to the realities of social discourse is not unlike that of
the Princess of Clèves. For if, in a first stage, the Princess's resistance
to connection with Nemours after her husband's death frees her is
based on guilt and homage to the memory of one she wounded with
her own innocence, ultimately she refuses Nemours's practical offer
because she understands that there would be no way for her to maintain herself intact within a society built upon the finite, on
circulation, on the codification of every human interaction. Her solution is an exit from the world as radical as Milly's: renunciation.

When the eighteenth-century novel is gynocentric, as it so often is,
the logic of narrative possibilities does not allow female protagonists to
wander beyond the confines of the boudoir and the salon. The dramas
of innocence and worldliness, as a result, are played out largely in these
"feminized" locales, with women, appropriately, dominating the scene.
In the nineteenth-century novel, however, as Robert Alter has noted:
"There is an obvious fascination . . . with the sheer mechanics of contemporary life—in politics, commerce, class relations, industry, crime
education, entertainment, virtually every sphere."[29] Consequently, initiation, apprenticeship, education, however *sentimentale,* however
mediated through erotic progress, are absorbed into broader preoccu-

pations. The innocent hero of the nineteenth-century *recherche,* unlike the heroines who preceded him, circulates in spaces that would be real; the world of fiction becomes a world of ambition, of money and professions. This shift in focus means that the loss of innocence and/or gain of experience will issue forth in androcentric paradigms. One has only to think of Balzac's *Illusions perdues.*

With Proust and James, however, there is a new shrinking of the fictional universe, and the themes of innocence and worldliness again become the province of an elite. Thus, Morton Densher's journalism, unlike Lucien de Rubempré's, serves only to explain, after the fact, his lack of funds and his encounter with Milly in America. His world, his education, are not located in a concretized, professional milieu. It is a place, rather, of expensive and highly coded conversation, of words. Indeed, for these authors, as for the novelists of the eighteenth century, "there is no human community worth considering (hence which demands expression in language) outside the circumference of the élite."[30] However, the metaphor of the self, of intersubjective relations, is no longer figured in simple terms of erotic polarization. Jamesian and Proustian fictions unfold under the sign of androgyny and the ambiguity of the text.[31] Densher's loss of innocence is not so much sexualized as textualized. The garden of difference gives way to the book. Thus Densher will say to Kate: "The women one meets— what are they but books one has already read? You're a whole library of the unknown, the uncut."[32] Densher will learn by reading and misreading, as did Mme de Tourvel. But his text is neither the letters of a correspondent, nor the letters of another, an earlier fiction (Mme de Tourvel reads *Clarissa*). Kate *is* his fiction: "He had compared her once, we know, to a 'new book,' an uncut volume of the highest, the rarest quality; and his emotion (to justify that) was again and again like the thrill of turning the page."[33]

Thus innocence and initiation in the novel are taken up by the allegory of fiction itself. Hence, Pansy, the sacrificial pawn in the power game of *The Portrait of a Lady* described in counterpoint to the agent of Isabel's revelation, the Countess Gemini:

> She was like a sheet of blank paper—the ideal *jeune fille* of foreign fiction. Isabel hoped that so fair and smooth a page would be covered with an edifying text.

> The Countess Gemini . . . was quite another affair. She was by no
> means a blank sheet; she had been written over in a variety of
> hands . . . a number of unmistakable blots were to be seen upon her
> surface. (*PL,* 257)

The power of worldliness is the subscription of the palimpsest, the
generations of texts against which the virgin surface of innocence is
measured and found inadequate:

> Pansy was really a blank page, a pure white surface . . . There was
> something touching about her . . . she would be an easy victim of
> fate. She would have no will, no power to resist . . . her force would
> be solely in her power to cling. (*PL,* 291–92)

So blank a page cannot underwrite a fiction, however modern; the
"easy victim" is only a *ficelle* in a larger textual strategy. Like Justine
and Cécile de Volanges, Pansy can do no more than cling to her ignorance. The story of these innocents, therefore, does not "wholly enlist
our sympathies." The novels of innocence that attach the reader require
the loss of illusions that comes from the sense of a text, of reading.

The heroine of *The Portrait,* Isabel Archer, is neither a blank sheet,
nor a palimpsest. In the paradigm of textuality, Isabel, as her sister
would have it, is an "original" and difficult to decipher. This status
would seem to overdetermine her destiny. As her brother-in-law puts
it: "Isabel is written in a foreign tongue. I can't make her out. She
ought to marry an Armenian, or a Portuguese" (*PL,* 29). Unlike
Pansy, who can only wait passively to be given her part in the script,
Isabel, despite her "bookish" reputation, is a seeker of experience:
"She had a great desire for knowledge, but she really preferred
almost any source of information to the printed page; she had an
immense curiosity about life . . ." (*PL,* 33). But her desire to know
has its limits:

> With all her love of knowledge, Isabel had a natural shrinking from
> raising curtains and looking into unlighted corners. The love of
> knowledge coexisted in her mind with a still tenderer love of igno-
> rance. (*PL,* 184)

Not surprisingly, then, the deception of which she is victim will be a
function of this partial knowledge, this selective vision; she misinter-

prets her (un-American) husband: "... she had mistaken a part for the whole. ... she had not read him right" (*PL,* 393). Isabel's misapprehension, in fine, like her knowledge, is not total but synecdochic. She can therefore survive disillusion to go beyond the printed page,[34] to resist the impulse for death and become both the agent and interpreter of her own fiction.

By the same token, if the systematic exposure of illusions, misprisions, misreadings is the linear text of innocence lost, it is also the locus of a movement toward mastery: our apprenticeship as readers. As Rousseau (and Sade) understood so well, we enter the world through these novels, fictions of loss from which we retrieve and interpret our experience. The thrill of turning the page that Densher experienced is no less ours; no less dangerous, no less erotic.

# Notes

## ONE Repairing the Tradition

1. Michel Foucault, *The History of Sexuality: Volume I: An Introduction*, trans. Robert Hurley (New York: Vintage Books, 1980). Page references are included in the text, indicated as *HS*. Throughout the text I use published translations when they are easily available; otherwise I provide my own and so indicate.

2. Denis Diderot, *Les Bijoux indiscrets* (Paris: Garnier Classiques, 1962). Page references are included in the text, indicated as *BI*.

3. James Creech, *Diderot: Thresholds of Representation* (Columbus: University of Ohio Press, 1986), 40.

4. Creech, 41.

5. Linda Williams, *Hard Core: Power, Pleasure, and the "Frenzy of the Visible"* (Berkeley: University of California Press, 1989), 3.

6. Adrienne Rich, "Compulsory Heterosexuality and Lesbian Existence," in *Blood, Bread, and Poetry* (New York: W.W. Norton, 1986); Monique Wittig, "On the Social Contract," in *The Straight Mind and Other Essays* (Boston: Beacon Press, 1992).

7. Naomi Schor, "Dreaming Dissymmetry: Barthes, Foucault, and Sexual Difference," in *Men in Feminism*, ed. Alice Jardine and Paul Smith (New York and London: Methuen, 1987), 107.

8. Luce Irigaray, *This Sex Which Is Not One*, trans. Catherine Porter (Ithaca: Cornell University Press, 1985).

9. Irigaray, "This Sex Which Is Not One," and 130–35.

10. Jane Gallop, *Thinking Through the Body* (New York: Columbia University Press, 1988). Page references are included in the text, indicated as *TTB*.

11. Williams, who also quotes this passage, takes issue with Gallop's interpretation of the reciprocal power arrangements between the two. She sees Mangogul's and Mirzoza's "romantic conflict" as typical of "couples porn" in which the "'truth'" of woman's desire finally is "too circumscribed by a larger patriarchal world" to be seen as truly emancipatory (Williams, 278). I think the remarks by Gallop that follow below, however, suggest the distance she herself takes from the 1977 reading.

12. *The Powers of Desire: The Politics of Sexuality*, ed. Ann Snitow, Christine Stansell and Sharon Thompson (New York: Monthly Review Press, 1983), 9, 10.

13. Schor, 109.

14. *Powers of Desire*, 10.

15. The exception to this rule is Graffigny's *Lettres d'une Péruvienne* collected under the lead title *Lettres portugaises et autres romans d'amour par lettres* (Paris: Garnier-Flammarion, 1983).

16. Raymond Trousson, ed., *Romans libertins du XVIIIe siècle* (Paris: Laffont, 1993).

17. René Etiemble, ed., *Romanciers du dix-huitième siècle* (Paris: Gallimard,1966, 1969).

18. See the catalogue from the Boucher show at the Metropolitan Museum of New York, February–May 1986, edited by Alastair Laing, J. Patrice Marandel, Pierre Rosenberg. The Catalogue of Paintings Section is signed by Alastair Lang. Entry 38, pp. 195–97.

19. Advertisement in *Le Nouvel Observateur* (1–7 July, 1993), 100–101.

20. In "The Political Economy of the Body in the *Liaisons dangereuses* of Choderlos de Laclos," Anne Deneys tries to make the case for a libertinism without pleasure. Although I think this position forces her to overstate the case against pleasure (especially on the level of the signifier), the argument that libertinism is a "structure that reinforces law at every level" is an interesting one for a feminist analysis of feminism with women. In *Eroticism and the Body Politic,* ed. Lynn Hunt [Baltimore: Johns Hopkins University Press, 1991], 42.

21. Trousson, xxxviii.

22. Trousson, xxxvii.

23. David Coward, "Up the *ancien régime*," *Times Literary Supplement,* 30 July, 1993, 9.

24. Boyer d'Argens, *Thérèse philosophe*, in *Romans libertins*, 590.

25. Kelly-Gadol, Joan, "Did Women Have a Renaissance?" in *Becoming Visible: Women in European History,* ed. Renate Bridenthal and Claudia Kanz (Boston: Houghton Mifflin, 1977).

26. Margaret C. Jacob, in "The Materialist World of Pornography," sees "the newly created female narrator" as essentially emancipatory. Jacob argues that both Thérèse and Fanny, although "invented to serve the needs of their invariably male, always anonymous authors, . . . escaped bondage and gave us timeless narrations because they were speaking out of a nascent social universe that was essentially modern." (Jacob, *The Invention of Pornography: Obscenity and the Origins of Modernity, 1500–1800,* ed. Lynn Hunt [New York: Zone Books, 1993], 165.)

Jacob makes her case brilliantly for the democratic uses of pornography, but I continue to resist the connection (always implicitly valued as somehow emancipatory) she makes (following Foucault) between modernity and the structures of this very particular pornographic imagination.

27. Lucienne Frappier-Mazur, "Marginal Canons: Rewriting the Erotic." *Yale French Studies,* 75 (1988): 119.

28. To be edited by Patrick and Roman Wald Lasowski. I am grateful to Pierre Saint-Amand for this information.

29. Jane Kramer, "Paris: Le Discours," in *The Europeans* (New York: Penguin, 1980), 149.

30. Jane Miller, "The Seductions of Women," in *Don Giovanni: Myths of Seduction and Betrayal,* ed. Jonathan Miller (New York: Schocken, 1990), 49–50.

31. Riccoboni, *Lettres de Mistress Fanni Butlerd,* ed. Joan Stewart (Geneva: Droz, 1979). Letter references are included in the text, indicated as *FB.*

32. Elizabeth Heckendorn Cook. "Going Public: The Letter and the Contract in *Fanni Butlerd,*" *Eighteenth-Century Studies* 24 (Fall, 1990), 1: 21–45.

33. Cook, 40.

34. Susan Sniader Lanser, *Fictions of Authority: Women Writers and Narrative Voice* (Ithaca and London: Cornell University Press, 1992), 34; Katharine A. Jensen, *Writing Love: Letters, Women, and the Novel, 1642–1776* (Carbondale: Southern Illinois University Press, 1994). Jensen comments: "Indeed . . . the novel portrays such fundamental incompatibility between men and women that change on a larger social scale is difficult, if not impossible, to contemplate." (Jensen, 130/140).

35. Riccoboni had already proven her gifts in this domain, not only as an actress but in her "Suite" to Marivaux's *La Vie de Marianne,* in which she "constructs a female voice that imitates a man's imitation of a female voice" (Lanser, 38).

36. Roland Barthes, *A Lover's Discourse,* trans. Richard Howard (New York: Noonday, 1990).

37. Judith Okely, *Simone de Beauvoir* (New York: Pantheon, 1986), 13.

38. Okely, 13.

39. Okely, 14.

40. Marina Warner, "Valmont—or the Marquise Unmasked," in *Don Giovanni: Myths of Seduction and Betrayal,* ed. Jonathan Miller (New York: Schocken, 1990), 105.

41. See Joseph Brami's "Mme de Merteuil, Juliette, and the Men: Notes for a Reading of Vadim's *Liaisons dangereuses 1960, Eighteenth-Century Life* 14 (May 1990): 56–66.

42. Warner, 105.

43. On the Marquise as Phallic Mother, see Warner, 99. For further discussion of the movies based on *Liaisons,* see Alan Singerman's "Variations on a Denouement: *Les Liaisons dangereuses* on Film," *Eighteenth Century Life* 14 (May 1990): 49–55.

44. Choderlos de Laclos, *Les Liaisons Dangereuses,* trans, Richard Aldington (New York: Signet, 1962). Letter references are included in the text, indicated as *LD.*

45. Quoted in Luc Sante's review of the play and the film in *The New York Review of Books,* August, 13, 1987.

46. "Sexy pas sexy!?" in *Actuel* (July, August 1993).

47. Claude Reichler makes the argument for libertine narrative as the introduction to our modernity, relying on Foucault in "Le récit d'initiation dans le roman libertin," *Littérature,* XII, 47 (October 1982): 100–112, 106.

48. Françoise Giroud, Bernard-Henri Lévy, *Les Hommes et les femmes* (Paris: Olivier Orban, 1993); Catherine Clément "Les princes de Marivaux," in *Le Magazine littéraire,* Juin 1993.

49. Clément, 89.

50. Giroud, Lévy, 74–75.

51. Eric Fassin, *The New Yorker,* November 29, 1993, under the heading "Different Strokes."

52. Fassin, 10

53. Fassin, 10.

54. *The New York Times,* December 26, 1993, "Playing by the Antioch Rules."

55. On the importance of defensiveness to women see Joan DeJean's analysis of *Les Liaisons dangereuses* in *Literary Fortifications: Rousseau, Laclos, Sade* (Princeton: Princeton University Press, 1984).

56. A letter to the editor in response to the November 29 comment gushes: "What woman or man on Antioch's campus, or elsewhere, wouldn't welcome the direct question 'May I kiss the hollow of your neck?' The possibilities are wonderful—pedagogic, even—as is the idea that language is choice." (*The New Yorker,* January 10, 1994), 8.

57. Fassin, 11.

58. On these visual representations and how to read them see Philip Stewart's *Engraven Desire: Eros, Image, and Text in the French Eighteenth Century* (Durham: Duke University Press, 1992), esp. 94–102.

59. *Mercure de France,* (April 1786), 191. For contemporary reviews see the bibliography provided by Joan Stewart and Philip Stewart in the edition prepared for *Texts and Translations* (New York: MLA 1993).

60. This was part of a late-century debate over the desirability of women's breastfeeding, and as such part of a complex process through which women's sexuality and bodily rights continued to be regulated. For an analysis of this phenomenon in England, see Ruth Perry's fascinating "Colonizing the Breast," *Journal of the History of Sexuality* 2 (October 1991): 204–34. Mr. B. also dilates on the question in *Pamela II.*

On these issues and their specific dialogue with Rousseau, see Nadine Bérenguier's paired reading, "From Clarens to Hollow Park, Isabelle de Charrière's Quiet Revolution," *Studies in Eighteenth-Century Culture,* 21 (1991): 219–43.

61. Isabelle de Charrière, *Letters of Mistress Henley, Published by Her Friend,* trans. Philip Stewart and Jean Vaché (New York: MLA, 1993), 5.

62. This is certainly the sense of Lanser's important chapter: "Dying for Publicity: Mistress Henley's Self-Silencing," in *Fictions of Authority.*

63. Charrière, 12.

64. Charrière, 39.

65. Charrière, 39–40.

66. Michael Warner, "Introduction: Fear of a Queer Planet," *Social Text* (29) 9 (4)(1991): 3–17, esp. 7.

67. It's tempting to play around with biography in these cases but ultimately frustrating. Does Rousseau idealize maternity and family life *because* he abandons his own children? Does Tencin in *Les Malheurs de l'amour* (In *Oeuvres complètes de Mmes Tencin, Lafayette, et Des Fontaines,* 5 [Paris: Moutardier, 1825]) picture Eugénie fixated on the future of her dead lover's child—born of another "forgetting"—because she abandoned d'Alembert? What about Riccoboni's childlessness? And Charrière's? Staël's many children?

68. Joan Stewart describes Ossery as being a virgin himself. I find this hard to support, but it's true that Ossery is not, like, say Duclos's Count, a reformed rake.

69. Riccoboni, *Lettres de Juliette Catesby,* (Paris: Desjonquères, 1983).

70. Riccoboni articulates throughout the novel a counter-discourse with more or less specific references to a male tradition. She concludes a discussion of "moralistes" and the failure of their vision with a typical self-denigrating remark: "You see the danger of these readings? I thought I was writing a book myself" (*Juliette Catesby,* letter XV).

71. Janet Todd comments of Riccoboni's treatment of friendship, which she sees as representative of the period: "More clearly than most, her works show how female relationships can nudge the romantic from center stage, while remaining incidental to the plot. At the same time her books summarize the categories of friendship, redefining and refreshing them where stagnant." (*Women's Friendship in Literature* [New York: Columbia University Press, 1980], p.358). Todd is probably right. Still, I think it's important to see female friendship as more than "an ointment for the social wounding of women" (Todd, 358); rather as the figuration of a plot that has yet to speak its name.

72. Riccoboni's precursor here may indeed be Richardson, who in *Pamela* gives Mr. B. an illegitimate daughter. Pamela and Mr. B. visit the little girl, Miss Goodwin, at the dairy before the wedding. Pamela's own pregnancy takes place in *Pamela II,* although that pregnancy is to be her fate is clear from the end of Part I.

73. There's something dizzying about the circulation of a handful of names: Sade's Juliette, and finally the pornographic, *Julie ou j'ai sauvé ma rose,* the title of an early female-authored novel.

74. Duclos, *Les Confessions du Comte de \*\*\*,* in the Bouquins edition, *Romans libertins* (see n. 16). Page references are included in the text, indicated as *LC*.

75. Crébillon, *The Wayward Head and Heart,* trans. Barbara Bray (New York: Oxford University Press, 1963), xix.

76. On the legitimacy of these views see Laurent Versini's judicious evaluation in his critical edition of the novel (Paris: Marcel Didier, 1969), 168.

77. Versini, 168.

78. For the long and theorized answer to this question, see Eve Kosofsky Sedgwick's complex analysis in *Between Men: English Literature and Male Homosocial Desire* (New York: Columbia University Press, 1985). See especially the introduction and Chapter 1.

79. I owe this expression to Elizabeth Dulong Galaznik, who in her article "Choreographing the Second Seduction: The Case of Prévan and Valmont" (ms.), coined it from her reading of letter LXXI in which Valmont, after a clever scene, receives kisses from two lovers: "I in my turn was embraced by them both. I had no more interest in the Vicomtesse's kisses; but I admit that Vressac's gave me pleasure." (Choderlos de Laclos, *Dangerous Liaisons,* trans. Richard Aldington [New York: New American Library, 1962], 152.)

80. Susan Winnett, *Terrible Sociability: The Text of Manners in Laclos, Goethe, and James* (Stanford: Stanford University Press, 1993). On the incommensurability of Meilcour's narrative and Merteuil's, see 76–77. This has to do with the limits of what Janie Vanpée calls "authoring gender." (Vanpée "Reading Differences: The Case of Letter 141 in *Les Liaisons dangereuses,*" *Eighteenth-Century Studies* [Winter 1993]: 85–110).

81. Claude Reichler, "Le récit d'initiation dans le roman libertin," *Littérature* XII, 47 (October 1982): 100–112, 111.

82. Lynn Hunt reflects on this problem in the introduction to *The Invention of Pornography: Obscenity and the Origins of Modernity, 1500–1800* (New York: Zone Books, 1993). Commenting on the gender blindness of Jean Marie Goulemot's analysis (in *Ces livres qu'on ne lit que d'une main: Lecture et lecteurs de livres pornographiques au XVIII siècle* [Aix-en Provence: Alinea, 1991]), Hunt remarks: "women were thought especially susceptible to the imaginative effects of the novel, while men were usually assumed—rightly or wrongly—to be the primary audience for pornographic writing, at least until the end of the eighteenth century" (36). Indeed, many engravings show women irresistibly overcome by sexual urges brought on by novel reading. See Philip Stewart's *Engraven Desire: Eros, Image, and Text in the French Eighteenth Century,* esp., 94–102. Everything remains to be said about women's (and women writers') interest in women's masturbation. A place to start is Eve Kosofsky Sedgwick's "Jane Austen and the Masturbating Girl," *Critical Inquiry* 17 (4) (Summer 1991): 818–37. Sally O'Driscoll has begun work on the representation of auto-eroticism in *Fanni Butlerd* as an emancipatory form of sexuality, in "Enlightened Autoeroticism" (ms.). But Jane Gallop probably is the first woman critic to speak of her own masturbatory reactions to (eighteenth-century) literature in *Thinking Through the Body* (Gallop, 18 [see n. 10]).

83. I'm referring here to Segal's provocative analysis, *The Unintended Reader: Feminism and Manon Lescaut* (Cambridge: Cambridge University Press, 1986),

and specifically to her reply to Lionel Gossman's question that follows. Gossman, in a footnote, asks himself about the narrative structure of Manon Lescaut: "On the common assumption that the readers—and increasingly, indeed, the writers—of novels were female, how can one explain that the central dilemma of a work intended for a female audience is . . . so profoundly masculine?" ("Male and Female in Two Short Novels by Prévost," *Modern Language Review* 77, Part I [January 1992], 32, note 4). Segal answers, following Judith Fetterley, "A woman reader is quite as radically alienated from the text as Gossman suggests. . . . [T]o read as a woman is to be forced into sympathies and antipathies that diametrically oppose women's interests and women's experience" (Segal, xiii).

84. This doesn't mean that repro-narrativity isn't at work. Saint-Amand writes of the bond between the two men: "The final conversion, this return to *virtue* (that sublimated region of passion that sealed their friendship), fails to conceal the eroticism of their relationship: '[I] gave him unexpected joy by declaring that the seeds of virtue he had sown long ago in my heart were beginning to bear fruit which he would approve of.' Des Grieux will bear Tiberge's child . . . ." (*The Libertine's Progress: Seduction in the Eighteenth-Century French Novel,* trans. Jennifer Curtiss Gage. [University Press of New England, forthcoming].)

85. This is also the solution Tencin arrives at for Eugénie and the marquis de La Valette, who chooses in *Les Malheurs de l'amour* to enjoy "the tender charms of the most solid friendship," rather than run the risk of marriage. That novel's heterosexual friendship is framed by the bonds between two women who live together in harmony and sympathy (Tencin, 145–46 [see n. 69]).

On reader response to Graffigny's ending and its relation to epistolary form, see Elizabeth MacArthur's "Devious Narratives: Refusal of Closure in Two Eighteenth-Century Novels." *Eighteenth-Century Studies* 21 (Fall 1987) (1): 1–20.

86. Joan Landes writes of published (but not fictional) correspondences: "Usually someone other than the author *constructed* the published work for a larger audience. Supplementing the author function, editors began to assume a much more assertive and self-conscious role. However, this vital function was rarely, if ever, performed by women," (*Women and the Public Sphere in the Age of the French Revolution* [Ithaca: Cornell University Press, 1988], 53.) So it's interesting to think about what the creation of the female publisher in fiction might tell us about women writers' desire to control the publication of their texts.

87. Laurent Versini sees this apostrophe (and others) as "a leit-motiv of the feminist novel" and as a reprise of Richardsonian tirades, notably in *Clarissa* (558). See Versini *Laclos et la tradition: Essai sur les sources et la technique des Liaisons Dangereuses* (Paris: Klincksieck, 1968). On the one hand, Riccoboni is denigrated for producing "pale imitations" of Richardsonian heroines (Versini, 557), and on the other, of writing, unimaginatively from her own, autobiographical experience (see "emotional biographicalism" in Cook, "Going Public," 27). Why it should be impossible to see Riccoboni as constructing an original fiction is a question with a rhetoric of its own.

88. Williams, *Hard Core,* 15.

89. Thus the class difference between Fanni and Alfred is eroded to be replaced—or at least superceded—by gender polarization.

I would like to thank Carolyn Heilbrun, Katharine Jensen, Sally O'Driscoll and Naomi Schor for their comments on earlier versions of this chapter.

## Two Rereading as a Woman

1. Johnathan Culler, *On Deconstruction: Theory and Criticism* (Ithaca: Cornell University Press, 1982), 50. The hypothesis of the female reader is Elaine Showalter's.

2. Wayne Booth, "Freedom of Interpretation: Bakhtin and the Challenge of Feminist Criticism." *Critical Inquiry* 9: 1 (September 1982): 74; emphasis added.

3. Booth, 68.

4. Of Booth's and Culler's recognition of the power of feminist theory to throw canonical assumptions into question, Elaine Showalter comments: "To women who have been writing feminist criticism this phenomenon must be gratifying and unsettling" ("Critical Cross-Dressing: Male Feminists and the Woman of the Year," *Raritan* 3:2 [Fall 1983]: 131). In many ways I share what I will call Showalter's "anxiety of recuperation," the concern—though we work with different metaphors—that male critics, speaking as men to other men, will recast and reappropriate (perhaps to equalize the codes, we could think of this process as a kind of laundering) the insights of a less glamorous practice, like ironing, the better to neutralize, through another sort of canonization, the disruption that feminism promises. But, at the same time, and specifically here in the case of Booth, I note first of all that the irony of the ironing is of course not lost on the rhetorician: "(!)." And perhaps most important, as Carolyn Heilbrun argues in "The Threshold of Gender," the fact remains that, "by testifying . . . Booth rendered it impossible for teachers of Rabelais to chuckle quite so mindlessly over that passage (there is now a text to refute that laughter)."(ms.)

5. Booth, 61, 65.

6. Laclos, *Les Liaisons Dangereuses*, trans. P.W.K. Stone (Harmondsworth: Penguin, 1961). There is, despite the insistence on the physical aspect of the action—producing "a letter written in bed, in the arms, almost, of a trollop"—a peculiar effacement of (the) woman's body in and as representation. It is curious to note that critics do not seem to agree, or rather do not seem to be able to *say* exactly what goes on here. Peter Brooks, in his presentation at MLA, imagined the letter written on Emilie's "bare backside." Jacques Bourgeacq argues (against "the literary tradition that limits Emilie's role in the composition of the letter to the use of her back") that Emilie actively participates in the action; that the "action external to the letter" as he euphemizes it, "organizes the text itself" ("A partir de la lettre XLVIII des *Liaisons dangereuses*: Analyse stylistique," *Studies in Voltaire and the Eighteenth Century* 182 (1980): 185–86). Thomas Fries, in "The Impossible Object: The Feminine, The Narrative (Laclos's *Liaisons dangereuses* and Kleist's *Marquise von O . . .*)" (*Modern Language Notes* 91:6 [1976]), deconstructively reads the modeling of sexual difference in the novel, assimilating the ambiguity implicit in the positioning of the woman's body to the general problematics of the novel, to the "figurality of language and more precisely in the figure Latin rhetoric

calls *dissimulatio*" (1308). For him this ambiguous manipulation of knowledge is the source of the pleasure of the text; he cites "one of the supposedly most scandalous pasages of this book, the famous letter *written from and on some lower part of Emilie's back,*" as a typical example (1309, emphasis added). The blockage of mimesis is, I think, tied to the narrative framing. By the use of a figure which is either periphrasis, or catchresis, or both—"in the arms, almost"—interpretation is both forced and inhibited. Paradoxically, this "undecidability" does not interfere with the reading effect which derives from the reading *process,* from the semiosis: one knows that a woman's body is being enlisted in a male production of language. The movie versions have removed the ambiguities.

7. I allude to and play with the distinctions in letter writing styles established by Janet Altman, in "Addressed and Undressed Language in *Les Liaisons dangereuses,*" in *Laclos: Critical Approaches to Les Liaisons dangereuses,* ed. Lloyd R. Free (Madrid: Studia Humanitatis, 1978).

8. Georges May, "The Witticisms of M. de Valmont," *L'Esprit Créateur* 3:4 (1963): 182–83; emphasis added.

9. Booth, 68.

10. Ronald Rosbottom, *Choderlos de Laclos* (Boston: Twayne, 1979), 108.

11. Rosbottom, 109.

12. "The juxtaposition of the lover's desire for sexual gratification and the writer's penetration into his subject is too strong to be overlooked" (Fries [see n. 6], 1309). And Michel Butor, enlisted by Fries, supplies a depressing and acute parenthesis on the subject of the lover as writer: "what is most surprising in Valmont's famous letter to the Présidente written using Emilie as a desk, is not that he interrupted it to 'commit a downright infidelity,' it's the transformation of the woman into a desk, into a means of writing to another [woman]; committed, he had nothing more pressing to do than to start writing again" (*Répertoire II.* [Paris: Minuit, 1964], 50). Male desire, then, originates not in the "arms" of a woman present, but in the desired absence of the woman to be written to. Would it not be possible to argue that the effacement of the woman's body in representation is here due precisely to its transformation into instrumentality? Emilie must remain invisible since her function is merely and classically to facilitate the exchange of women and/or signs . . . between men.

13. I am playing here with the phrase Sandra Gilbert and Susan Gubar have constructed—against Harold Bloom's model of a male "anxiety of influence"—to account for the psychological posture of the female artist: her "need for sisterly precursors and successors, her urgent sense of her need for a female audience" (*The Madwoman in the Attic: The Woman Writer and the Nineteenth-Century Literary Imagination,* [New Haven and London: Yale University Press, 1979], 50).

14. In "'The Blank Page' and the Issues of Female Creativity," Susan Gubar summarizes the history of this figuration: "This model of the pen-penis writing on the virgin-page participates in a long tradition identifying the author as a male who is primary and the female as his passive creation—a secondary object lacking autonomy, endowed with often contradictory meaning but denied intentionality" (*Critical Inquiry* 8: 2 [Winter 1981]: 247). It's interesting to note that where she

writes "virgin," we can substitute "whore" and leave the meaning of the argument intact.

15. Jean Biou, in "Une lettre au-dessus de tout soupçon," underscores the oppressive power of this representation: "Letter XLVII supplies in effect an imaginary scenario founded on two opposed but not contradictory principles: on the one hand, the division of women—in the double sense of the division of labor and the breakdown of a potential solidarity—on the other, the unique employment of women, sexual employment" (*Laclos et le libertinage: 1782–1982, Actes du Colloque du Bicentenaire des Liaisons dangereuses* [Paris: Presses Universitaires de France, 1983], 197.

16. Judith Fetterley, *The Resisting Reader: A Feminist Approach to American Fiction* (Bloomington: Indiana University Press, 1978), xx, xxi.

17. Jane Austen, *Persuasion* (Harmondsworth: Penguin, 1975), 239.

18. Austen, 237.

19. Austen, 239. I am indebted here to Nancy Nystul for her critical insights about Austen's revisionist incorporation of older literary models.

20. Austen, 239.

21. I thank Carolyn Heilbrun, who remembered it for me. In their groundbreaking work on women writers, Gilbert and Gubar have forcefully documented the power of this account of literary paternity, and the damage it has done to the female imagination. My argument operates here at an angle to their poetics, with the emphasis falling on the metonymic, or literal valences of the penis as pen, on the one hand, and the pen as metaphor beyond the phallus on the other.

22. I allude here to Eve Kosofsky Sedgwick's refinement of the concept of male bonding that makes it possible, through the use of the term "homosocial," to understand the continuum of social and genital arrangements that structure male power relations in Western culture. Sedgwick, *Between Men* (see chap. 1, n. 61).

23. Gilbert and Gubar, *Madwoman in the Attic,* 179.

24. This portrait of the male artist in love perhaps rewrites, by feminizing, an earlier, more virile dropping of the pen. I am thinking of the prelude to the celebrated scene in Clarissa in which Lovelace, "writing on" to his friend Belford, is surprised at 5 0'clock in the morning by a fire alarm: "My pen (its last scrawl a benediction on my beloved) dropped from my fingers" (Richardson, *Clarissa, Or the History of a Young Lady* [London, New York: Dent, Dutton, 1968]; Letter CXXVI, Vol. II, p. 500). This pretext allows Lovelace to penetrate into Clarissa's room to encircle "the almost disrobed body of the loveliest of her sex." Clarissa picks up a "pair of sharp-pointed scissors" to prepare a Portia-like defense. These are the classical penetrations of Western culture.

25. Austen, 240.

## THREE  Men's Reading, Women's Writing

1. Frances [Fanny] Burney, *Camilla,* ed. Edward A. and Lillian D. Bloom (Oxford: Oxford University Press, 1983), 606.

2. Burney, 949–50.

3. I am grateful to Rachel Brownstein for bringing this note to my attention.

4. An account of the translation history is provided by Gianni Nicoletti in his critical edition of the novel. Françoise de Graffigny, *Lettres d'une Péruvienne*, ed. Gianni Nicoletti (Bari: Adriatica Editrice, 1967).

5. Joan Kelly-Gadol, "The Social Relation of the Sexes: Methodological Implications of Women's History," *Signs* 4 (Summer 1974): 809–24. Reprinted in *Women, History, and Theory: The Essays of Joan Kelly* (Chicago: University of Chicago Press, 1984), 1–18. This is also part of the territory mapped by Peter Brooks in his *Novel of Worldliness: Crébillon, Marivaux, Laclos, Stendhal* (Princeton: Princeton University Press, 1969).

6. Georges May, *Le Dilemme du roman au XVIIIe siècle: Etude sur les rapports du roman et de la critique (1715–1761)* (New Haven: Yale University Press, 1963), 1.

7. Joan DeJean, "Classical Reeducation: Decanonizing the Feminine," in *Displacements: Women, Tradition, Literatures in French,* ed. Joan DeJean and Nancy K. Miller (Baltimore: Johns Hopkins University Press, 1991), 23.

8. René Etiemble, *Romanciers du XVIIIe siècle,* 2 vols. (Paris: Gallimard, Pléiade, 1966, 1969.) Page references are included in the text, indicated as *R.*

9. In *Encyclopédie de la Pléiade. Histoire des Littératures,* ed. Raymond Queneau (Paris: Gallimard, 1958), vol. 3, *Littératures françaises, connexes et marginales,* ed. René Etiemble, 849. These two titles often appear in the incorrect form Etiemble has chosen here: following Sainte-Beuve, this models Graffigny's title on Montesquieu's (de-emphasizing the singular of female subjectivity: "d'une Péruvienne") and adds an *s* to Tencin's *Comminge,* succumbing to the seduction of another "geographical" analogy that also erases a mark of difference: the old "comté de Comminges." When "1735" (in this volume) was published in *A New History of French Literature,* ed. Denis Hollier (Cambridge: Harvard University Press: 1989) the *s* was added to the name; and so the footnotes continue.

10. Thus in his massive *La Destinée féminine dans le roman européen du dix-huitième siècle* (Paris: Armand Colin, 1972), in the chapter called, "La Romancière," Pierre Fauchery states categorically: "In the eighteenth century, the myths of feminine destiny, of masculine creation, are for the most part accepted whole cloth by the women novelists. The latter, moreover, far from claiming their autonomy, take shelter behind the authority of the great writers of the other sex" (93).

11. Susan Winnett, "Coming Unstrung: Women, Men, and Principle(s) of Pleasure," *PMLA* 105; 3 (May 1990): 505–18.

12. Nancy K. Miller, *Subject to Change: Reading Feminist Writing* (New York: Columbia University Press, 1988).

13. Rachel DuPlessis, *Writing Beyond the Ending: Narrative Strategies of Twentieth-Century Women Writers* (Bloomington: Indiana University Press, 1985).

14. *Lettres de Mistress Fanni Butlerd* offers perhaps the clearest instance of a feminist critique of masculine advantage: when Alfred (Mylord Charles Alfred, Comte d'Erford) abandons the woman in love with him to move on to the next and make a fashionable marriage, the woman goes public with their story; her letters, like the

narrative of *L'Histoire du Marquis de Cressy,* reveal the psychic and social cost to women of a socially unregulated male sexual "freedom." Both Riccoboni's *Cressy* and Tencin's *Mémoires du Comte de Comminge* rewrite the masculine suffering embodied by Des Grieux as a form of blindness and narcissism. Thus, in the end, both Comminge and Cressy are forced to witness the spectacular death of the superior woman they have failed. Unlike Manon, however, Adélaïde and the marquise de Cressy are neither mythical nor enigmatic; it is instead their human complexity *as women* that the men in love with them prove unable to comprehend.

15. *Littérature française,* vol. 5, *De Fénelon à Voltaire,* ed. René Pomeau and Jean Ehrard; vol. 6, *De L'Encyclopédie aux Méditations,* ed. Michel Delon, Robert Mauzi, and Sylvain Menant (Paris: Arthaud, 1984). Page references are included in the text, indicated as *LF.*

16. The masterpiece model, which assumes that a work both exemplifies and transcends its historical moment, seems particularly inappropriate to the eighteenth-century novel, since its "most important" instance, Rousseau's *Nouvelle Héloïse* is not a novel which is often reread.

17. Jane Tompkins, *Sensational Designs: The Cultural Work of American Fiction: 1790–1860.* (New York: Oxford University Press, 1985), xv.

18. Sainte-Beuve, we might say, finished off Graffigny for several generations of readers. In his caustic portrait of her in *Lettres de Madame de Grafigny ou Voltaire à Cirey* (written in 1850 and published in *Causeries du lundi* [Paris: Garnier, 1858], vol. 2) the critic, in another instance of literary criticism as male bonding, reviews Turgot's reservations about the novel's ending. Having commented enthusiastically and at length on the novel's ideas, ideas that inspired writings of his own, he concludes: "All these pages of Turgot are excellent, and I recommend reading them, as much as I can't recommend rereading [*rouvrir*] the *Lettres péruviennes*" (224).

19. On "overreading," see "Arachnologies: The Woman, the Text, and the Critic," in my *Subject to Change* (see n. 12); on the "intersextual," see Naomi Schor, "La Pérodie: Superposition dans *Lorenzaccio,*" *Michigan Romance Studies* 1 (1982): 73–86.

20. Choderlos de Laclos, "Le Roman: Cecilia," in his *Oeuvres complètes,* ed. Maurice Allem (Paris: Gallimard, 1959), 501. Page references are included in the text, indicated as *LR.*

21. See May's discussion of the coexistence of this discourse on women's special aptitude for novel writing with an undisguised misogyny (May, 218ff.).

22. In "Idealism in the Novel," in *Displacements: Women, Tradition, Literatures in French,* ed. Joan DeJean and Nancy K. Miller (Baltimore: Johns Hopkins University Press, 1991), Naomi Schor, citing the Riccoboni-Laclos exchange, argues that the mapping of idealism onto femininity, and the identification of masculinity with realism, play a crucial role in canon-formation in the history of the nineteenth century novel.

23. Donatien-Alphonse-François Sade, "Idée sur les romans," (Paris: Palimugre, 1946), 27–28.

24. Sade, 28.

25. Susan Lanser and Evelyn Beck, "[Why] Are There No Great Women Critics? And What Difference Does It Make?" in *The Prism of Sex: Essays in the Sociology of Knowledge,* ed. Julia A. Sherman and Evelyn Torton Beck (Madison: University of Wisconsin Press, 1979), 79–91. It is here that the much cited feminist formulation of women's "double-voiced discourse" is first articulated. "The writings of women who are struggling to define themselves but have not yet given up a patriarchal frame of reference may betray a tension so strong as to produce a virtually 'double-voiced' discourse" (86). The essay was originally presented as a paper in 1977.

26. Lanser and Beck, 87.

27. Frances [Fanny] Burney, *Evelina, Or The History of A Young Lady's Entrance Into the World* (New York: Norton, 1965) no page number. Burney's novel is framed by an "Original Dedication: To the Authors of the Monthly and Critical Reviews," in which the authorial persona is that of a young writer without a name—the gender is implicitly one constructed on a continuity with the gentlemen of the press—and a preface.

    In Riccoboni's second letter to Laclos she rejects the title of "un auteur" and denies any self-importance: "I am so barely an author that in reading a new book I would find myself quite unjust and foolish if I compared it to the trifles that issue from my pen and thought my ideas qualified to guide those of others." She writes instead, she says, as a woman, a French woman (*LR, 689*).

28. Graffigny, *Letters From a Peruvian Woman,* trans. David Kornacker (New York: MLA, 1993), 3.

29. Myra Jehlen, "Archimedes and the Paradox of Feminist Criticism," *Signs* 6 (Summer 1981): 585.

30. Janet Todd's *Sensibility* (London: Methuen, 1986) provides a stimulating account of these issues as they emerge in eighteenth-century England.

31. George Eliot, "Woman in France: Madame de Sablé," *The Essays of George Eliot,* ed. Thomas Pinney (London: Routledge & Kegan Paul, 1963), 55.

32. On the relation of *Corinne* to women and the history of the French novel, see Joan DeJean's "Staël's *Corinne:* The Novel's Other Dilemma," *Stanford Literature Review* 10, no. 1 (Spring 1987): 77–88.

33. Margaret Switten and Elissa Gelfand have already conceived and taught such a course at Mount Holyoke called "Gender and the Rise of the Novel" (which I have appropriated for the subtitle of this essay) in which the notion I describe earlier as "reading in pairs" is imaginatively enacted. I am grateful to them for sharing their materials with me.

    Following several introductory sessions on the beginning of the *roman* in the Middle Ages, the *querelle des femmes,* early poetics, and contemporary feminist criticism, the students of "Gender and the Rise of the Novel" read Tencin's *Comminge,* Prévost's *Manon Lescaut,* Graffigny's *Lettres d'une Péruvienne,* Rousseau's *Nouvelle Héloïse,* Diderot's *Jacques le fataliste,* Charrière's *Caliste,* Riccoboni's *Fanni Butlerd,* Laclos's *Liaisons dangereuses,* and the correspondence between Laclos and Riccoboni.

    In the same spirit, one could also imagine reading Montesquieu's *Lettres persanes* or Prévost's *Histoire d'une grecque moderne* with *Lettres d'une Péruvienne;*

the *Lettres portugaises* with the Graffigny; Duclos's *Les Confessions du comte de\*\*\** with Riccoboni's *Histoire du marquis de Cressy* or *Lettres de Milady Juliette Catesby*. Finally, to circle back to the question of *Corinne,* and as a move into questions of the nineteenth-century novel, one could reread the canonical tropes of the "psychological" novel *Adolphe* in the light of a male subjectivity brilliantly supplied by *Caliste* and *Corinne.* Switten and Gelfand's own account of the course they taught at Smith College appears in the *French Review* 61, no. 3 (February 1988): 443–53 under the title "Gender and the Rise of the Novel." Nadine Bérenguier has also taught such a course at Harvard University.

## FOUR  Cultural Memory and the Art of the Novel

1. An earlier version of this essay appeared in French under the title "La Mémoire, l'oubli et l'art du roman: textes libertins, textes sentimentaux," in the collection *Femmes et pouvoirs sous l'ancien régime,* ed. Danielle Haase-Dubosc and Eliane Viennot (Paris: Rivages, 1991), 238–58. I would like to thank Sally O'Driscoll for translating the primary and critical material from the French; page numbers refer to the French originals.

2. Henri Coulet, *Le Roman jusqu'à la revolution,* (Paris: Armand Colin, 1967), 378. Coulet is the clearest about the category. The adjective sentimental only entered the French language with the translation of Sterne's 1768 *A Sentimental Journey.* The Arthaud manuals (see chap. 3, n. 15), use variants of sensibility, the language of the period to describe the works of women writers: *romans pour coeurs sensibles.* In the 1986 edition of Hachette's manual for secondary school teaching (Xavier Darcos and Bernard Tartayre, *Le XVIIIe siècle en littérature* [Paris: Hachette, 1986]), the authors of the volume combine women and sensibility by devoting part of a chapter on the eighteenth-century novel to "Women's Writing" ("L'écriture au féminin"). In it they include excerpts from Riccoboni, Tencin, Graffigny, and Deffand. What is interesting, and even surprising, is the characterization of this writing as having a "feminist character" which is described as "a very conscious determination to give a voice to woman, to her demands, in a society called upon to evolve" (223). To my knowledge, this is the first inclusion of women writers in manuals at this level; it is also the first general description of women's writing in the eigtheenth century as feminist, rather than the usual clichés of the sentimental. The writing, moreover, through the internal apparatus of the manual, is specifically contrasted to excerpts of men's writing—Prévost, Rousseau, Diderot, etc.—within the volume. Despite the marginalizing gesture of the women's chapter—as opposed to an account of named authorship ("The Libertine Novel" with Crébillon and Duclos, for instance), recognition by the signature—this represents significant progress and compares favorably to manuals designed for university students and the general public like the Arthaud volumes.

3. Coulet, 386.

4. Charles Pinot-Duclos, *Les Confessions du Comte de\*\*\*,* ed. Laurent Versini (Paris: Didier, 1976), xxxviii.

5. Crébillon, *Les Egarements du coeur et de l'esprit,* ed. Etiemble (Paris: Folio, 1977), 28.

6. Crébillon, *Les Egarements du coeur et de l'esprit,* ed. Etiemble (Paris: Garnier-Flammarion, 1985), 57.

7. Duclos, *Mémoires pour servir à l'histoire des moeurs du XVIIIe siècle* (Paris: Desjonquères, 1986), page references for this novel are included in the text, indicated as M; [Riccoboni, *Lettres de Milady Juliette Catesby A Milady Henriette Campley, Son Amie* (Paris: Desjonquères, 1983), letter references for this novel are included in the text, indicated as JC.] Both of these novels had been out of print since the nineteenth century. This fact, however, gives the two novels a certain false symmetry. On the one hand, Riccoboni's novel was extremely popular at the time of publication; there were twenty editions by 1800, several translations and more printings of any novel before *La Nouvelle Héloïse.* The blurb on the back jacket bears Diderot's praise, etc. But then Riccoboni becomes, we might say, a woman author. Subsequently, she is most generally referred to as having written the suite to Marivaux's *La Vie de Marianne* and as having had a correspondence with Laclos that is published with his novel in the Pléiade edition. She is also referred to as the wife and daughter-in-law of famous actors of the Comédie Italienne.

The *Mémoires,* unlike Duclos's other works, were not successful, perhaps Duclos's least successful work, but Duclos, on the other hand, remains in the tradition; most famously by anthologization in Pléiade, *Romanciers du XVIIIe siècle,* edited by Etiemble (Paris: Gallimard, 1966). Secretary of the Académie française, admired by Stendhal, Duclos is remembered for his *style* and through it part of the French cultural mainstream. Thus Versini maintains that we should see in Duclos, "a witness to his time and an indispensable link in the chain between the seventeenth-century *moralistes* and a Laclos or a Stendhal" (Duclos, liv).

Neither of these texts belongs to the "masterpiece theater" model of literary history; they do not bear the famous signatures of the Enlightenment figures. Duclos is considered one of the *minores,* or as belonging to the category of books described by Emile Henriot—as on the second shelf down—in the title of the classic *Les Livres du second rayon. Irréguliers et libertins.* (Paris: Grasset, 1948). I make use of these categories only as a familiar shorthand because it isn't my purpose here to show all the ways in which canon-formation is dependent on a politics of taste.

8. This is in some sense a double education. As Geoffrey Bennington argues, in *Sententiousness and the Novel: Laying Down the Law in 18th-century Fiction* (Cambridge: Cambridge University Press, 1985), naming what he calls the "pré-monde": "What goes on before high society . . . is also a scene of education" (67).

9. Sylvain Menant, *Juliette Catesby,* Preface VII.

10. Joan Stewart, *The Novels of Madame Riccoboni* (Chapel Hill: University of North Carolina Press, 1977); "Sex, Text, and Exchange: *Lettres neuchâteloises* and *Lettres de Milady Juliette Catesby,*" *Eighteenth-Century Life.* 13 (1) (February 1989): 82.

11. Susan Sniader Lanser's *Fictions of Authority: Women Writers and Narrative Voice* (Ithaca: Cornell University Press, 1992), by its brilliant readings of ideology in women's narratives, has greatly influenced my understanding of this difficult text.

12. The language Henri Coulet uses in the language of his preface to the *Mémoires* is in this sense symptomatic when he describes the narrator as "libertine by imitation and a sentimentalist caught between *Tendre-sur-estime* (love-respect) and *Tendre-sur-reconnaissance*" (love-gratitude) (*M*, ix).

13. *Romanciers du XVIIIe siècle,* xvii.

14. Emily Crosby, *Une romancière oubliée, Madame Riccoboni* (Paris: Rieder, 1924). (The title may have been an echo of a study devoted to another neglected woman writer: *Mme de Graffigny: Une "Primitive" oubliée de l'école des coeurs sensibles.* G. Noël [Paris: Plon-Nourrit, 1913]).

    Thus, in the introduction to the *Egarements* (Paris: Garnier Flammarion, 1985): "L'abbé Sabatier de Castres, who was never considered prophetic, writes in *Les Trois Siècles de la Littérature française* (1775) . . . Most of his works are hardly read today except by young officers in the garrisons. Now we know a certain young officer who . . ." and we rejoin memory with Laclos.

    The shaping of literary traditions has largely been managed by male readers, who build on a male tradition of poeticians, critics and grammarians (not to mention military officers!) of the period. Feminist traditions will have other genealogies and identifications.

15. Once again, the question of point of view is key. Riccoboni, for instance, describes another of her novels precisely as a novel of manners: "The manners [*moeurs*] of our aristocracy, that is our polite [*honnête*] aristocracy, the tone of our court, easy to overdo and seldom caught exactly—that is the whole merit of *Lettres de Madame de Sancerre*" (in Stewart, "Sex, Text, and Exchange," 86).

    In commentary on the publication of a Pléiade edition of Rétif de la Bretonne's memoirs, Michel Braudeau questions the relation between memory, sexuality, and the representation of *moeurs:* "In his *Calendrier,* published together with *Monsieur Nicolas,* he gives a list of the women who meant the most to him, putting one on each day of the year, a little like an almanac; he admits to fathering about a hundred and fifteen children. How much truth, how much fantasy is there in a list of this type. There is no way to know exactly, and anyway, does it matter? Rétif's work has been praised for its description of the manners of his time. It is true that there are many juicy or realistic details in his innumerable adventures and one can stumble upon the price of a furnished room in Revolutionary Paris. But we must not delude ourselves about the realism of this document, which is greatly influenced by an imaginary strongly directed by the 'grand narrator,' as Nicolas calls himself." (*Le Monde,* December 22, 1989, 14).

16. The expression is Janet Todd's, whose book, *Sensibility* (London: Methuen, 1986), interestingly analyzes many of these issues as they are expressed in the English novel.

# FIVE 1735

1. Tencin is also said to be portrayed in the character Madame de Tonins in Duclos's *Les Confessions du Comte de* \*\*\*. She's shown, among other things, as making the Count into an author against his will ("auteur malgré moi"). The Count drops

her and her "bureau de l'esprit" as is his habit. His play, a comedy, was a flop. It's not a very attractive portrait.

2. Philip Stewart, *Imitation and Illusion in the Memoir-Novel, 1700–1750: The Art of Make Believe* (New Haven: Yale University Press, 1969).

3. Prévost, *Manon Lescaut,* trans. Donald Frame (New York: New American Library, 1961). Page references are included in the text, indicated as *ML.*

4. Tencin, *Les Mémoires du Comte de Comminge,* ed. Jean Decottignies (Lille: René Giad, 1969), 21.

5. Tencin, 195.

6. On the suffering that love brings in Tencin's novels, see Chantal Thomas's "Les Rigueurs de l'amour: Etude sur Mme de Tencin et Stendhal," *L'Infini* (Automne 1985) 12: 77–89.

7. Katharine A. Jensen has developed these themes in "The Inheritance of Masculinity and the Limits of Heterosexual Revision: Tencin's *Les Mémoires du Comte de Comminge,*" *Eighteenth-Century Life* 16 (May 1992): 44–58. When the lovers finally embrace, it's *as men:* dressed as men, at least, just like Manon and Des Grieux at the end of *Manon Lescaut* (Manon dies wrapped in Des Grieux's clothes).

## SIX "I's" in Drag

1. "Introduction," in *Lettres portugaises,* ed. Frédéric Deloffre and Jacques Rougeot. (Paris: Garnier, 1962), 3.

2. *Lettres portugaises,* v; emphasis added.

3. Only La Bruyère and Sainte-Beuve refer specifically to the text of the "Portuguese Nun."

4. I owe the term and its implications to Peggy Brawer, who forged this expression to account for the masculine appropriation of the feminine in writing.

5. *Lettre à d'Alembert sur les spectacles,* ed. Léon Fontaine (Paris: Garnier, 1889), 239. Fontaine comments: "Whatever he may say, it's still a woman, Marianne Alcaforada, a nun in a convent of Beja (Alentejo) who wrote the famous letters to the Marquis of Chantilly" (240).

6. This second translation can be taken, I think, as part of what will become standard operating procedures of the eighteenth-century epistolary novel, a strategy of authentication and exculpation. If the letters were conceived elsewhere, they must be real; if they show virtue threatened by the disorders of passion, the threat is also elsewhere. Thus, what can be read as a more worldly and less passive version of the nun's story of seduction and betrayal, Riccoboni's anonymously published one-way correspondence *Lettres de Mistriss Fanni Butlerd*—often and paradoxically seen as both the rewriting of the *Portuguese Letters* and as *autobiography*—is identified in its title as letters translated from the English. And there is the more general use of national displacement common to Lesage, Montesquieu, Voltaire, Prévost, Diderot, et. al. A foreign origin codes, then, an anxiety not only of gender but of genre.

7. I refer to the line of argument shared by Ian Watt in *The Rise of the Novel*, Georges May in *Le Dilemme du roman au dix-huitième siècle*, and Pierre Fauchery in *La Destinée féminine dans le roman européen du dix-huitième siècle*.

8. Julia Kristeva, *Le Texte du roman*, (The Hague: Mouton, 1970), 160.

9. Duclos, *Les Confessions*, in *Romanciers du XVIIIe siècle* (Paris: Gallimard, 1966), 199. In the count's first reference to his wife he describes her as "un ami fidèle, qui partage ma solitude" (199).

10. Duclos, 300.

11. Duclos, 218.

12. Duclos, 218.

13. Leo Braudy, "Fanny Hill and Materialism," *Eighteenth-Century Studies* 4 (1970): 37.

14. Cleland, *The Memoirs of Fanny Hill*, (New York: Signet, 1965), 14.

15. Cleland, 220–21.

16. In "Memoirs of a Woman of Pleasure: Pornography and the Mid-Eighteenth Century Novel," Michael Shinagel, citing the concluding passage of the novel, argues that this initiation/education is meant to be the reader's as well "so that we can appreciate more fully the role of sexual pleasure in our lives" (217). True, but whose pleasure, whose life? As he subsequently remarks, "Cleland is writing from a male point of view for a male audience" (225). (In *Studies in Change and Revolution 1640–1800*, ed. Paul Korshin [Menston: Scholar Press, 1972]).

17. Shinagel counts about "fifty variations, all more or less elegant, on the male sexual organ," but finds Cleland "equally inventive, though less quantitative, in his euphemisms for the vagina. There are roughly half as many references to the female sexual organ" (225).

18. Cleland, xiii–xiv.

19. Virginia Woolf, *A Room of One's Own* (New York: Harcourt Brace Jovanovich, 1929), 36.

20. Cleland, 94–95.

21. Sade, *Juliette, or the Prosperities of Vice*, trans. Austryn Wainhouse (New York, Grove Press, 1968), 185.

22. Helen Buckingham, a prostitute writing in the newsletter of the National Task Force on Prostitution, cited in Deirdre English, "The Politics of Porn," *Mother Jones*, 49 (April, 1980); emphasis added.

23. Roland Barthes, *A Lover's Discourse*, trans. Richard Howard (New York: Noonday, 1990), 13–14.

24. Barthes, 19.

25. Barthes, 19.

26. *Lettres portugaises*, 61; emphasis added.

27. *Lettres portugaises*, 69.

28. Ovid, *The Heroides,* trans. Grant Showerman (Cambridge: Harvard University Press, 1971), 99.

29. *Lettres portugaises,* 37.

## SEVEN  *L'Histoire d'une Grecque moderne*

1. Roland Barthes, *S/Z.* trans. Richard Miller (New York: Hill and Wang, 1974). Page references are included in the text, indicated as *S/Z.*

2. Roland Barthes, "Analyse textuelle d'un conte d'Edgar Poe," in *Sémiotique narrative et textuelle,* presented by Claude Chabrol (Paris: Larousse, 1973), 30.

3. Ibid., 11. In "Fiction as Interpretation/Interpretation as Fiction," Naomi Schor describes Barthes's position here as "ecumenical hermeneutics." The label is apt but, as we will see, Barthes does not retain his favorite pew. In *The Reader in the Text: Essays on Audience and Interpretation,* ed. Susan R. Suleiman and Inge Crosman (Princeton: Princeton University Press, 1980).

4. In her acute deconstructionist reading of *S/Z,* "The Critical Difference," Barbara Johnson identifies the subtending polarity of Barthes's agenda as the opposition of the classic text and the text of modernity (plurality), the readerly and the writerly. She shows by rereading *Sarrasine* with *S/Z,* that "the traditional value system which Barthes is attempting to reverse is . . . already mapped out within the text he analyses"; and then asks whether Balzac's story really does "uphold the unambiguousness of the readerly values to which Barthes relegates it" (6). Ultimately she answers that "the readerly text is itself nothing other than a deconstruction of the readerly text" (8). Although Johnson's emphasis differs from mine, her penetration of Barthes's critical investment—particularly in her insistence upon Barthes's ambivalence toward the truth of/in sexual difference—has helped me clarify the stakes of my reading. (In *Diacritics* [Summer 1978], 2–9; reprinted in *The Critical Difference* [Baltimore: Johns Hopkins University Press, 1980]).

5. Prévost, *L'Histoire d'une Grecque Moderne* (Paris,1965), introduction by Robert Mauzi. Page references are included in the text, indicated as *GM.* Pagination for the English edition, (*The Story of a Fair Greek of Yesteryear,* trans. James. F. Jones, Jr. [Potomac, Maryland: Scripta Humastica, 1984]), will follow, in parenthesis.

6. I refer here to a mode of reading practiced by Luce Irigaray and defined to somewhat different ends in her *Ce Sexe qui n'en est pas un* (Paris: Minuit, 1977), 73–74.

In Barthes's lexicon, readerly refers to the classic text, writerly to the modern.

7. A lexia is an arbitrary fragment (unit) carved out of the text for the purpose of analysis.

8. To superimpose this "sentence" as a grid creates a slightly distorting (homogenizing) effect. But it is neither my purpose, nor possible within this limited space, to replicate Barthes's procedures.

9. For, Barthes, I should specify, oxymoron (paradox) and antithesis are not strictly speaking interchangeable terms: "the Antithesis is the figure of the given opposi-

tion . . . Every joining of two antithetical terms . . . constitutes a transgression; to be sure, rhetoric can reinvent a figure designed to name the transgressive; this figure exists: it is the *paradoxism* (or alliance of words)" (*S/Z*, 27).

10. In this sense the status of the narrator is that of an "interpretant," as Schor defines that function in "Fiction as interpretation, interpretation as Fiction." His activity is peculiarly modern: "via the interpretant the author is trying to tell the interpreter [the interpreting critic] something *about* interpretation and the interpreter would do well to listen and take note." (170). Which is what I argue at the end of this essay.

11. Naomi Schor, "Smiles of the Sphinx: Zola and the Riddle of Femininity," in *Breaking the Chain: Women, Theory, and Realist Fiction* (New York: Columbia, 1985), 32–33. Schor's analysis of nineteenth-century novels leads her to add a subcode (peculiar to the feminocentric text) to Barthes's hermeneutic code: the hieratic code (44).

12. On the status of the "Z" and the "ph" in the European alphabet, see Jean Starobinski's *L'Invention de la liberté* (Geneva: Skira, 1964) 22, and Barthes in *S/Z*. On the etymological meaning of Théophé's name, Julia Douthwaite writes: "The neologism Théophé combines the Greek symbol of divinity *theo*, with *phé*, derived from the Greek *phema* (voice, rumor, reputation), from *phanai*, to speak. Hence Théophé means "God's voice" or "divine reputation," the ultimate signifier for this eighteenth-century woman who so fervently desires a good reputation." (*Exotic Women: Literary Heroines and Cultural Strategies in Ancien Régime France* [Philadelphia: University of Pennsylvania Press, 1992], 53).

13. "Expectation thus becomes the basic condition of truth: truth, these narratives tell us, is what is *at the end* of waiting" (*S/Z*, 32). Waiting is also the founding condition of the love plot. As Barthes writes in *A Lover's Discourse:* "The lover's fatal identity is precisely: *I am the one who waits.*" (Trans. Richard Howard [New York: Noonday, 1990], 40).

14. Johnson, 7.

15. Synese, who had claimed to recognize his long-lost sister, after several weeks of shared familiarity with Théophé under the ambassador's paternal aegis, suddenly declares that he is no longer convinced that she is in fact his sister. The narrator comments: "I knew him well enough to know that he was capable of disguising something quite easily, and the Selictar's proverb about being wary of the good will of the Greeks had not slipped my mind" (*GM*, 117; 160). The Selictar himself, however, becomes an object of suspicion, suspicion which contaminates Théophé: "if so, I said to myself, if he had hidden in my house since that night, is it unreasonable to assume that he was not acting in concert with Théophé?" (*GM*, 127; 169). On the lover as "interpretant" see "The Uncertainty of Signs," in *A Lover's Discourse* (see n.13), 214–15, and passim.

16. Mauzi also makes the point in his introduction, (*GM*, viii).

17. Théophé, in transit from East to West, is courted by a Count who assumes that she is the narrator's *daughter;* when disabused, he then assumes that she is his mistress, etc. The rest of the novel plays itself out in the equivocality of this neither/nor.

18. Point eight, "the suspended answer (after having been begun)" (*S/Z*, 210) is not characteristic of Prévost's novel in terms of local analysis. One can say that it is always an implicit figure, but eclipsed concretely by Point nine, "*partial answer,* which consists in stating only one of the features whose total will form the complete identification of the truth" (*S/Z*, 210).

19. Barthes, "Analyse textuelle d'un conte d'Edgar Poe," 53.

20. Johnson, 11.

21. In a paired reading which interestingly contrasts Prévost's novel with Lafayette's *Zaïde,* Julia Douthwaite emphasizes the narrator's "masculine blindness" and the ways in which "male authors' seeming obliviousness toward issues of sexual politics" distinguishes their orientalism from the analysis of cultural difference in the works of women writers. *Exotic Women* (64).

22. Jacques Derrida, "Becoming Woman," in *Sémiotext(e)* 3(1) (1978), 134.

## EIGHT *Justine,* Or, the Vicious Circle

1. In "Sade, or Text as Fantasy," *Diacritics,* 2 (1972): 2–9, Michael Riffaterre takes a similar point of departure. He concludes, however, that since Sade's "writing differs in no way from poetic language," linguistic analysis provides the only pertinent metalanguage. (9)

2. All references to the novel are drawn from *Justine, or Good Conduct Well Chastised,* trans. Richard Seaver and Austryn Wainhouse (New York: Grove Press, 1966). Page references are included in the text, indicated as *JGC*. Pagination for the French edition, (Paris: Union Générale D'Editions, 1969), will follow in parenthesis.

3. Henri Coulet, "La Vie intérieure dans *Justine,*" in *Le Marquis de Sade,* ed. Jean Fabre (Paris: Armand Colin, 1968), 92.

4. Henri Coulet, *Le Roman jusqu'à la Révolution* (New York: McGraw-Hill-Armand Colin, 1967), 488.

5. Jean Fabre, "Sade et le roman noir," in *Le Marquis de Sade,* 273.

6. Phillippe Sollers, "Sade dans le texte," *L'Ecriture et l'expérience des limites* (Paris: Seuil, 1968), 52.

7. Sollers speaks of a "reversal" performed upon our definitions of madness and sanity, 52–53.

8. Gérard Genette, "Vraisemblance et motivation," *Figures II* (Paris: Seuil, 1969), 74.

9. Pierre Fauchery, *La Destinée féminine dans le roman européen du dix-huitième siècle* (Paris: Armand Colin, 1972), 317.

10. For a theoretical discussion of the pictorial code, see Roland Barthes "Painting as a Model," in *S/Z,* trans. Richard Miller (New York: Hill & Wang, 1974), 54–56.

11. Voltaire, "The Maid of Orleans," in *The Works of Voltaire,* vol. xx, trans. William F. Fleming (1901), 38.

12. Voltaire, *Candide, Zadig, and Selected Stories,* trans. Donald M. Frame

(Bloomington: Indiana University Press, 1961), 4. Cited by Jean Sareil in his *Essai sur Candide* (Geneva: Droz, 1967), with the comment that this purely physical description "explains her fatal power of attraction." (72).

13. Voltaire, "The Maid of Orleans," 69.

14. Sareil (see n. 12), 73.

15. Henri Coulet, *Le Roman jusqu'à la Révolution*, 488.

16. Denis Diderot, *The Nun*, trans. Leonard Tancock (London: The Folio Society, 1972), 168.

17. Jean Paulhan, "The Marquis de Sade and His Accomplice," in *The Marquis de Sade* (New York: Grove Press, 1965), 13.

18. Tzvetan Todorov, *The Poetics of Prose*, trans. Richard Howard (Ithaca: Cornell University Press, 1977), 66–80.

19. "A character trait is not simply the cause of an action, nor simply its effect: it is both at once, just as action is. X kills his wife because he is cruel; but he is cruel because he kills his wife," (Todorov, 69).

20. Genette, 75.

21. Sade, *Juliette* (Paris: Pauvert, 1969), V, 79, cited by Jean Biou, in "Deux oeuvres complémentaires: *Les Liaisons dangereuses* et *Juliette*," Fabre, ed., *Le Marquis de Sade* (see n. 3), 103–14.

22. Todorov, *Poetics of Prose*, 68.

23. Roland Barthes, *Sade, Fourier, Loyola*, trans. Richard Miller (Berkeley: University of California Press, 1989), 168–69.

24. Riffaterre, 5.

25. For a discussion of spatial circularity in Sade, I refer the reader to Jean-Jacques Brochier's "La Circularité de l'espace," Fabre, ed., *Le Marquis de Sade* (see n.3), 717–84.

26. Todorov, 74.

27. Voltaire, "The Maid of Orleans," 296.

28. Curiously, although Mario Praz defends the opposite point of view ("The cycle of possible chemical disaggregations which constitute . . . [the libertine's] . . . tortures is soon exhausted, because as Proust remarks, nothing is more limited than pleasure and vice."), he is seduced nonetheless by the metaphor of the vicious circle: "and—to make a play on words—it may be said that the vicious man moves always in the same vicious circle" (*The Romantic Agony* [Cleveland: Meridian Books, 1968], 105).

## NINE *Juliette* and the Posterity of Prosperity

1. That this is, moreover, a narrative cliché of the period is well documented by Ronald Brissenden, in his excellent and illuminating article: "*La Philosophie dans le boudoir;* or, a Young Lady's Entrance into the World," *Studies in Eighteenth-Century Culture. Irrationalism in the Eighteenth Century,*" Vol. 2 (1972), 113–42.

On the coincidence of the erotic and the spiritual, see also Barry Ivker's remarks in "Towards a definition of libertinism in 18th-century French fiction," *Studies on Voltaire and the Eighteenth Century,* LXXII (1970), 231.

2. Ellen Morgan, "Humanbecoming: Form and Focus in the Neo-Feminist novel," *Images of Women in Fiction: Feminist Perspectives,* ed. Susan K. Cornillon (Bowling Green: Popular Press, 1972), 184.

3. I use Michael Riffaterre's definition of genre: "The perception of genre is analogous to that of the cliché: the reader reads it and recalls having read it elsewhere. . . . It's a phantom form that only exists in the reader's mind; it's only a standard measurement against which he tests real works. In a word, a structure of which texts are the variants." ("Système d'un genre descriptif," *Poétique,* 9 [1972], 16).

4. *Juliette,* translated Austryn Wainhouse (New York: Grove Press, 1968); page references are included in the text, indicated as *J.* Pagination for the French edition, drawn from Sade's *Oeuvres complètes* (Paris: Cercle du Livre Précieux, 1967), V. 7–8, 9–10, will follow in parenthesis.

5. Roland Barthes, *Sade, Fourier, Loyola,* trans. Richard Miller (Berkeley: University of California Press, 1989), 24; emphasis added.

6. For an analysis of the implications of the term *narratee,* as used by Gerald Prince, see his article, "Introduction à l'étude du narrataire," *Poétique,* 14 (1973), 178–96. The footnotes are directed specifically at a female narratee when the matter at hand bears on Juliette's behavior as a *woman;* general (anthropological, historical) comments are not gender oriented.

7. I would like to maintain a distinction between genre—a problem of abstraction that lends itself to formalization—and conventions. While it is true that many aspects of Juliette's progress renew clichés of libertine fiction (cf. Brissenden's work), I am more interested in disengaging structures which point to what T. Todorov has called "the relays by which the work places itself in relation to the universe of literature," (*Introduction à la littérature fantastique* [Paris: Seuil, 1970], 12). In this sense, I found David Miles's article most useful: "The Picaro's Journey to the Confessional: The Changing Image of the Hero in the German Bildungsroman," *PMLA,* Vol. 89, no. 5 (Oct. 1974), 980–82.

8. Susan Suleiman, "Pour une poétique du roman à thèse: l'exemple de Nizan," *Critique,* 330 (Nov. 1974), 1006.

9. Brissenden cites the analogous scene of Eugénie's mutilation of her mother in *La Philosophie dans le boudoir,* and comments on its "Electral . . . structure," (Brissenden, 131–132).

10. Phillipe Sollers notes the analogues, Julie/Juliette, Claire/Clairwil, to emphasize a more generalized intertextual relation: "Literary history is therefore in its turn unmasked." ("Sade dans le texte," *L'Ecriture et l'expérience des limites* [Paris: Seuil, 1968], 60).

11. Having opted to follow the thread of linearity and thematic progression, I do not discuss Juliette's activities abroad; they are constructed on the principle of hyperbole and repetition and deserve a separate study. For an analysis of the problem of libertine education in its temporal aspect, see Jean-Jacques Brochier's comments in

"La circularité de l'espace," *Le Marquis de Sade,* ed. Jean Fabre (Paris: Armand Colin, 1968), 173.

12. A.J. Greimas and François Rastier, "The Interaction of Semiotic Constraints," *YFS,* 41 (1968), 93–94.

13. Merteuil's behavior is condemned as transgression of the fundamental Code of eighteenth-century society, i.e., (public) male sexual activity + vs. (public) female sexual *in*-activity +. Thus, Prévan's reputation is based on vaunted sexual aggression, Merteuil's upon its apparent absence; Prévan is thought to be irresistible, Merteuil, invincible. As a result of the information disclosed at the end of the novel (Merteuil's expression of desire in the form of *advances*), Prévan is reinstated and Merteuil destroyed.

14. This distinction is indeed crucial: "And here, where Laclos's Merteuil was searching for a difficult equilibrium between what is and what appears to be, concerned about being herself, but also about safeguarding her reputation, the Sadian heroine with neither mask nor concern for public opinion, without boundaries, accepts the richness of her nature, *unconditionally*" (Maurice Tourné, "Les mythes de la femme," *Europe* [Oct. 1972], 80, emphasis added). But I take exception to it being an unconditional acceptance. Femaleness, rather, is itself a *condition* of freedom (Tourné, fn. 15).

15. Miles, "The Picaro's Journey," (see n. 7) 984.

16. Tourné, 87.

17. "The submission of Juliette to Noirceuil-Sade is primarily that of the character to her author; it is, however, also that of a woman to her partner; finally equal in the conquest of liberty" (Tourné, 87). The juxtaposition of the terms *submission/liberty* poses a serious problem of interpretation, and suggests the famous Orwellian formula that some are more equal than others. As Catherine Claude (in "Une lecture de femme," *Europe,* Oct. 1972, 64–70) rightly points out, Sade's presentation of male/female relations, where maleness reigns supreme should be a caution to those who would promote Sade as a revolutionary. In this optic, there should be nothing surprising in the final reinscription of the writer as Father, and the return of the family.

18. Miles, 984.

19. Barthes, 31; emphasis added.

20. Naomi Schor, "For a Restricted Thematics: Writing, Speech, and Difference in *Madame Bovary,*" in *Breaking the Chain: Women, Theory, and French Realist Fiction* (New York: Columbia University Press, 1985), 17.

21. Sollers, 65.

22. Thus, I must finally disagree with Barthes, despite his great powers of seduction: "Juliette, 'proud and fresh in the world, soft and submissive in pleasure,' is enormously seductive; however, the one who seduces me is the paper Juliette, *the storyteller who makes herself a subject of the discourse,* not a subject of 'reality'" (37; emphasis added). The subject of *speech,* however, is not the subject of *writing;* Juliette's voice is narrated.

## TEN  The Exquisite Cadavers

1. Pierre Fauchery, *La Destinée Féminine dans le roman européen du dix-huitième siècle: essai de gynécomythie romanesque* (Paris: Armand Colin, 1972). This book was the subject of the review essay written for this special number of *Diacritics* (Winter 1975): "Textual Politics: Feminist Criticism." The editors—Nelly Furman, Caren Greenberg, Peggy Kamuf de Magnin, Lucille Kerr, Catherine Porter—signed the following statement. I reproduce it here, almost two decades later, to give the flavor of that moment:

> Contemporary criticism recognizes that critical neutrality is a fiction. The affirmation of position, the display of methodology, the posture of critical self-consciousness mask, however, an unexamined assumption of sexual/textual neutrality which feminist criticism calls into question. To qualify criticism as feminist is not merely to create another rubric, an alternative position from which some (female) critics may choose to speak. Such qualification is rather a (dia)critical gesture which discloses the false neutrality of the unmarked term "critic" and cuts across the modernisms by posing a radical challenge to prevailing notions of gender, identity, the speaking subject and the critical object. The criticism represented in these essays, while seeking to render visible/give voice to the feminine, supplements such corrective measures with theoretical elaboration insisting upon the sexual import of textual politics. The deconstruction of the (culturally overdetermined) process of textual composition opens the text not only to comprehension of its phallogocentrism but also to transformation of the structures of power inscribed within it. (1)

2. Georges May, *Le Dilemme du Roman au XVIIIe siècle: Etude sur les rapports du roman et de la critique (1715–1761)* (Paris: P.U.F., 1963), 209.

3. Fauchery's language knows one figure: metaphor (preferably expanded); one register: hyperbole. In this it is reminiscent of Norman Mailer at his worst, that is, cloyingly rich without the pangs of metalinguistic conscience. Mailer (in *The Prisoner of Sex,* [New York: Signet, 1971]), at least, will admit his guilt: "Purple metaphor, but he was not a prisoner for nothing" (43). I juxtapose the two writers here, however, not so much for their general linguistic excess but for its locus: as if the very *act* of writing about women generated and justified the purplest (and juiciest) of prose; as if the challenge to understand women—real or fictional, awesome creatures all—stimulated a mimetic (stylish and stylized) reproduction of the qualities women are *thought* to possess. The mechanism at work is a variant of the phenomenon Mary Ellman has so aptly described as the problem of "sexual analogy" (*Thinking About Women,* [New York: Harcourt Brace, 1968], 2–26). Mailer concludes his apology in the comforting embrace of its apparent subject: "(And so saying he realized he had been able to end a portentous piece in the soft sweet flesh of parentheses)" (169). Even punctuation does not escape the strictures of gender. My writing in this period showed many of the same tics, of course.

4. Laurent Versini, *Laclos et la tradition* (Paris: Klincksieck, 1968), 564.

5. The verb is indeed Fauchery's and the coincidence led me inevitably to Diderot's

*Entretien entre d'Alembert et Diderot,* in *Oeuvres philosophiques* (Paris: Garnier, 1964), 263.

6. The pun on Kristevan terminology was developed by Naomi Schor in a rather different context; see her "For a Restricted Thematics: Writing, Speech, and Difference in *Madame Bovary,*" in *Breaking the Chain: Women, Theory, and French Realist Fiction* (New York: Columbia University Press, 1985).

7. This question of timing is not specifically bound to the feminine. As Philip Stewart has pointed out, "the typical narrator begins his real story, not at birth, but at the time he becomes a socially functioning individual" ("The Child Comes of Age," *Yale French Studies,* 40 [1968], 134–35). To function socially is to function sexually.

8. Ian Watt, *The Rise of the Novel* (Berkeley: University of California Press, 1971); Daniel Defoe, *Moll Flanders* (New York: Modern Library, 1950), 22.

9. Simone de Beauvoir, *The Second Sex,* trans. H.M. Parshley (New York: Bantam, 1970), 174.

10. Julia Kristeva, *Le Texte du roman* (The Hague: Mouton, 1970), 160; emphasis added.

11. Beauvoir, 174.

12. Ruth Yeazell, "Fictional Heroines and Feminist Critics," *Novel* (Fall 1974), 30.

13. The comparative luxury of this stance assumes of course the "compensatory" phase of investigation (as it is called in current feminist terminology) which identifies and valorizes images of women writers as *pertinent* objects or subjects of analysis; a phase of the research process admirably achieved by the construction of Fauchery's "corpus."

14. Elaine Showalter, "Review Essay: Literary Criticism," *Signs* (Winter 1975) 1 (2), 436.

15. Julia Kristeva, "Le sujet en procès (suite)," *Tel Quel,* 53 (1973), 24.

16. This is precisely the loss of manpower that male heroes of the eighteenth-century novel congenitally fear; see Patricia Spacks, "Early Fiction and the Frightened Male." *Novel* (Fall 1974), 8.

17. Paul Hoffmann, "Aspects de la condition féminine dans *Les Liaisons dangereuses.*" *L'Information littéraire* (March–April, 1963), 48.

18. Mailer, *The Prisoner of Sex* (see n. 2), 86; emphasis added.

19. Diane Alstad, "*Les Liaisons dangereuses:* Hustlers and Hypocrites," *Yale French Studies,* 40 (1968), 166.

20. I thus find myself, on this very sore point in Laclos canon, in the curious company of Martin Turnell, who, however, places the problem of the ending and the origin of complicity squarely in the author's lap. Citing Merteuil's previous victories for her sex, Turnell conlcudes: "The novelist's personal jealousy is aroused and he revenges himself on his greatest creation by covering her with shame and ignominy. She is deprived of wealth, reputation and looks—of all the things which enabled her to use her great intellectual powers to the detriment of Laclos' own sex—and she flies to Holland, a fugitive from male justice." (*The Novel in France* [New York: Vintage, 1958], 77).

21. Cynthia Sutherland Matlack, "'Spectatress of the Mischief Which She Made': Tragic Woman Perceived and Perceiver," *Studies in Eighteenth-Century Culture,* 6 (1976): 317–30, 319.

22. Staël concludes her essay, "Des femmes qui cultivent les lettres," in much the same manner. The plight of the *femme extraordinaire* is to bear her "singular existence like the Pariahs of India . . : object of curiosity, perhaps of envy, and in fact deserving only pity." (*De la littérature* [Paris: Charpentier, 1860], 316).

## ELEVEN Tender Economies

1. Mme de Lafayette, *Histoire de Madame Henriette d'Angleterre, La Princesse de Montpensier, La Comtesse de Tende* (Paris: Editions des Femmes, 1979), 9. Herrmann's judgment has an oddly hard edge to it here. After all, Mme de Villedieu supported herself by her writing, and thus was dependent both on public favor and royal pleasure. She had no other identity, precisely, on which to draw. Dorothy Backer's *Precious Women: A Feminist Phenomenon in the Age of Louis XIV* (New York: Basic Books, 1974) provides a gritty version of these differing materialities: "Mlle Desjardins catered to an enormous public of not very refined sentiments. She was constantly working under financial pressure and had no time to write a masterpiece like *La Princesse de Clèves,* (251). "This emancipated girl" (249), as Backer glosses her status, lived "without fear of appearances, without means, without moral support. . . . by her wits and sustained only by a romantic image of love . . . a 'seventeenth-century George Sand'" (251).

2. Thus, Bruce Morrissette, author of the only full-length study of Mme de Villedieu's work in English, concluding his discussion of *Les Désordres de l'amour* affirms: "That she was moving in a direction which might have led to real artistic achievement is illuminated significantly by the lesser work. The plain fact is that the talent of Mlle Desjardins was not of the quality necessary to produce a masterpiece." (*The Life and Works of Marie-Catherine Desjardins (Mme de Villedieu), 1632–1683* [Saint Louis: Washington University Studies, 1947], 116). "We like her bravery and enthusiasm . . . ," Backer exclaims, "what a pity she did not write at least one good book" (*Precious Women,* 251).

3. In 1970, some 200 years after its last publication, a critical edition of Mme de Villedieu's *Les Désordres* appeared (Geneva: Droz, 1970). Page references to this edition are included in the text, indicated as *LD.* Micheline Cuénin, the editor, provides extremely useful information—to which I am much indebted—about Mme de Villedieu's sources, and thus helps situate Villedieu in a complex literary tradition.

4. The implications of Valincour's analysis of narrative economy and economic reasoning for modern criticism have been drawn by Gérard Genette in "Vraisemblance et Motivation," *Figures II* (Paris: Seuil, 1969).

5. Morrisette, 107.

6. Henri Coulet, *Le Roman jusqu'à la Révolution* (Paris: Armand Colin, 1967), 267. Michel Mercier, in his overview of women's writing, *Le Roman féminin* (Paris: P.U.F., 1976), thematizes their differences in terms of their attitudes towards love,

"In Mme de Villedieu's works . . . an abandonment to love, leading to its 'disorders' and to death contrasts with the refusal to surpass love in Mme de Lafayette . . . All these milestones—novel or *nouvelle galante,* novel of manners or psychological novel—prepare and assure the dawn of the novel in the eighteenth century" (230; see n. 11 infra).

7. Mme de Lafayette, *The Princess of Clèves,* trans. Walter J. Cobb (New York: Meridian, 1989), 1.

8. Why was Mme de Maugiron invented, or rather what does she *figure as fiction?* (Cuénin comments: "The character of Maugiron thus seems invented for novelistic reasons" [*LD,* 121, n. 7]). She shares with Mme de Bellegarde, and indeed Mme de Villedieu, the ambiguous status derived from a "marriage" for love in which, "the word exchanged between the married couple constituted the whole ceremony" (*LD,* 121). In all three cases, perhaps because the unions were only illicit fictions, the women ultimately find themselves alone—not young enough to be cast as innocent maidens in a story of seduced and abandoned—but at least embittered and disappointed. Mme de Villedieu keeps writing (it might also usefully be remembered that Mme de Villedieu was also—and perhaps first—a poet); Mme de Maugiron, "the too constant," will die.

9. On the relationship of ambitious and erotic wishes to the logic of female plot, see my "Emphasis Added: Plots and Plausibilities in Women's Fiction," *PMLA* 96 (January 1981), 36–48; reprinted in *Subject to Change: Reading Feminist Writing* (New York: Columbia University Press, 1988).

10. Of this friendship, we learned earlier: "They were intimate friends, and had never concealed anything from one another" (*LD,* 128–29). This male bond is homologous, in its status as fiction, to the creation of Mme de Maugiron. Cuénin comments: "Givry and Bellegarde were only comrades in arms: they were found 'with all the galants of the army' at the foot of the rampart. This friendship is a novelistic invention that adds to Givry's unhappiness and makes the tragic results more plausible" (129, n. 18).

11. In the same way, Givry had pondered the princess's motivation in versifying; were the *Maximes* written "in private or in general conversation?" (*LD,* 136). Cuénin underlines: "An important question: is this a matter of a society game as they were played in the salons, or is this a singular intended act, which would be more flattering for Givry? This uncertainty inspires his mad hope" (136, n. 33). One could also read here an oblique commentary on the status of women's writing in seventeenth-century France; see, for example, the discussion of the "Question galante" and *La Princesse de Clèves* in Maurice Laugaa's *Lectures de Mme de Lafayette* (Paris: Armand Colin, 1971).

12. Cuénin, in Villedieu, 206–207. Tallemant, earlier, reproduces the letter in the *historiette* which bears the title "La Princesse de Conty." Tallemant des Réaux, *Historiettes* (Paris: Gallimard, 1960), I, 35. Cuénin suggests that Mme de Villedieu might have seen the original. Did the original generate the story or does the story accommodate history? The enigma, bound precisely to the problem of genre, history or fiction, remains insoluble.

13. A. Kibédi-Varga, "Romans d'amour, romans de femmes, à l'époque classique," *Revue des sciences humaines,* 168 (octobre–décembre 1977), 523.

14. Lafayette, 152.

15. The feminist investment in this genderization of plot can be read unambiguously in Mme Riccoboni's *Histoire du Marquis de Cressy* (1758), cited by René Godenne as a "renewal" of the seventeenth-century *nouvelle,* and worthy of comparison with the works of Mme de Lafayette. *Histoire de la nouvelle française aux XVIIe et XVIIIe Siècles* (Geneva: Droz, 1970), 195. The novels of Mme de Tencin, particularly *Les Malheurs de l'amour* (1747), are another case in point; though in the eighteenth century, the state gives way to the slightly more diffuse prerogatives of the *estate.*

16. The actual disbursement of funds only took place some seven years later, however, in 1676, when Mme de Villedieu had stopped writing, and at half the sum awarded. Nevertheless, Cuénin observes, "in a period of budgetary restriction, this royal warrant was distinctly rare." (*Roman et Société sous Louis XIV: Mme de Villedieu (Marie-Catherine Desjardins 1640–1683)* [Lille: Université de Lille III, 1979], 54).

17. See Morrissette, 115; Cuénin, 215.

## TWELVE  "Tristes Triangles"

1. Charles-Augustin Sainte-Beuve, *Portraits contemporains* (1882), 2: 256–57; as cited by Moïse Le Yaouanc in his introduction to *Le Lys dans la vallée* (Paris: Garnier, 1966), x.

2. Honoré de Balzac, *Lettres à l'Etrangère* (Paris: Calmann-Lévy), 1: 186; as cited by Le Yaouanc (see n. 1), xi.

3. Balzac, xi.

4. André Vial, "De *Volupté à L'Education Sentimentale:* Vie et avatars de thèmes romanesques," *Revue d'histoire littéraire de la France* 57 (1957): 194.

5. M. Le Yaouanc has the longest list of possible suspects (xxxv), but he is not alone in his speculations. See, for example, Jacques Borel's chapter on Mme de Mortsauf in *Le Lys dans la vallée et les sources profondes de la création balzacienne* (Paris: Corti, 1961) chap. 4.

6. Nicole Mozet, preface to *Le Lys dans la vallée* (Paris: Garnier Flammarion, 1972), 21–22; emphasis added. The enigma of female sexuality constitutes a problem that of course is not restricted to Balzac's fiction. For a mapping of the territory in Zola, see Naomi Schor's "Le Sourire du sphinx: Zola et l'énigme de la féminité," *Romantisme* 13–14 (1976): 183–95; reprinted as "Smiles of the Sphinx: Zola and the Riddle of Femininity," in *Breaking the Chain: Women, Theory, and French Realist Fiction* (New York: Columbia University Press, 1985).

7. See Maurice Serval's "Autour d'un roman de Balzac: *Le Lys dans la vallée*," *Revue d'histoire littéraire de la France* 33 (October–December 1926), 574–76.

8. English translations from Marguerite de Navarre, *The Heptameron,* trans. P.A. Chilton (Middlesex: Penguin Books Ltd., 1984). Page references are included in the text, indicated as *H.* Pagination for the French edition, taken from *L'Heptaméron* (Paris: Garnier, 1967), will follow. When only one page number appears, that reference is taken from the French edition.

9. English translations from Jean-Jacques Rousseau, *La Nouvelle Héloïse: Julie or the New Eloise* trans. Judith H. McDowell (University Park: The Pennsylvania State University Press, 1968). Page references are included in the text, indicated as *NH*. Pages numbers for the French edition, taken from *La Nouvelle Héloïse* (Paris: Garnier, 1960), will follow. When only one page number appears, that reference is to the French edition.

10. English translations from *The Lily in the Valley* trans. Lucienne Hill (London: Elek Books, 1957). Page references are included in the text, indicated as *LV*. Page numbers for the French edition, taken from *Le Lys dans la vallée*, the Garnier edition (see note 2), will follow. When only one page number appears, that reference is to the French edition.

11. André Wurmser, *La Comédie inhumaine* (Paris: Gallimard, 1964), 625. See too his remarks on Mme de Mortsauf's sexuality and the variants, 624–25.

12. Schor (see n. 6), 189; *Smiles*, 39.

13. M. Le Yaouanc in his commentary on variants, 446.

14. Ibid., lxxiii; emphasis added.

15. In particular, the famous letter 18 of part 3, Julie's first letter as Mme de Wolmar.

16. Peter Brooks, "Virtue-Tripping: Notes on *Le Lys dans la vallée*," *Yale French Studies* 50 (1974): 158–59.

17. Of two sorts: Le Yaouanc footnotes the obvious reference to Mme de Rênal (LV, 317); and Brooks describes the kisses as "a memory trace that she was never able to exorcise," an event that has "determined the rest of her life, all the counter-cathexes she has been obliged to form" (Brooks, 157–58).

18. Perhaps the only use of hair that rivals this unromantic, *unheimlich* one is George Sand's in *Indiana* (where the hair fetishized belongs to a dead woman).

19. Brooks, 157.

20. Brooks, 155–56. "Mme de Mortsauf's final illness is patterned as a conversion hysteria, that is, as a flight into illness in which the somatic symptoms are symbolic of the repressed."

21. Le Yaouanc, for example, concludes from the symptoms described (251 n. 2, 288 n. 1, and elsewhere) that such is her illness. But his diagnosis is an interpretation and not a textual fact.

22. Brooks, commenting on these lines in the context on his analysis of Mme de Mortsauf's conversion hysteria, points out: "But the terms of the denial make it textually inevitable that the repressed will take its revenge"—which it does (156).

23. Petrarch, Sonnet 294; see title page of the Garnier edition.

24. René Girard, *Deceit, Desire and the Novel: Self and Other in Literary Structure*, trans. Yvonne Freccero (Baltimore: The Johns Hopkins Press, 1965), 308.

25. Brooks, 161.

26. Girard, 175.

## THIRTEEN Novels of Innocence

1. Harry Levin, Foreword to *Les Liaisons Dangereuses* (New York: Signet, New American Library, 1962), ix.

2. R.F. Brissenden, *Virtue in Distress: Studies in the Novel of Sentiment from Richardson to Sade* (New York: Barnes and Noble, 1974), 276.

3. In more formal terms one might say that loss of innocence and entrance into the world are grammatical corollaries of each other from the perspective of genre. As Michael Riffaterre writes in "On Deciphering Mallarmé," "a genre . . . has a grammar and this grammar merely develops a very limited number of matrix sentences. The Gothic novel, for example, is built upon the expansion of sentences linking innocence and a threat to that innocence, and linking the threat and the past with the corollary that the past is secret" (*Georgia Review*, 29 [Spring 1975], 80). Peter Brooks also makes the James connection: "Like all his contemporaries . . . [James] was undoubtedly ignorant of the eighteenth-century French novel. Yet from the models of a novel of manners he did possess, equipped with his hypersensitivity to questions of social comportment and psychology, ways of acting and knowing, he wrote novels that often seem the true posterity of the novel of worldliness" (*The Novel of Worldliness* [Princeton : Princeton University Press, 1969], 283); see also Brooks's remarks on *The Portrait of a Lady* and *The Wings of the Dove*.

4. Brooks, (see n. 3), 4.

5. Gilles Deleuze, *Proust and Signs*, trans. Richard Howard (New York: George Braziller, 1972), 4.

6. Henry James, *The Wings of the Dove* (New York: Charles Scribner's Sons, 1909), 405.

7. My own thinking intersects here with Leo Bersani's analysis in "The Jamesian Lie," *Partisan Review*, 26 (Winter 1969), 53–82. Bersani, however, favors the *visual* metaphor: "Apparently nothing is more stimulating, more exhilarating for James's characters than the act of recognition which they constantly and somewhat breathlessly confirm. But seeing can be dangerous as well as thrilling. James's fiction is full of visual shocks which constitute crucial turning points for his heroes and heroines" (58).

8. Ruth Yeazell, "Talking in James," *PMLA*, 91 (January 1976), 71–72; emphasis added.

9. Claude Bremond, *Logique du Récit* (Paris: Seuil, 1973), 263.

10. The prospects for applying models of communicational theory to eighteenth-century fiction from a psychological/behavioral perspective have been explored by Ronald Rosbottom in *Choderlos de Laclos* (Boston: Twayne, 1979).

11. This intimate relationship between sexual and social identities is inevitable in a society that sees "the erotic situation as the limit term in human relationships, a final confrontation of two beings, an ultimate metaphor for what people do to one another" (Brooks, 22). This vision attains paroxysmal dimensions in Clarissa's moment of truth, to cite the obvious example.

12. What I mean by illusions, simply, is unexamined, or rather, *untested* notions of the self, and the status of that self in relation to others.

13. English translations from Madame de Lafayette *The Princesse de Clèves*. trans. Walter J. Cobb (New York: Meridian Classic, 1989). Page references are included in the text, indicated as *PC*. The French pagination follows, taken from *La Princesse de Clèves* (Paris: Garnier-Flammarion, 1966).

14. The unexpected result of the Princess's confession would probably be coded by Bremond as an "involuntary action": "characterized by the roles of the type: *agent tending involuntarily to commit action x while undertaking task y*" (240). However, the roles that would correspond to this action do not seem to apply: "*Voluntary* informer, if he is sincere, takes on the role of the voluntary revealer: but if he is in error, he tends to play the role of the involuntary deceiver at the same time" (263). For the Princess is both "in good faith" about herself and "in error" about her husband. As a result, Bremond's disjunctive (Aristotelian) categories do not work here.

15. Abbé Prévost *Manon Lescaut,* trans. Donald M. Frame. (New York: Meridian Classic, 1983). Page references are included in the text, indicated as *ML*. The French pagination, from *Manon Lescaut* (Paris: Garnier, 1967) will follow.

16. Prévost; 143, 147.

17. As Lovelace sees it: "A *jest,* I call all that has passed between her and me; a mere jest to die for—for has not her triumph over me, from first to last, been infinitely greater than her suffering from me?" (Richardson, *Clarissa: or, The History of a Young Lady,* [New York: Everyman's Library, 1932], IV, 261).

18. Richardson, 262.

19. Percy Lubbock, *The Craft of Fiction* (New York: Viking, 1957), 183.

20. Frederick C. Crews, *The Tragedy of Manners: Moral Drama in the Later Novels of Henry James* (New Haven: Yale University Press, 1957), 77.

21. Richardson, 306.

22. Laclos, *Les Liaisons dangereuses* (Paris: Gallimard, 1959), letter CLXV.

23. Brooks, 214.

24. Brooks, 214.

25. Brooks, 4.

26. Brissenden, 284.

27. This is, of course, a simplification. The concept of a self that is not coded in fact constitutes another code of the self; roughly, the code of an innocent, unknown self versus the code of a worldly, known self. However, the fiction *alone* is capable of registering this interaction. The characters themselves have no words adequate for the overflow, beyond the labels of ineffable *difference.* Leo Braudy has an interesting discussion of these problems as they emerge in the English novel in "Penetration and Impenetrability in *Clarissa,*" *New Approaches to English Literature,* ed. Philip Harth (New York: Columbia University Press, 1974), 177–206.

28. Crews, 75.

29. Robert Alter, "History and Imagination in the Nineteenth-Century Novel," *Georgia Review,* 29 (Spring 1975), 45–46.

30. Brooks, 4.

31. For a discussion of the androgynous project in James, see Carolyn Heilbrun, *Toward a Recognition of Androgyny* (New York: W.W. Norton, 1973), 94–97.

32. James, *Wings of the Dove,* 62.

33. James, 222.

34. For Dorothy Van Ghent, *The English Novel: Form and Function* (1953, 1961; rpt. New York, 1967), Isabel's trajectory is a movement from knowledge to freedom: "*The Portrait* identifies life with the most probing, dangerous responsible awareness—identifies, as it were, the two 'trees,' the tree of the Fall and the tree of Resurrection. The knowledge [Isabel] has acquired has been tragic knowledge, but her story does not stop here, as it would if it were a tragedy—it goes on out of the pages of the book, to Rome, where we cannot follow it" (260–61).

# INDEX

Alstad, Diane, 226n
Alter, Robert, 196, 233n
Altman, Janet, 209n
Ancien régime fiction, 5–15, 28, 30, 35, 72
Argens, Boyer d'
  *Thérèse philosophe,* 7, 10–11, 202n
Arnaud, François Thomas Marie d', 88
Austen, Jane, 51–52, 210n
Authorship
  canon, 7–15, 81–83
  female, 53–68, 93–95
  and gender, 3–15, 45–52, 69–79, 81–83
  literary history, 3–15
  male, 45–52
  universal, 58, 63, 71

Backer, Dorothy, 227n
Bakhtin, Mikhail, 46
Balzac, Honoré de, 56, 105–20, 173, 197, 219n, 229n
  *Le Lys dans la vallée,* 173–85
Barthes, Roland, 14, 101–102, 103, 128, 219n, 224n

*A Lover's Discourse,* 102, 203n, 218n, 220n
*Sade, Fourier, Loyola,* 128–29, 222n, 223n
*S/Z,* 105–20, 219n, 220n, 221n
Beauvoir, Simone de, 20, 24, 153, 154, 226n
Beck, Evelyn, 64, 213n
Bennington, Geoffrey, 215n
Bérenguier, Nadine, 204n
Bersani, Leo, 231n
*Bildungsroman,* 133–34, 143
Biou, Jean, 210n, 222n
Bloom, Edward A., 54
Bloom, Harold, 209n
Bloom, Lillian D., 54
Booth, Wayne, 46, 51, 208n, 209n
Borel, Jacques, 229n
Boucher, François, 8
Bourgeacq, Jacques, 208n
Brami, Joseph, 203n
Braudeau, Michel, 216n
Braudy, Leo, 218n, 232n
Brawer, Peggy, 217n
Bremond, Claude, 190, 231n, 232n

Brissenden, Ronald, 187–88, 195, 222n, 223n, 231n, 232n
Brochier, Jean-Jacques, 222n, 223n
Brooks, Peter, 45, 179, 184, 188, 195, 208n, 230n, 231n, 232n, 233n
Brownstein, Rachel, 15, 211n
Buckingham, Helen, 218n
Burney, Frances (Fanny), 53, 64, 213n
   Camilla, 53–54, 210n
   Cecilia, 62
Butor, Michel, 209n

Charrière, Isabelle de, 33, 36, 40, 204n, 205n, 213n
   Lettres de Mistress Henley, 33, 34, 40
Claude, Catherine, 224n
Cleland, John, 7, 218n
   Fanny Hill, 7, 97–99, 100
Clément, Catherine, 30, 204n
Cook, Elizabeth, 13, 203n
Coulet, Henri, 69, 72, 162, 214n, 216n, 221n, 222n, 227n
Coward, David, 10, 202n
Crébillon, Claude Prosper Jolyot de (Crébillon fils), 8, 29, 39, 49, 56, 206n, 214n, 215n
   Les Egarements du coeur et de l'esprit, 70–71, 72
Creech, James, 4, 201n
Crews, Frederick C., 195, 196, 232n
Crosby, Emily, 216n
Cuénin Micheline, 163–64, 228n, 229n
Culler, Jonathan, 45, 208n

Dagen, Jean, 71
DeJean, Joan, 55, 204n, 211n, 213n
Deleuze, Gilles, 105, 231n
Deneys, Anne, 202n
Denon, Vivant, 8

Derrida, Jacques, 20, 120, 221n
Diderot, Denis, 3–7, 13, 41, 56, 59, 84, 124, 149, 213n, 215n, 217n, 222n, 225n
   Les Bijoux indiscrets, 3–7, 39, 201n
Douthwaite, Julia, 220n, 221n
Dressing, 27–29
Duclos. See Pinot-Duclos.
DuPlessis, Rachel, 58, 211n

Eliot, George, 23, 66, 213n
Ellman, Mary, 225n
Etiemble, René, 8, 55–57, 66, 67, 202n, 211n, 215n

Fabre, Jean, 221n
Fassin, Eric, 31, 204n
Fauchery, Pierre, 147–49, 153, 156, 158, 211n, 218n, 221n, 225n
Female impersonation, 65
Feminism, 19, 42, 46
   American, 5, 6
   erotics and, 13
   French, 5
Feminist
   criticism, 5–6, 156, 157–58
   writing, 57–62, 171
Fetterley, Judith, 207n, 210n
Fontaines, Marie-Louise de, 82
Forman, Milos, 26
Foucault, Michel, 3–6, 12, 133, 201n, 204n
Fragonard, Jean Honoré, 32
France, Marie de, 22
Frappier-Mazur, Lucienne, 11, 203n
Frears, Stephen, 26, 27
Fries, Thomas, 208n

Galaznik, Elizabeth Dulong, 206n
Gallop, Jane, 4–6, 201n, 206n
Gelfand, Elissa, 213n, 214n

Gender, 53–68, 69–79. *See also*
    Masculinity; Women.
genre, 69–79, 81–89
and the memoir–novel, 81–89
and power, 79
and reading, 3–15, 38–42
Genette, Gérard, 123, 127, 221n,
    222n, 227n
Genre. *See* Libertine literature;
    Memoir-novel; Sentimental lit-
    erature.
Gilbert, Sandra M., 51–52, 209n,
    210n
Girard, René, 184, 185, 230n
Giroud, Françoise, 30, 204n
Godenne, René, 229n
Gornick, Vivian, 18
Gossman, Lionel, 207n
Graffigny, Françoise d'Issembourg
    d'Happencourt de, 34, 36–37,
    54, 56, 64–65, 207n, 211n,
    212n, 213n, 214n, 216n
    *Lettres d'une Péruvienne*, 7, 40,
    61, 63, 202n
Greimas, A.J., 140–42, 224n
Greuze, Jean-Baptiste, 32
Gubar, Susan, 51–52, 209n, 210n

Hampton, Christopher, 26, 29
Heilbrun, Carolyn, 208n, 210n,
    233n
Henriot, Emile, 215n
Hite, Shere, 5
    *Hite Report*, 5–6
Hoffmann, Paul, 226n
Hunt, Lynn, 206n

Identity
    in drag, 93–103
    moral, 72–73
    social, 73
Irigaray, Luce, 5, 6, 201n, 219n
Ivker, Barry, 223n

Jacob, Margaret C., 202n–203n
James, Henry, 187–90, 195, 231n,
    233n
Jehlen, Myra, 65, 213n
Jensen, Katharine, 14, 203n, 217n
Johnson, Barbara, 114, 120, 219n,
    220n

Kelly, Joan, 55, 202n, 211n
Kibédi-Varga, A., 171, 228n
Kramer, Jane, 12, 203n
Kristeva, Julia, 95, 153–54, 156,
    218n, 226n

Labé, Louise, 22
Lacan, Jacques, 6, 20
Laclos, Pierre Choderlos de, 15, 16,
    24, 48, 62–63, 208n, 212n,
    213n, 215n, 224n
    *Les Liaisons dangereuses*, 25–29,
    35, 41, 47, 49–50, 84, 156–59,
    202n, 204n, 209n, 232n
Lafayette, Marie-Madeleine de, 22,
    34, 56, 70, 81, 82, 171, 185,
    221n, 227n, 229n
    *La Contesse de Tende*, 33
    *Histoire de Madame Henriette
    d'Angleterre*, 161
    *La Princesse de Clèves*, 82, 162,
    191–94, 232n
    *The Princess de Clèves* (English
    translation), 192–94, 228n,
    232n
La Fontaine, Jean de, 49
La Harpe, Jean François de, 82
Landes, Joan, 207n
Lanser, Susan, 14, 64, 76, 203n,
    205n, 213n, 215n
*Letters of a Portuguese Nun*, 15–16,
    23, 93–95, 102, 103
Levin, Harry, 187, 231n
Lévi-Strauss, Claude, 20, 140–42

Lévy, Bernard-Henri, 30, 204n
Le Yaouanc, M., 230n
Libertine literature, 9–17, 38–42,
    69–70, 76–79, 202n
  and sentimental literature, 69–79
Louvet de Couvray (Jean-Baptiste),
    57
Lubbock, Percy, 194, 232n
Lyttleton, George, 54

MacArthur, Elizabeth, 207n
Mailer, Norman, 18, 158, 225n,
    226n
Marivaux, Pierre Carlet de, 56, 84,
    215n
Marriage, 34, 38, 76
Masculinity, 34, 93–103
  construction of, 38, 69–79
  male bonding, 46–47, 66
  privilege and, 3–15, 34, 41, 76
Matlack, Cynthia Sutherland, 227n
May, Georges, 47–48, 55, 56, 148,
    209n, 211n, 212n, 218n, 225n
Méheust, Mme de, 85
Meilhan, Sénac de, 56, 66–67
Memoir-novel, 81–94
Mercier, Michel, 227n
Miles, David, 223n, 224n
Miller, Henry, 158
Miller, Jane, 12, 203n
Miller, Nancy K.
  The Heroine's Text, 21, 23–24
  Subject to Change, 58, 211n, 212n
Millett, Kate, 18, 19, 21, 158
Montesquieu, Charles de Secondat,
    56, 211n, 213n, 217n
Morgan, Ellen, 223n
Morrissette, Bruce, 162, 227n
Mozet, Nicole, 229n

Navarre, Marguerite de
  L'Heptaméron, 174–75, 182, 184,
    229n

Nicoletti, Gianni, 61, 211n
Nystul, Nancy, 210n

O'Driscoll, Sally, 206n
Okely, Judith, 24–25, 203n
O'Reilly, Jane, 20
Ovid
  Heroides, 102, 103

Paulhan, Jean, 222n
Perry, Ruth, 204n
Petrarch, 183–84, 230n
Pinot-Duclos, Charles, 8, 29, 39, 56,
    214n, 215n, 218n
  Les Confessions du comte de***,
    37–42, 70, 72, 205n
  Mémoires pour servir à l'histoire
    des moeurs du XVIIIe siècle,
    71–79
Praz, Mario, 222n
Prévost, Antoine François (abbé),
    81, 83, 85, 213n, 214n, 217n,
    221n, 232n
  Histoire du chevalier des Grieux
    et de Manon Lescaut, 85–89,
    96–97, 130, 193
  L'Histoire d'une Grecque mo-
    derne, 105–20, 219n
Prince, Gerald, 223n
Proust, Marcel, 222n

Queneau, Raymond, 211n
Quenell, Peter, 99

Rabelais, François, 46
Rastier, François, 140–42, 224n
Reading
  overreading, 61–62
  in pairs, 62, 71–79, 83–89
  rereading, 8–15, 45–52
  and sexuality, 3–15, 38–42
  women, 45–52
Reichler, Claude, 39, 204n, 206n

Rétif, or Restif de la Bretonne, Nicolas Edme, 56, 216n
Riccoboni, Marie-Jeanne, 13–15, 29, 32, 35, 36, 41, 56, 63, 203n, 205n, 207n, 212n, 213n, 214n, 215n, 216n, 217n, 229n
  *Lettres de Milady Juliette Catesby A Milady Henriette Campley, Son Amie,* 40, 55, 58, 59, 72–79
  *Lettres de Mistress Fanni Butlerd,* 13, 14, 31, 40, 41, 42, 203n
Rich, Adrienne, 5, 201n
Richardson, Samuel, 60
  *Clarissa,* 7, 210n, 231n, 232n
  Clarissa (character), 150, 151–52, 194, 195, 196
  *Pamela,* 205n
  Pamela (character), 117, 149, 150, 152
Riffaterre, Michael, 128, 221n, 222n, 223n, 231n
*Roman sentimental. See* Sentimental literature.
Rosbottom, Ronald, 48, 209n, 231n
Rousseau, Jean-Jacques, 34, 49, 56, 59–60, 71, 72, 83, 183–84, 214n
  *Letter to d'Alembert,* 94–95
  *La Nouvelle Héloïse,* 39, 175, 179, 180, 181, 182, 183, 213n, 230n

Sade, Donatien Alphonse François, marquis de, 63, 101, 152, 187, 199, 205n, 212n, 224n
  *Juliette,* 133–44, 218n, 222n, 223n
  *Justine, ou les malheurs de la vertu,* 121–31
  *Justine, Or Good Conduct Well Chastised* (English translation), 122–31, 221n

Sagan, Françoise, 9
Sainte-Beuve, Charles-Augustin, 61, 174, 211n, 212n, 217n, 229n
Sand, George, 230n
Sareil, Jean, 222n
Schor, Naomi, 5, 7, 62, 110, 201n, 202n, 212n, 219n, 220n, 224n, 226n, 229n, 230n
Scudéry, Madeleine de, 56, 172
Sedgwick, Eve Kosofsky, 206n, 210n
Seduction
  and betrayal, 189
  consequences, 30–36
  strategies, 30–31
Segal, Erich
  *Love Story,* 147–48
Segal, Naomi, 39, 206n–207n
Sentimental literature, 71, 77–78, 83, 191–99
  definition of, 69
Serval, Maurice, 229n
Sexuality
  heterosexuality and plot, 37–39
  history and power, 3–7, 8–15
  and knowledge, 5–7
  repro-narrativity, 34, 207n
Shinagel, Michael, 218n
Showalter, Elaine, 155, 208n, 226n
Singerman, Alan, 203n
Sollers, Phillipe, 122, 221n, 223n, 224n
Spacks, Patricia, 226n
Staël, Germaine de, 22, 36, 66, 67, 83, 154–55, 205n, 227n
Starobinski, Jean, 220n
Stendhal (Marie Henri Beyle), 56, 215n
Stewart, Joan Hinde, 79, 204n, 205n, 215n
Stewart, Philip, 84, 204n, 206n, 217n, 226n
Suleiman, Susan, 223n
Switten, Margaret, 213n, 214n

Tencin, Claudine Alexandrine
 Guérin, marquise de, 81, 205n,
 207n, 211n, 212n, 213n, 214n,
 216n, 229n
 *Les Mémoires du comte de
 Comminge*, 56, 81–89, 217n
Thibaudet, Albert, 67
Thomas, Chantal, 217n
Todd, Janet, 205n, 213n, 216n
Todorov, Tzvetan, 127, 130, 222n
Tompkins, Jane, 60, 212n
Trousson, Raymond, 9–10, 202n
Turnell, Martin, 226n

Vadim, Roger, 25, 26, 27
Van Ghent, Dorothy, 233n
Vanpée, Janie, 206n
Versini, Laurent, 70, 148, 206n,
 207n, 215n, 225n
Vial, André, 229n
Villedieu, Mme de (Desjardins,
 Marie-Catherine), 161–72,
 227n, 228n, 229n
Voltaire, 124, 217n, 221n, 222n

Warner, Marina, 25–26, 203n
Warner, Michael, 34, 205n
Watt, Ian, 218n, 226n

Williams, Linda, 4–5, 42, 201n,
 202n, 207n
Winnett, Susan, 39, 45, 206n,
 211n
Wittig, Monique, 5
Women, 107, 196. *See also*
 Feminism; Women's writing.
 adolescent heroine, 150–51
 children, 34–36, 49–50
 death, 147–49, 152, 176–79,
 181–82, 183–85, 189
 desire, 40, 99
 friendship, 40–42
 marriage, 34, 38, 76
 masturbation, 7–8, 39
 misogyny, 9–10
 pregnancy, 30–36
 rape, 75–76, 152, 196
 sexuality, 13, 18
 and subjectivity, 45–52
Women's writing
 history of, 53–68, 81–83
Woolf, Virginia
 *A Room of One's Own*, 99–100,
 218n
Wurmser, André, 230n

Yeazell, Ruth, 189–90, 226n, 231n

*For Product Safety Concerns and Information please contact our EU representative GPSR@taylorandfrancis.com Taylor & Francis Verlag GmbH, Kaufingerstraße 24, 80331 München, Germany*

T - #0108 - 270225 - C0 - 229/152/14 - PB - 9780415903226 - Gloss Lamination